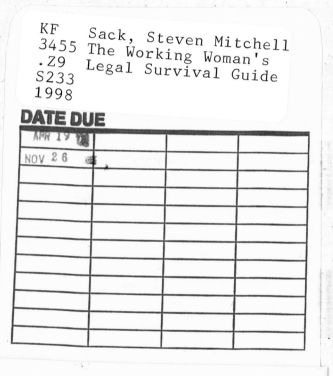

THE WORKING WOMAN'S LEGAL SURVIVAL GUIDE

Steven Mitchell Sack
Attorney at Law

PRENTICE HALL PRESS

Library of Congress Cataloging in Publication Data

Sack, Steven Mitchell.
    The working woman's legal survival guide : know your workplace rights
before it's too late / Steven Mitchell Sack.
      p. cm.
    Includes index.
    ISBN 07352-000X-5
    1. Women—Employment—Law and legislation—United States—Popular
works. I. Title.
    KF3455.Z9S233 1998
    344.7301'4—dc21   97-31552
                                                    CIP

This publication is designed to provide accurate and authoritative information in
regard to the subject matter covered. It is sold with the understanding that the
publisher is not engaged in rendering legal, accounting, or other professional service. If legal advice or other expert assistance is required, the services of a competent professional person should be sought.

—From a Declaration of Principles jointly adopted by a Committe of the American
Bar Association and a Committee of Publishers and Associations.

Printed in the United States of America
10 9 8 7 6 5 4 3 2 1

ISBN 07352-000X-5

ATTENTION: CORPORATIONS AND SCHOOLS
Prentice Hall books are available at quantity discounts with bulk purchase for
educational, business, or sales promotional use. For information, please write
to: Prentice Hall Special Sales, 240 Frisch Court, Paramus, New Jersey 07652.
Please supply: title of book, ISBN, quantity, how the book will be used, date
needed.

 PRENTICE HALL PRESS
Paramus, NJ 07652

A Simon & Schuster Company

On the World Wide Web at http://www.phdirect.com

Prentice Hall International (UK) Limited, *London*
Prentice Hall of Australia Pty. Limited, *Sydney*
Prentice Hall Canada, Inc., *Toronto*
Prentice Hall Hispanoamericana, S.A., *Mexico*
Prentice Hall of India Private Limited, *New Delhi*
Prentice Hall of Japan, Inc., *Tokyo*
Simon & Schuster Asia Pte. Ltd., *Singapore*
Editora Prentice Hall do Brasil, Ltda., *Rio de Janeiro*

DEDICATION

To Women Everywhere

To Gwen, With Love Always

ALSO BY STEVEN MITCHELL SACK

The Salesperson's Legal Guide

Don't Get Taken!: How To Avoid Everyday Consumer Rip-offs

The Complete Legal Guide To Marriage, Divorce, Custody and
Living Together

The Employee Rights Handbook: Answers to Legal Questions From
Interview To Pink Slip

From Hiring To Firing: The Legal Survival Guide for Employers in
the 90's

The Complete Collection of Legal Forms For Employers

The Lifetime Legal Guide

ABOUT THE AUTHOR

Steven Mitchell Sack maintains a private law practice in New York City devoted to severance negotiations of terminated workers and executives, discrimination lawsuits, contract negotiations, representation of salespeople and employees in breach of contract and commission disputes, and general labor law. He is a Phi Beta Kappa graduate of the State University of New York at Stony Brook and Boston College Law School.

Mr. Sack is the author of fifteen legal books for the American public. His views on employment law have been reported in *The Wall Street Journal*, *The New York Times*, *Fortune* magazine, and dozens of other publications. He has appeared on *The Oprah Winfrey Show*, *Jenny Jones*, and *The Sally Jessy Raphael Show* (three times discussing unjust firings and sexual harassment), and has made numerous appearances on CNBC's *Smart Money* and *Steals and Deals*.

Mr. Sack is the president of Legal Strategies, Inc., a publishing firm. He is a member of the American Bar Association Labor and Employment Sections and is admitted to practice before the U.S. Tax Court. He also serves as a commercial and labor arbitrator for the American Arbitration Association and as general labor counsel for many trade organizations. In addition to regularly conducting seminars on employment issues for both employee and employer groups, he is engaged by law firms throughout the United States to strategize cases and testify as an expert witness.

Mr. Sack is married and has two sons. He enjoys boating and sports in his spare time.

ACKNOWLEDGMENTS

I would like to thank many individuals for assisting me in the preparation of this book.

First, gratitude is extended to my publicist Donna Gould at Phoenix Media. Her enthusiasm for my work has never wavered through the years and I appreciate her talent and wisdom. She is the best in the business.

I also thank my literary agent, Alex Hoyt, for his capable efforts and talents, Faith Hansen for her great copy editing skills, and Susan McDermott, acquisitions editor at Prentice Hall, for her support and interest in the project.

Kudos are also extended to Carolyn Porter and Alan Gadney at One-On-One Book Production and Marketing for their various efforts and Blanche Mackey for the jacket photograph.

I offer my warmest appreciation to friend and fellow attorney Stanley A. Spiegler, who taught me more about the practice of labor and employment law than he could ever realize and Faye DeWitt, President of Book Call in New Canaan, Connecticut and her staff for their efforts in timely and efficiently fulfilling all book orders through the 1-800-255-2665 service.

Thanks are given to my brother and law partner Jonathan Scott Sack, Esq., for his love and interest in my work. Of course, personal gratitude is extended to my wife Gwen, who provides the nourishment and support to enable me to work such long hours "stress free" during my writing activities.

I also acknowledge Dr. Subhi Gulati, who literally saved my life, my mother, Judith, and my extended family and friends for their constant love and encouragement.

Gratitude is given to my sons Andrew and David for future dreams.

As always, I wish to express my appreciation and gratitude to my father, Bernard, whose insights and dreams helped make this book a reality.

Finally, special thanks must be given to those legislators, lawyers, judges and others who have enacted and enforce legislation to protect women in the workplace.

AUTHOR'S NOTE

The information in this book is my attempt to reduce complex and confusing law to practical general legal strategies. These strategies are meant to serve as helpful guidelines and concepts to think about in all legal decisions affecting your job. They are not intended as legal advice per se, because laws vary considerably throughout the 50 states and the law can be interpreted differently depending on the particular facts of each case. Thus, it is important to consult experienced counsel regarding the applicability of any strategy or point of information contained herein.

In addition, this book is sold with the understanding that the publisher is not engaged in rendering legal, accounting, or other professional service. If legal advice or other professional assistance is required, the services of a competent professional must always be sought. Finally, fictitious names have been used throughout the work and any similarity to actual persons, places or events is purely coincidental.

CONTENTS

CHAPTER FOUR   83
On-the-Job Benefits and Policies, Including Pregnancy and Family Leave

CHAPTER FIVE   119
On-the-Job Rights and Conduct

CHAPTER SIX 147

Sex Discrimination, Sex Harassment, and Other Forms of Discrimination

CHAPTER SEVEN 201

What to Do If You Are Fired

AGREEMENTS, FORMS, AND SAMPLE LETTERS INCLUDED IN THIS BOOK

INTRODUCTION

Female workers enjoy a unique status in the eyes of the law. As a protected class, you cannot be discriminated against on the basis of your sex or harassed on the job. In many instances, the law requires employers to offer equal pay for similar positions when compared to male counterparts. You are protected against unfair firings and retaliation as a result of becoming pregnant or caring for a newborn child. These are just a few of the many legal protections women possess.

Unfortunately, most women are not aware of these rights and do not know how to use them effectively. As a practicing labor lawyer, I see the mistakes people make. Many don't receive promised benefits, such as year-end bonuses, commissions, health insurance, and overtime pay. Others do not know how to react when asked discriminatory questions at a hiring interview. Still others are fired without cause or notice through no fault of their own and do not know how to successfully negotiate a severance package. Many often make hasty, uninformed decisions.

One of the most frustrating aspects of practicing law is telling a client she waited too long before taking action or that a case could have been worth a great deal of money if the right moves had been made. In fact, millions of dollars are lost each year by female workers who have valid claims, but who fail to take appropriate action.

That is the purpose behind *The Working Woman's Legal Survival Guide*. Because it is essential to know how to protect your job and livelihood, this book is intended to serve as a visit to a lawyer's office where you will find valuable information, advice, and counsel. Whatever your experience or the type of job or industry you work in, this book offers practical advice and numerous preventive steps to take to avoid problems before being hired, while working, and after a firing or resignation. *It was written to give women the edge.*

I am consulted by hundreds of female clients each year. To make this book relevant and useful, I have addressed specific job issues that pertain primarily and sometimes exclusively to women. Instead of making this book a treatise on general employee rights, I focused my attention on the key topics my female clients typically seek guidance. Consequently, the practical strategies contained in this book cover areas where women are commonly misinformed and exploited, including pregnancy, child care, and maternity issues, discrimination problems, sex harassment, equal pay and overtime issues, part-time positions, and problems affecting consultants and independent contractors.

The idea to write *The Working Woman's Legal Survival Guide* arose from the strong interest generated by my previous title *The Employee Rights Handbook: Answers To Legal Questions From Interview To Pink Slip.* As a result of this book I appeared on countless television and radio shows throughout the country to discuss employee rights and spoke to millions of Americans with job problems. It became clear that many female workers do not possess the legal knowledge necessary to protect their rights.

This book contains practical strategies and tips for virtually all the legal decisions you will make concerning a job. It will help you detect problems before they occur and make you aware of the legal consequences of your acts. If litigation becomes necessary, your chances of success and the value of a claim will increase substantially because you will recognize potential exploitation and know what to do about it. For example, the Equal Employment Opportunity Commission recently obtained a $1.185 million settlement in a sexual harassment case on behalf of a group of 10 women who worked for the same company. You will learn what action these women collectively took before filing a claim to preserve and strengthen a case.

These guidelines were written to give you a practicing employment lawyer's guidance when you need it. For example, in addition to knowing the key terms to discuss during employment negotiations, you will learn the proper steps to take if you resign or are fired from your job. I've included strategies to protect on-the-job and post-termination benefits as well as your reputation after a firing. All this information will assist you in anticipating and avoiding legal hassles before they occur.

I have tried to make the text easy to read and often include checklists with suggestions of questions to ask or think about. Where appropriate, I have included sample letters you can send without a lawyer to protect your rights, plus actual agreements and documents used by employment lawyers. The book also contains lists of important public and private agencies, groups, and organizations to contact for additional assistance. The glossary will help you understand the meaning of important legal terms and concepts.

This is a practical easy-to-follow legal guide I've dreamed about writing for women. In the course of writing 14 other legal books mostly dealing with labor subjects, it has become clear that many workers, unlike my business clients, are unable to obtain valuable legal strategies at a low cost. The desire to provide such information for the people who most need it prompted me to write *The Working Woman's Legal Survival Guide.*

This book was not meant to replace a lawyer, but it will help you decide if your problem requires a lawyer's assistance. If you currently have a lawyer, the information can help you work more effectively with that person and make more intelligent choices. Typically I suggest numerous courses of action to take before consulting a lawyer; such actions can prove to be invaluable once you retain one.

Many of my suggestions can be followed without the help of a lawyer to obtain satisfaction on your own. For example, you will learn what to do when:

- a company unfairly changes your compensation package
- you receive an unfair performance review or evaluation
- a male with weaker credentials and job performance is promoted to a desired position instead of you
- overtime or a strenuous job you can perform is being offered to males only
- you suspect you are being treated differently after announcing your pregnancy
- you are being retaliated against after notifying your boss about a sex harassment claim

These strategies can help prove your case, protect your job, and increase the value of a claim. If you want to maximize your efforts to collect benefits at an unemployment compensation hearing, Department of Labor or OSHA investigation, small-claims court, mediation, arbitration proceeding, or discrimination trial, information in this book will discuss how.

Numerous cases of women winning large verdicts for sex discrimination have been reported recently. For example, Chevron reportedly agreed to pay more than $8 million to settle a class action filed by 777 female employees who claimed they were discriminated against in terms of pay, promotions and assignments. A New Jersey judge upheld a $7.1 million sex discrimination jury verdict against a company after the plaintiff successfully alleged that senior managers removed her from accounts she had helped build and gave them to male brokers. After 12 years with the company, the woman was accused of poor productivity and fired. The verdict included a $5 million punitive damages award.

Publix reportedly agreed to pay $81.5 million to settle a class action lawsuit by 150,000 women who accused the big grocery chain of relegating them to dead-end, low paying jobs. The settlement applies to all women who worked at any of the 535 Publix stores in Florida, Georgia, South Carolina and Alabama since 1981. The suit was brought in 1995 by eight women who accused Publix of passing them over for raises and repeatedly denying them management jobs. They and four others who quickly joined the case said they watched as men with less experience and less seniority got promotions. Some said their requests were met with unwanted sexual advances from managers. The EEOC later joined the suit, and it was expanded to a class action covering past and current employees.

Although the Publix settlement is the largest involving supermarket chains, Lucky Stores allegedly paid $107 million to 14,000 women to settle similar allegations, and Albertson's allegedly paid a $29.4 million settlement to women and Hispanic workers. It was also reported that Safeway Stores settled for $7.5 million in a 1994 sex discrimination suit covering 20,000 employees in California.

$250 million was reportedly paid in 1992 in a suit against State Farm for a class of women who said they were denied or deterred from positions as insurance agents. And Home Depot faces a similar challenge from more than 200,000 current and former female employees who filed a class action lawsuit claiming the company's personnel structure is set up to limit their access to sales jobs, supervisor and manager positions. The lawsuit claims women are placed in positions with fewer opportunities while men are given jobs with greater advancement potential. The suit also alleges a pattern of sexual harassment and unequal pay. The case is currently proceeding to a jury trial.

I have provided you with all the practical information my clients receive, at a fraction of the cost. Keep this guide in an accessible place and refer to it before a matter arises. For example, read the applicable sections before negotiating the terms of an employment agreement. Examine and use the valuable sample forms, agreements, and sample letters to gain insights into protecting or strengthening your position. It's that simple.

The benefits of applying this information can be significant, as the following true case demonstrates:

A client recently heard me discuss the subject of employee rights on a national television show. She came to my New York City law office for a consultation. After working many years, she told me she was suddenly fired from a prestigious job with little prospect of obtaining immediate employment at her previous rate of pay. Based on something she heard me say, she believed she had been treated unfairly. After investigating the facts, I determined that although my client had been fired legally, the severance package offered to her (one week per year) was inadequate based on industry standards and offers made to comparable terminated male executives at her company.

I was hired and contacted the ex-employer. Almost immediately, the company offered an enhanced package, including paid out-placement services, extended medical benefits, $85,000 more in additional severance (equivalent to three weeks of severance per year of employment), and a favorable letter of reference. I later learned that the client initially did not think she had a case and was prepared to accept the company's offer and go away meekly after being fired. Fortunately, she saw me on television and that made all the difference.

The experience of this woman is not unique. Although no one should take a job expecting the worst, this book can help you recover money for your efforts when you have been wronged. I have tried to reduce complicated court rulings, regulations, and labor laws to simple strategies you can understand and follow. Knowledge is power. That is the concept behind *The Working Woman's Legal Survival Guide*. Knowing your job rights as a woman in all phases of your working career can enhance and protect you and your family. Thus, know the law, and above all, good luck!

Steven Mitchell Sack, Esq.
New York City

CHAPTER ONE

INITIAL CONCERNS

Significant abuses women sometimes experience prior to being hired involve being asked illegal questions during job interviews and exposure to subtle forms of sex discrimination, job misrepresentation, phony employment schemes, and problems with employment agencies.

Discrimination in employment based on gender, as well as on race, national origin, religion, age, and disability is prohibited by numerous state and federal laws, such as Title VII of the Civil Rights Act of 1964, the Age Discrimination in Employment Act, and the Americans With Disabilities Act of 1990, among other laws. These laws protect women from discrimination during various stages of the pre-employment selection process including screening and job requirements, responding to advertisements and brochures, and during the interview.

SCREENING AND JOB REQUIREMENTS

Screening takes place before job applicants are formally interviewed. Proper screening procedure begins with the development of an accurate, detailed job description so that applicants know the type of job that is being offered. Any action that directly or indirectly places limitations on women because of gender is unlawful, especially when it deprives a disproportionate number of women from applying for a position. Some employers illegally screen women from potential jobs on the basis of a perception of physical inability to perform the job offered. For example, an ad or brochure may say "women need not apply." This is probably illegal. Only in certain limited situations are bona fide occupational qualifications (called BFOQs) deemed to be genuine considerations in hiring. Sometimes women are beneficiaries of BFOQs, for example, being offered a job as a clothing model.

A female applicant cannot be automatically screened out because a job involves physical labor, such as heavy lifting beyond the capacity of the average woman; nor can gender be used as a factor for determining whether an applicant will be satisfied with a particular job. BFOQs have been narrowly construed by the courts and the federal Equal Employment Opportunity Commission (EEOC), so an employer must be sure that any qualifications imposed in the screening process are significantly and directly related to successful job performance (i.e., a men's restroom attendant is a job solely for men).

Although employers cannot set a higher requirement than is needed for a job simply to attract a higher-caliber applicant, they can establish basic job requirements and work standards if these do not discriminate. However, as a result of cultural obstacles and practices, women, older applicants, and persons belonging to minority groups may be affected unfairly by job standards based on poor or nonexistent credit (many elder women have never established credit on their own) or level of educational achievement. Courts and anti-discrimination agencies insist that all requirements be related to the successful performance of the job at hand. For example, refusing to hire single custodial parents may discriminate against women, since women are more likely to have physical custody of their children.

This is also true with respect to pre-determined height and weight standards. In one case, the New York State Human Rights Commission awarded $225,000 in wages and $95,000 in emotional distress damages to four female job applicants who previously worked for Pan American World Airways and sought jobs with Delta. As part of the hiring process, the flight attendants were required to take preemployment medical examinations and answer questions pertaining to their place of birth and use of birth control devices. Most significant, woman candidates, unlike males, were required to meet "personal appearance" requirements.

Four otherwise qualified female applicants who exceeded the maximum weight permitted under the height/weight chart were rejected while males with excess weight were accepted. The women claimed that the use of sex-based appearance standards, which imposed more stringent weight and height requirements on females than males and resulted in the denial of employment, violated federal and state discrimination laws.

At the hearing, the complainants' expert testified that the airline's sex-differentiated weight standards had no medical or occupational justification, The airline could not show that this standard was a necessary BFOQ. In fact, the employer lost its case when it was discovered it had abandoned this requirement after the initiation of the lawsuit but prior to the Commission's decision.

> **TIP:**   If you believe a company's job requirements are not directly job-related and penalize you because you are a woman, consult a labor lawyer or regional EEOC office immediately. Except in rare instances, employers are forbidden from denying employment to women because of their gender, and it is not sufficient to show a lack of discriminatory intent when a company's selection process favors one class of applicant over another.

ADVERTISEMENTS

Employers are not permitted to place ads in newspapers that declare preferences on the basis of gender, such as "Help Wanted-Male" or "Young, Attractive Receptionist Wanted." The Department of Labor and the EEOC state that help wanted notices or advertisements containing any reference to sex or age (such as "age 25 to 35 preferred" or "recent male college graduate") violate the law. However, requesting an experienced, mature female worker in an advertisement is not illegal since this does not discriminate against older female workers. If you seek to apply for a job through an illegal ad that affects you adversely, speak to a lawyer immediately.

ILLEGAL INTERVIEW QUESTIONS

During the interview, women are often the target of illegal hiring questions. Years ago, employers could ask almost any question they wanted of a job candidate. Questions could be asked about marital status, credit history, childbearing plans, and age. Such questions are now illegal. Questions pertaining to marital status, sexual preference, pregnancy, future childbearing plans, unwed motherhood, child care, and the number and ages of children (for example, "Who will look after your child if you are hired?" "Do you have children under the age of five?" "Do you have a boyfriend?" "What form of birth control, if any, do you use?" "If you become pregnant while working would you continue to work?" "Are you married?" "Does your husband support your decision to work?") are illegal.

Employers are allowed to ask questions to learn about a candidate's motivation and personality. Such questions can relate to former job responsibilities and outside interests. However, inquiries into an applicant's sex life are illegal, and this applies to all private employers, employment agencies, labor organizations, and training programs. In addition, each state has its own discrimination laws, which often go further in protecting the rights of female applicants during job interviews.

Job interviews must be conducted in accordance with formal objective guidelines for evaluating a job applicant's qualifications. Skills, experience, motivation, ambition, and interests are generally permissible subjects of preemployment inquiries. However, women are often singled out because of their gender, and it is a violation of Title VII for employers to require information about child care arrangements from female applicants only. Saying to a female applicant, "Joy, given the fact that you've got one child entering kindergarten and another in junior high school, do you really want to take on a job with so much overtime?" is illegal. It is better for the employer to state that the job involves a lot of overtime and ask all applicants if they have a problem working in excess of 40 hours per week.

> **TIP:** The same is true with respect to an inquiry relating to an applicant's anticipated duration of stay on the job or anticipated absences. Such questions are allowed only if both male and female applicants are asked the same questions.

Innocent questions often result in employers having to defend charges of discrimination filed with the EEOC and various state agencies, including the Human Rights Commission and the Attorney General's Office. When charges of discrimination are filed, the burden of proof usually falls on the employer to show that all preemployment questions are job-related and not discriminatory. If discrimination is found, an applicant may be awarded damages, including a job offer, attorney costs, and other benefits. Following enactment of the Civil Rights Act of 1991, successful claimants may also demand jury trials and receive compensatory damages (i.e., money paid for emotional pain and suffering) of up to $300,000, depending on the employer's size, and punitive damages, plus legal fees and money for expert witnesses who testify at the trial. Thus, employers face lost productivity, poor publicity, and expensive legal fees costs and verdicts for sloppy pre-employment interviewing techniques.

Although the federal Americans With Disabilities Act of 1990 has been in existence for more than seven years, many employers are not knowledgeable about the law's sweeping effects in the area of pre-employment inquiries. The ADA is designed to eliminate discrimination against persons with disabilities in connection with a wide range of activities. The employment provisions apply to employers with 15 or more employees (state law often reduces that number). The ADA expressly forbids employers from conducting preemployment medical examinations or making preemployment inquiries about disabilities. The EEOC enforces the ADA through investigators who are trained to uncover whether employers ask questions at the pre-offer stage that are likely to elicit information about a disability. Such questions, whether asked in person or on an employment application, are illegal.

Additionally, according to the Older Workers Benefit Protection Act, employers are forbidden from discussing or asking any questions pertaining to a person's age. Thus, if you are an older (i.e., over 40) job applicant and are told that you "lack formal education credits," "are overqualified," "are overspecialized," or that the company is "looking to hire someone with a more recent college degree," speak to a labor lawyer if you are denied a job. Recent cases demonstrate it may be illegal for a company to refuse to hire an older female applicant by arguing that being overqualified for a position means that the applicant is unqualified for the position. (Note: Simply showing that a younger individual was hired over a qualified older applicant does not prove age discrimination if the employer can demonstrate the decision was based on an honest evaluation of the candidate's qualifications, e.g., the prospective employee would be bored or likely to leave upon finding a better job, or both.)

The chart beginning on page 7 illustrates interview questions that are legal, as well as those found illegal under EEOC guidelines and state regulations. Note that the same questions may be either legal or illegal depending on the employer's intent in asking. For instance, asking a woman her maiden name is legal if the employer needs the information to verify past employment records, but not if the intent is to check family background. Thus, the chart should be viewed only as a guide since some questions that are indicated as being illegal may be asked in certain situations (for example, where the applicant is applying for a security-sensitive job).

The potential illegality of such questions must always be examined in the context in which they are asked. (Note: And once you are hired, an employer may have a legitimate business reason for asking your marital status, since it may be relevant for family health insurance coverage and tax deduction purposes.) However, the chart is instructive because female applicants often do not understand the illegality of commonly asked questions.

Looking at the questions in this chart, it is apparent that many female job applicants are exploited, since employers often ask illegal questions routinely. It is also illegal for an employer to ask for photographs or references from clergy before hiring and to ask discriminatory questions after the formal interview has concluded (e.g., during lunch after the interview but before the decision to hire has been made, when saying good-bye, or when talking to the applicant in the waiting area).

TIP: Answers to post-interview questions are not supposed to be considered during the hiring process, but the ramifications of asking illegal questions in informal settings are just as serious. Avoid volunteering information in such informal settings where possible.

STEPS TO TAKE TO AVOID BEING A VICTIM

Review the chart to understand what questions are illegal. Examine all employment applications and forms that contain discriminatory questions. If you feel that a question is discriminatory, such as if you are asked if you have any plans to raise a family, point this out to the interviewer. Be tactful. Explain that you believe the question is illegal and that you decline to answer it for that reason. Some

INTERVIEW QUESTIONS AND THE LAW

Subject	Legal	Illegal
Name	■ What is your full name? ■ Have you ever worked under a different name? If so, what name? ■ What is the name of your parent or guardian? (but only in the case of a minor job applicant) ■ What is your maiden name? (but only to check prior employment or education)	■ Have you ever changed your name by court order or other means?
Residence	■ What is your address? ■ How long have you been a resident of this state? of this city? ■ What is your phone number?	■ Do you rent or own your home? ■ How long have you lived in the US? ■ Do you live with someone? If so, what is your relationship with that person?
Marital Status	■ What is your marital status?	■ Are you married, single, divorced, separated, engaged, or widowed? ■ Are you the head of the household? ■ Are you the principal wage earner? ■ Should we call you Mrs., Miss, or Ms.? ■ Where does your spouse work? ■ What does your spouse do? ■ When do you plan to marry? ■ Do you plan on having children? ■ Who will care for the children while you work?

INTERVIEW QUESTIONS AND THE LAW (CONTINUED)

Subject	Legal	Illegal
Marital Status (cont'd)		▪ What is your spouse's health insurance coverage? ▪ How much does your spouse earn? ▪ What is your view on ERA? ▪ What is your view on abortion? ▪ Are you a feminist? ▪ Do you advocate the use of birth control or family planning?
Child Care	▪ Is there any reason that you will not be able to report to work on time each day? (only if asked of all applicants)	▪ Do you have any young children at home? ▪ Do you have a baby-sitter? ▪ How old are your children?
Credit	▪ If hired, would you allow us to order a credit report to confirm statements made on your employment application (provided you receive a copy)?	▪ Do you have any credit problems? ▪ Have you recently filed for personal bankruptcy? ▪ Is your salary presently subject to legal attachment or wage garnishment?
Disability	▪ Do you currently use illegal drugs? ▪ Have you ever been convicted for driving under the influence? ▪ Would you submit to a company-paid physical or provide a doctor's certificate of health after being offered the job?	▪ What medications are you currently taking? ▪ Have you ever been treated for drug use? ▪ How often did you use drugs in the past? ▪ Are you an alcoholic? How much and how frequently do you drink?

INTERVIEW QUESTIONS AND THE LAW (CONTINUED)

Subject	Legal	Illegal
Disability (cont'd)		▪ Do you have a disability that would interfere with your ability to perform the job? ▪ Have you ever filed for workers' compensation benefits? ▪ Have you ever been injured on the job? ▪ Do you have AIDS? ▪ Do you have cancer? ▪ Have you ever been treated for mental health problems? ▪ Have you ever been unable to handle work-related stress? ▪ How many sick days were you out last year? ▪ Why were you sick so often? ▪ Have you ever been compensated for injuries?
Job Requirements	▪ Can you lift heavy objects with or without reasonable accommodations? (only if the job directly requires this)	
Organizations	▪ List all organizations in which your membership is relevant to this job.	▪ List all clubs, societies, and lodges to which you belong.
Age	▪ Are you old enough to work? ▪ Are you between 18 and 65 years of age? If not, state your age.	▪ How old are you? ▪ What is your date of birth? ▪ Why did you decide to seek employment at your age?

INTERVIEW QUESTIONS AND THE LAW (CONTINUED)

Subject	Legal	Illegal
Religion		▪ What is your religion? ▪ Are you available to work on the Sabbath? ▪ What religious holidays do you observe? ▪ What church do you attend?
National Origin		▪ What is your ancestry? Place of birth? ▪ What is your maiden name? ▪ What is your spouse's nationality? ▪ What is your mother's native language?
Color		▪ What is your skin coloring? ▪ Do you date men outside of your religion or color?
Language	▪ Do you speak a foreign language? If so, which one?	▪ What is your native tongue? ▪ How did you acquire the ability to read, write, and speak a foreign language?
Relatives	▪ Names of relatives already employed by this company.	▪ Names, addresses, ages and other pertinent information concerning your spouse, children, or relatives not employed by the company. ▪ What type of work does your mother/father do?
Arrest Record	▪ Have you ever been convicted of a crime within the past seven years? ▪ Do you have a valid driver's license?	▪ Have you ever been arrested? ▪ Have you ever pled guilty to a crime? ▪ Have you ever been in trouble with the law?

employers will appreciate your candor and may be impressed by your knowledge of the law. Others may feel you are a threat and may decline to offer you the job. If you believe you were denied a job based on a refusal to answer discriminatory questions or if you gave an answer to a discriminatory question because you feared that failure to do so would jeopardize your chances of employment, you can file a complaint with an appropriate agency to protect your rights. These agencies include a state or local human rights office or a regional office of the Equal Employment Opportunity Commission. You may also wish to contact a private lawyer for advice and guidance.

One job candidate did just that and was awarded $15,000 in compensatory damages and $30,000 in punitive damages by the EEOC from an employer who asked an improper question during a job interview and failed to hire the applicant as a result of her answer.

If you believe you were victimized, document your complaint by writing a letter similar to the one on the following page. Follow up the letter by contacting the agency to confirm that action is being taken to protect your rights. Speak to a lawyer to determine your options if you are not satisfied with the progress of the investigation. You should also consider filing a formal discrimination lawsuit through either a private attorney (after an investigation by a state agency or the EEOC) if you were denied a job by refusing to answer discriminatory questions or furnishing answers to illegal questions. Sometimes it is not necessary to hire a lawyer because a state agency or EEOC will sue on your behalf.

COUNSEL COMMENTS: Some applicants innocently provide illegal information. Employers are trained to circumvent the law at an interview by asking the applicant a general question such as "Tell us about yourself." The applicant then volunteers personal information the employer has no right to hear, such as "Well, I'm married to a teacher, we have two young children, and I desire a position with your firm because I'm bored of being a housewife and want to wait several years before having more children."

Thus, try to limit what you say and avoid volunteering personal information at an interview where possible.

Sample Letter to File Complaint of Discrimination During a Job Interview

Your Name
Street Address
Telephone Number
Date

Name of Official
Title
Name of Agency
Address

Re: Charge of Discrimination By ABC Employer

Dear (Name),

This letter is a formal protest against certain hiring practices of (name of Employer) which I believe are illegal.

On (date), I was interviewed by (name and title of employee) for the position of (state). The interview took place at (specify). During the interview (name of employee) asked the following questions which I believe were illegal under federal and state law: (specify).

I explained to the interviewer that such questions were improper and refused to answer them. The interviewer told me that such questions were routinely asked of all job candidates and that the interview would be terminated immediately if I chose not to answer them.

The interviewer then told me I had "an attitude problem" and that the position was no longer available. Based on this, I believe I have been victimized by discrimination since I am highly qualified for the job in question and was never given an adequate opportunity to display my qualifications.

I authorize you to investigate this matter on my behalf if it is determined that my charges have merit. You may also institute legal proceedings if appropriate. I am available to meet with you at your office at a mutually convenient date to furnish you with additional details and can be reached at (provide available telephone numbers).

Thank you for your cooperation and attention in this matter.

Very truly yours,

Your Name

Send certified mail, return receipt requested

PHONY EMPLOYMENT SCHEMES

Many women seek to work part-time from their homes and are often exposed to phony advertisements and employment scams promising large income for part-time work or offering jobs with unlimited earning potential. The following is an example of a typical ad:

OVER $1000 PER WEEK possible by working at home.

Manage your own time; no prior experience necessary.

Newspapers are filled with ads for such jobs. However, many of these ads are misleading, Applicants sometimes travel great distances at their own expense to apply. They then learn that a large amount of some product (for example, $5,000 worth) must be purchased in order to sell and be hired.

TIP: As a general rule, be skeptical of work-at-home employment ads. Many ads turn out to be envelope-stuffing pyramid schemes requiring people to purchase introductory mailing lists. These lists actually cost more than you can possibly earn from work-at-home activities.

Always beware of companies you can't communicate with by telephone, especially those that only list a post office box address. This is because there may be no one to reach when you have questions about the work or have not received agreed-upon payments.

It is also a good idea to understand how much money and time you will be required to expend to get started and whether the job requires special training or skills. Inquire about refund policies. Once a finished product is completed by you, who is required to sell it?

Most importantly, never commence work at home until you understand the amount of compensation and how often you will be paid. Avoid working for long periods of time without being paid; demand to receive payment on a regular basis (never less than once a month). That way you can cut your losses if the company misses a payment.

Finally, if you are buying a work-at-home franchise, demand to review all the written documents concerning the venture, including the prospectus, before you invest. Speak to your lawyer, accountant and similar franchise owners for advice whenever possible.

If you believe you have been victimized by an employment scam or a work-at-home advertisement, you have options. You can contact a lawyer or Legal Aid service to protect your rights and take action on your behalf. Such action could include filing a private lawsuit based on fraud and misrepresentation. Some lawsuits even allow you to sue the officers of an employer in their individual capacities. If the amount of money is relatively small, e.g., under $3,000, and the employer is located nearby, you might consider suing the company yourself in small-claims court in the county where the company maintains a principal office.

Additionally, you can contact the nearest regional office of the Federal Trade Commission, the Better Business Bureau, or the U.S. Post Office. Numerous federal and state laws have been enacted, including the Uniform Deceptive Trade Practices Act, the Racketeer Influenced and Corrupt Organizations Act (RICO), and other mail and labor statutes, preventing organizations from engaging in a variety of phony employment schemes or using the mails to further such schemes.

The Federal Trade Commission has the authority to investigate claims and impose cease and desist orders prohibiting the continuation of illegal activity by phony employers. Each state's attorney general's office maintains a division for labor fraud and other related deceptive employment practices. In certain cases, the U.S. Post Office has the power to issue a court order preventing employers from using the mails or receiving mail.

Whenever you are in doubt about a particular employer or an individual representing an employer offering a potentially lucrative work-at-home proposition, contact your local Better Business Bureau. Explain the proposal to a representative. Ask for his or her opinion. Inquire whether anyone has complained about the organization in the past. Most Better Business Bureaus maintain lists of employers and individuals accused of engaging in phony employment-related practices. Obtaining such information before spending money in a dubious venture is a wise move.

JOB MISREPRESENTATION

Job misrepresentation typically occurs before the offer is made. Statements and comments are made to female applicants concerning job security, promised benefits, and exemplary working conditions that never materialize. For example, to induce a female job candidate to leave her current company, she is told, "We offer flexible hours and child care assistance." Impressed by such a statement, the candidate resigns from her position and accepts employment, only to later learn that no assistance is available.

Promising benefits or earnings that never materialize can cause an employer to be liable under various legal causes of action. If the person making a statement of fact knew the comment was false when made, and the applicant relies on such a statement to her detriment (such as resigning a lucrative position and relocating to the new employer in a different state), the employer may be held accountable for damages under theories of fraud, fraud in the inducement, misrepresentation, and negligent misrepresentation. A legal trend called truth-in-hiring is emerging in some states that holds employers accountable for promises made at the interview. Additionally, some employees are suing employers for breach of contract and breach of an implied contract when promises are made concerning job security that are never kept. For example, if a statement is made such as "We never fire anyone around here except for cause," but you are terminated suddenly for no reason, you may have a valid breach of contract claim.

When applicants are exposed to exaggerated earning claims (such as, "If you come to work for us you will make $75,000 in commissions this year, based on what our other salespeople make.") that are untrue, the Federal Trade Commission considers such statements to be an unfair and deceptive trade practice when promises of earnings exceed the average net earnings of other employees or sales reps at the company.

> **TIP:** Be on the alert when a potential employer makes claims regarding guaranteed earnings, job security, or conditions of employment. Ask the employer to put all claims in writing for your protection. Talk to other employees who currently work there to see if the company delivers on its promises. Document all promises and write down the date, time, location, and names of all witnesses who overheard such statements. This may help your lawyer if you are asserting a lawsuit to enforce such promises.

With respect to guaranteed earning claims, ask to see the wage statements (for example, W-2s or 1099s) of other people at the company to confirm such claims. If the employer tells you such information is confidential, suggest that the names of the employees be concealed. If the employer refuses to do this or cannot provide factual information to support such claims, think twice before accepting the job.

Smart applicants thoroughly investigate potential employers before accepting employment. By learning facts about the employer's business reputation, credit rating, financial standing, rate of employee turnover, morale problems with workers, and whether the company has recently been involved in any employee-related lawsuits, you may be able to detect whether you will be working for a dishonest employer who doesn't care much about its workforce. Information on how to investigate employers is discussed in Chapter Three, *Getting Hired*.

PROMISES OF JOB SECURITY

Courts in some states are ruling that employees have the right to rely on representations made before hiring. In a growing number of recent cases throughout the country, some discharged employees are suing and winning lawsuits against ex-employers for breach of oral agreements promising secure employment and even jobs for life. While courts have generally recognized that employers may be bound by written assurances and statements made in employee manuals, handbooks, and work rules, they are now increasingly willing to consider oral contracts extended by management and company officers having the apparent authority to make such promises.

In some states, informal off-the-cuff oral assurances can bind the company. For example, a Michigan jury in one case awarded $1.1 million to a worker based on a claim of an oral promise of lifetime employment. In that case, the jury found the existence of a valid, oral contract and ruled that the company unjustifiably breached that contract when the employee was terminated.

> **TIP:** Interviewers, recruiters, and other intake personnel are often advised never to say anything at the hiring interview that can be construed as a promise of job security. Try to remember all statements that imply anything other than an at-will relationship. For example, if you hear the words "permanent employment," "job for life," or the requirement that "just cause only" must be shown

Allison was invited to apply for a job as the marketing director at a large corporation. During the interview, Allison made it clear how happy she was at her present position. In front of several people, a senior vice president assured her that if she resigned from her present position she would have secure employment as long as sales increased.

Relying on this promise, Allison accepted the position and worked very hard. Although sales increased dramatically every year after she came aboard, she was suddenly fired without cause or notice.

The company offered Allison a small severance package. She consulted an employment lawyer who sued the company for breach of contract. The parties settled out of court for a substantial settlement (two years' salary plus other benefits) after the senior vice president admitted under oath at a pretrial deposition what he promised Allison.

before being terminated, or are given broad assurances regarding job longevity, continued employment, or promises regarding career opportunities, write these statements down, including the time and place the words were spoken (and in front of whom) for future reference if applicable.

Even when employee handbooks and written personnel guidelines make it clear that no employee's job is guaranteed, there are circumstances when an oral assurance of secure employment may bind the employer assuming:

1. The discharged employee can prove such a statement was made;
2. The statement was a crucial factor in the decision to accept the job or decline another job with a competitor; and
3. The employee reasonably relied on such a promise and suffered damages as a result.

These were the facts with a national sales manager for a New Jersey company who worked four years and then was fired. At the trial she claimed that four months before getting fired the president had persuaded her to turn down a job offer from a competitor by a promise of lifetime employment. Although the company argued that the words were merely friendly assurances and weren't enforceable, the court ruled that the president's remarks had persuaded the employee to stay and could constitute a contract. In this case it was proved that a better employment opportunity was turned down based on the employee's reliance on an oral promise of permanent employment.

> **COUNSEL COMMENTS:** Companies are protected to a certain extent in this area because many employees have difficulty proving such statements were made, or that although made, no approval came from the company's president or board of directors (the only ones with legal authority to bind the company to an important promise). However, when a supervisor or officer who allegedly made such a statement has died, no longer works for the company and can't be located, or left under unpleasant terms, companies may be unable to rebut the employee's statements if a lawsuit is commenced. Some courts have ruled that conversations conducted in an atmosphere of critical one-on-one negotiation regarding terms of future employment may give rise to a contract of lifetime employment. One court held that an employee could be terminated only "for cause" (i.e., a good reason like insubordination or stealing but not for inadequate work performance) where the employee had inquired about job security during the job interview and the employer had agreed that the employee would be employed "as long as she does the job."

However, recognize that promises of permanent or lifetime employment from low- or middle-level company officials may not legally bind the employer. In many cases even the president does not have the authority to give a lifetime contract without the written approval of the company's board of directors; in some states (e.g., California) employment contracts that exceed a specified number of years are unenforceable.

> **TIP:** Try to get the company to offer you a secure job so that you can't be fired without adequate notice or an opportunity to correct deficient performance. This is discussed in Chapter Three, *Getting Hired*.

CHECKING REFERENCES

The majority of states limit an employer's ability to make preemployment inquiries regarding criminal arrests and convictions beyond a certain number of years and restrict the use of such information. Some employers have been held legally liable to applicants for defamation, intentional infliction of emotional distress, and violations of the implied covenant of good faith and fair dealing when references are not investigated properly or are leaked to nonessential third parties. In one case, someone terminated from an insurance company several years ago discovered that his former boss, in responding to reference checks, had called him "untrustworthy, disruptive, paranoid, hostile, irrational, a classic sociopath." He sued, and a jury decided those characterizations were out of line, a mistake that cost the company $1.9 million.

Laws have been enacted to protect women in this area. For example, as a result of the 1990 Americans with Disabilities Act (ADA), the review and investigation of a person's medical history has been virtually eliminated. According to the Bankruptcy Code, no private employer may deny employment to someone who filed for bankruptcy or who is married to someone who has been or is bankrupt. Also, the EEOC has stated that refusal to hire candidates with poor credit (often minorities and women) is illegal since such groups are more likely to be unable to pay their bills and such a policy effectively excludes a class of applicant from the job market.

In the majority of states and under the federal Consumer Credit Protection Act, it is illegal for a company to fire a person being sued for the nonpayment of a debt or when the company is instructed to cooperate in the collection of a portion of the person's wages through garnishment proceedings for any one indebtedness. Enforcement of this federal law is tough and violations are punishable by a fine of up to $1,000 and imprisonment for up to one year. Discharge for garnishment for more than one indebtedness is not prohibited. However, such a policy may be restricted by Title VII of the Civil Rights Act of 1964 when it has a disproportionate effect on minority and female workers.

TIP: Under the federal Fair Debt Credit Reporting Act, employers are generally forbidden to use credit reports for hiring or employment decisions unless the job is security-sensitive or the financial integrity of the applicant is essential to successful job performance. If such a report is made, ask for a copy to be sure it is accurate, together with the name and address of the credit agency supplying it. This way you may immediately be able to explain important errors that sometimes need to be corrected on credit reports.

TESTING

A great percentage of large employers now routinely test job applicants before hiring. Pre-employment drug and alcohol tests have generally been upheld as legal when all applicants must submit to such tests and are warned in advance that the failure to take the test will cause them not to be considered for the position. For certain types of jobs involving airline pilots, railroad employees, and motor carriers who operate commercial motor vehicles in interstate commerce, drug testing is required by the U.S. Department of Transportation.

> **TIP:** Pre-employment drug and alcohol testing is prohibited in some states as violating a person's right to privacy, so check your local state's law where applicable. Also, the ability to test does not give potential employers the right to handle test results carelessly. Some states impose strict guidelines as to the manner in which job applicants can be tested (for example, by giving reasonable notice before the test is administered and stating how specimens will be handled and safeguarded). Unwarranted disclosure of test results can result in huge damages by successfully asserting legal claims of wrongful discharge, slander, defamation, and invasion of privacy, especially if you are denied a job on the basis of an alleged failure and it is later determined there was a mistake with the test results. Consult a competent lawyer when you believe you have been exploited or injured in this area.

The federal Polygraph Protection Act of 1988 prohibits applicants from submitting to lie detector tests before hiring. Additionally, most states have enacted laws protecting job applicants from stress tests, psychological evaluator tests, and other honesty tests. In one reported case, a large retailer required thousands of applicants to take a detailed psychological test as a prerequisite to being hired. The test contained questions designed to elicit information about an applicant's sexual orientation and preference. One question asked a candidate to state whether the person had indulged in "unusual" sex practices or preferred members of their same sex as partners. A class action lawsuit was filed, alleging violations of privacy and discrimination laws. The retailer admitted wrongdoing in an out-of-court settlement, and agreed to pay $1.3 million to more than 2,000 applicants who took the test, and destroy all test results.

> **COUNSEL COMMENTS:** Although legitimate psychological tests may exist, they may still be discriminatory. The EEOC has ruled that any test with a hidden bias or which unfairly penalizes women is illegal.

EMPLOYMENT AGENCIES, CAREER COUNSELORS, AND SEARCH FIRMS

The main purpose of an employment agency is to find a job for you. Career counselors and search firms offer additional services such as resume and letter preparation, training in interview techniques, and providing job leads. Career counselors typically do not obtain jobs for applicants.

Inexperienced applicants can be exploited by dishonest employment agencies. While some applicants are charged exorbitant placement fees, others pay large, non-refundable fees for job interviews that do not result in jobs. Still others are asked discriminatory questions at the initial interview or are told to register for courses (for which the agency gets a fee) before they are sent out on interviews.

A search firm placed an ad in a nationally known newspaper that read:

> *We Use Our Contacts, Methods, Experience, Research Facilities, and Equipment To Obtain Interviews For You in the Unpublished, Unadvertised Job Marketplace. Positions are Available for qualified executives, managers and professionals in the $20,000 to $60,000 range in corporations, associations and foundations.*

The ad attracted several hundred individuals, who reportedly paid advance fees ranging from $500 to $8,000. Most of these people never received any placement assistance or contacts.

To avoid being exploited, understand fully the terms of any arrangement. Ask the following questions before you agree to be represented by an employment agency, search firm, or career counselor:

Questions to Ask Before Beginning Working With an Employment Agency, Search Firm, or Career Counselor

- Is the firm licensed? (Note: In some states, employment agencies are licensed and regulated by the Department of Consumer Affairs. To obtain a license, the agency must fill out a detailed application, post a performance bond, maintain accurate financial records, and avoid engaging in illegal acts. Career counselors and search firms generally are not required to be licensed to conduct business.)

- What are the precise services the firm or individual will render?

- What is required of the job applicant (prepare a resume, buy interviewing attire, etc.)?

- When will the firm or individual earn its fee: When you are offered a job by an acceptable employer, when you accept the job, or when you have worked a minimum amount of time?

- What is the maximum fee to be charged?

- Who will pay for the fee, you or the employer? When is it payable?

- What happens if you decide not to accept a job that is offered?

- Is a deposit required once a job is accepted?

- Will you receive a detailed description of each potential employer before you go on an interview, including the name, address, kind of work to be performed, title, amount of wages or compensation, hours, whether the work is temporary or permanent?

- Will the agency investigate whether the potential employer has defaulted in the payment of salaries to others during the past five years?

- What happens to the fee if you resign or are fired within a short period of time?

- Will the agency help you obtain another job if you are terminated?

- Does the agency have the right to represent you on an exclusive basis?

- What happens to the fee if you become disabled and cannot work?

Confirm everything in writing to avoid problems. Reputable firms will generally provide you with a written retainer agreement. Don't sign any document that is presented to you unless you understand it. If an agreement is long and complicated, discuss it with a family member, lawyer or advisor before signing.

Never pay money in advance of results. In most states it is illegal for employment agencies to charge fees before they have found a job for an applicant. Although career counselors and search firms are allowed to charge up-front fees, resist this because many people pay money to firms but never receive promised results.

Recognize common abuses before they occur. Check with your local bar association or Better Business Bureau for a description of what employment agencies, career counselors, and search firms are allowed to do and what prohibitions exist. For example, under the laws in many states, it is illegal for an employment agency to:

- induce you to terminate your job so the agency can obtain new employment for you
- publish false or misleading ads
- advertise in newspapers without providing the name and address of the agency
- send you to an employer without obtaining a job order from the employer
- require you to subscribe to publications, pay for advertising or mailing costs, enroll in special courses, or pay for additional services
- charge a placement fee when the agency represents that it was a fee-paid job
- discriminate on the basis of sex, age, or race
- require you to complete application forms that obtain different information from male and female applicants
- make false representations or promises

TIP: Don't procrastinate if an employment agency or career service takes advantage of you. The longer you wait, the harder it may be to prove your case and collect damages. If you believe you have been exploited, send a letter to the firm to document your protest. The letter should state the reasons for your dissatisfaction and the manner in which you would like the problem resolved. The letters on the following pages illustrate this. If the financial exploitation is significant, contact a lawyer immediately. In any event, if your problem is not resolved amicably, contact your local Department of Consumer Affairs or Better Business Bureau, outlining your complaint in writing. In many states these agencies have the power to investigate charges and take action, including revoking licenses, when wrongdoing is proven. If you are still dissatisfied with the outcome, you can consider suing in small-claims court or through formal litigation.

Sample Complaint Letter to Job-Search Firm

Your Name
Address
Telephone Number
Date

Name of Officer
Name of Firm
Address

Dear (Name),

On (specify date) I responded to an advertisement your firm ran in (specify newspaper or magazine). The ad specifically promised that your firm could find a job for me as a salesperson in the cosmetics industry. The ad stated that a ($XXX) advance was fully refundable in the event I could not obtain a job paying more than $20,000 per year.

Per your request, and after several telephone conversations, I sent you a check for ($XXX) which was cashed. That was four months ago. Since that time I have received one letter from you dated (specify), which states you are reviewing my employment history.

In view of the fact that you have not obtained full-time employment on my behalf, I hereby demand the return of ($XXX), per our agreement.

If I do not receive the money within 14 days from the date of this letter, be assured that I shall contact the Department of Consumer Affairs, Better Business Bureau, the frauds division of the attorney general's office, and my lawyer to commence a formal investigation.

Hopefully this can be avoided and I thank you for your immediate cooperation in this matter.

Very truly yours,

(your name)

(Send certified mail, return receipt requested.)

Follow-up Letter to Department of Consumer Affairs
(or appropriate agency)

Your Name
Address
Telephone Number
Date

Commissioner
Department of Consumer Affairs
Address

Re: Formal Complaint Against ABC Employment Agency, License
#XXXXX

Dear Commissioner,

I hereby make a formal complaint against (specify name of firm). I believe the firm has committed the following illegal acts (specify).

The facts on which I base my allegations are as follows: (state the facts in detail).

On (specify date), I sent the agency a formal demand letter requesting the return of my deposit. This letter was sent by certified mail, was received by the firm, yet I have received no response. I enclose a copy of the letter for your review together with all pertinent documentation from my files.

I request that you convene a formal investigation regarding this matter. Feel free to contact me at the above address if you need further assistance or information.

Thank you for your cooperation and attention.

Very truly yours,

(your name)

(Send certified mail, return receipt requested)

cc: the employment agency, your lawyer, Better Business Bureau
      and the frauds division of the state attorney general's office

INDEPENDENT CONTRACTORS, CONSULTANTS, SALES REPRESENTATIVES, AND STATUTORY NONEMPLOYEES

Millions of women earn their livelihood not as employees but as independent contractors. Special legal and tax rules apply to independent contractors—many of whom function as consultants, sales representatives (also called agents or brokers), and statutory non-employees. The author is consulted by countless women every year who operate as independents and who wish to learn more about protecting their job security, billings, and commissions. This chapter will offer guidance to protecting yourself properly if you are an independent contractor.

EMPLOYEE VERSUS INDEPENDENT CONTRACTOR STATUS

The IRS generally opposes independent status because companies who retain independents don't have to withhold income or employment taxes. Since a contractor can manipulate earnings by claiming all business-related expenses on Schedule C (where expenses offset gross business income), the IRS believes that many dollars of compensation go unreported. Additionally, if you are an independent contractor who is injured while working, you are not bound to collecting workers' compensation damages for your injuries. This is advantageous since larger awards typically go to claimants who commence private lawsuits for injuries than workers' compensation benefits.

As an independent contractor, however, you are not permitted to file for unemployment benefits after a job has ended or you are terminated unless it is determined at the unemployment hearing that you are legally an employee. You probably cannot avail yourself of employer-provided disability and health insurance plans, and may have to establish your own retirement and pension plans. Since you will receive an IRS Form 1099 and not a W-2 form with deductions withheld, you are responsible to pay all applicable social security, unemployment insurance, state and local income taxes, and workers' compensation insurance benefits for any people you employ. Under the laws of many states, you probably will have a more difficult time asserting discrimination claims. Furthermore, you cannot assert claims for overtime since wage and hour laws apply only to employees. (Note: In a recent ruling however, the 9th U.S. Circuit Court of Appeals rejected Microsoft's attempt to withhold benefits from workers it said were freelancers rather than employees. The Court stated that the practice of hiring temporary employees or independent contractors as a means of avoiding payment of certain employee benefits was troubling. Microsoft has appealed the decision.)

No precise legal definition of an independent contractor exists, and each state has its own laws to determine whether an individual is an employee or an independent contractor. When the courts attempt to determine the difference, they analyze the facts of each particular case. Significant factors courts look for when making this distinction are:

1. The company's right of control over the worker;

2. Whether the individual works exclusively for the company or is permitted to work for others at the same time;

3. Whether the parties have a written agreement that defines the status of the worker and states she is not considered an employee for the purposes of the Federal Contributions Act and the Federal Unemployment Tax Act and that the individual must pay all self-employment and federal income tax;

4. Whether the individual controls her own work schedule and the number of working hours; and

5. Operates from her own place of business (or pays rent if an office is provided) and supplies her own stationery and business cards not at the company's expense.

Typically, employees undertake to achieve an agreed result and to accept an employer's directions as to the manner in which the result is accomplished, while independent contractors agree to achieve a certain result but are not subject to the orders of the employer as to the means that were used. In each case, the court looks at the specific facts in making its determination. For instructive purposes, the company's right of control is best explained by the use of examples. Courts have found workers to be employees if companies:

- have the right to supervise details of the operation
- require salespeople to collect accounts on its behalf
- provide workers with an office, company equipment, company car, and/or reimbursement for some or all expenses
- require workers to call on particular customers
- deduct income and FICA taxes from their wages or salary
- provide workers with insurance and workers' compensation benefits
- restrict their ability to work for other companies or jobs and require full-time efforts

This list is not meant to be all-inclusive, but rather to help you determine what classification you fall under. Since the law is quite unsettled, the IRS follows a summary of rules used to determine proper status. According to the IRS, an employer-employee relationship for tax purposes exists when the person for whom the services are performed has the right to control and direct the individual who performs the services, not only as to the result to be accomplished by the work, but also as to the details and means by which the result is accomplished. In this connection it is not necessary that the employer actually direct or control the manner in which services are performed; it is sufficient if the firm had the *right* to do so. The designation or description of the relationship of the parties in a written agreement other than that of an employer and employee is immaterial if such a relationship exists, and the IRS will disregard other designations (such as being called a partner, agent, consultant or independent contractor) in the agreement.

On page 31 you will find a summary of rules used by the IRS to determine proper status. Courts do consider other relevant facts and circumstances not contained in the list and may overrule initial IRS and state tax determinations where warranted.

> **TIP:** The odds of finding employee status become lower when you form a corporation and receive compensation from your corporation. The IRS may also be impressed when your corporation works for several companies and not just one.

When an initial determination is made by the IRS finding employee status, costly damages, penalties, and interest can ensue to you and the company hiring you. Speak to a competent lawyer or accountant immediately upon receiving an initial IRS or state taxing agency notice of determination or request for facts. Competent tax advice and guidance is crucial in this area.

STEPS TO TAKE TO AVOID PROBLEMS

If you are not a statutory or common law employee (which includes leased employees, part-time workers, and temporaries, all of which will be discussed in Chapter Three) you legally may be considered an independent contractor. This is so even if you call yourself a consultant or subcontractor. As an independent contractor, it is crucial to discuss all the terms and conditions of your working relationship with a company or individual. This must be done before commencing work, no matter what your trade or profession. All key terms of the relationship, including the services to be rendered, payment, stages of payment, whether expenses are to be reimbursed (and to what extent), and the length (also known as the term) of the arrangement, should be understood and agreed upon to reduce misunderstandings.

The Sample Consulting Agreement beginning on page 32 illustrates many of the points to be contained in a document. Both parties should sign the agreement to avoid future problems.

After you have come to terms, it is essential to confirm the arrangement in writing. A handshake, or oral agreement, only indicates that the parties came to some form of agreement; it does not prove what the agreement was. Failure to spell out important terms often leads to misunderstandings and disputes. Even when key terms are discussed, the same spoken words that are agreed upon have different meanings from each party's perspective; written words limit this sort of misunderstanding.

> **COUNSEL COMMENTS:** Be sure that all changes, strikeouts, and erasures are initialed by both parties and that all blanks are filled in. If additions are necessary, include them in a space provided or attach them on a separate piece of paper but refer to it in the body of the contract.

Summary of IRS Rules to Determine Employee vs. Independent Contractor Status

- **Instructions.** Employees generally follow instructions about when, where, and how work is to be performed; contractors establish their own hours and have no instructions regarding how the job should be completed.
- **Training.** Employees typically receive training via classes and meetings regarding how services are to be performed; contractors generally establish their own procedures and receive no training.
- **Services performed personally.** Services are typically performed personally by the employee; contractors may utilize others to perform job tasks and duties.
- **Supervision.** Most employees are supervised by a foreman or representative of the employer; contractors generally are not.
- **Set hours of work.** An employee's hours and days are set by the employer; contractors dictate their own time and are often retained to complete one particular job.
- **Full time required.** An employee typically works for only one employer; contractors may have several jobs or work for others at the same time.
- **Work on premises.** Employees work on the premises of an employer or on a route or site designated by the employer; contractors typically work from their own premises and pay rent for their own premises.
- **Manner of payment.** Employees are generally paid in regular amounts at stated intervals; contractors are paid upon the completion of the job or project, in a lump sum or other arrangement (such as on a commission basis).
- **Furnishing of tools and materials.** Employees are usually furnished tools and materials by employers; contractors typically furnish and pay for their own tools, materials, and expenses.
- **Profit.** Employees generally receive no direct profit or loss from work performed, while contractors do.
- **Job security.** Employees may be discharged or quit at any time without incurring liability; contractors are typically discharged after a job is completed and are legally obligated to complete a particular job to avoid liability.

(**Author's Note:** Many of these rules are followed by the IRS when determining employee or independent contractor status. Speak to an accountant or other professional for more advice when applicable.)

Sample Consulting Agreement

This Consulting Agreement (the "Agreement") is entered into this (specify date) by and between (specify parties; "Consultant" and "Company").

WHEREAS, the Company is in need of assistance in (specify area); and

WHEREAS, Consultant has agreed to perform consulting work for the Company.

NOW, THEREFORE, the parties hereby agree as follows:

1. *Consultant's Services.* Consultant shall be available and shall provide the following efforts (specify) as requested.

2. *Consideration.* The Company will pay Consultant (specify payment such as at an hourly rate, flat fee, or a commission). If for an hourly rate, then state: Consultant will submit written, signed reports of the time spent performing consulting services, itemizing in reasonable detail the dates on which services were performed, the number of hours spent on such dates, and a brief description of the services rendered. The Company will receive such reports not less than once a month and the total amount of work will not exceed (specify $). The Company shall pay Consultant the amounts due within (specify) days after such reports are received.

3. *Expenses.* Additionally, the Company will pay Consultant for the following expenses incurred while this Agreement exists: (specify, such as all travel expenses to and from work sites, meals, lodging, and related expenses). The Consultant shall submit written documentation and receipts itemizing the dates on which such expenses were incurred and the Company will pay for such expenses by separate check no later than (specify) days after receipt of same.

4. *Independent Contractor.* Nothing herein shall be construed to create an employer-employee relationship between the parties. The consideration set forth above shall be the sole payment due for services rendered. It is understood that the Company will not withhold any amounts for payment of taxes from the compensation of Consultant and that Consultant will be solely responsible to pay all applicable taxes from said payments, including payments owed to its employees and subagents.

5. *Consultant's Warranties.* The taxpayer I.D. number (or social security number) of the Consultant is (specify). The Consultant is licensed to perform the agreed-upon services enumerated herein and covenants that it maintains all valid licenses, permits, and registrations to perform same and on behalf of its employees and subagents.

6. *Competent Work.* All work will be done in a competent fashion in accordance with applicable standards of the profession and all services are subject to final approval by (specify) prior to the Company's payment.

7. *Representations and Warranties.* The Consultant will make no representations, warranties, or commitments binding the Company without the Company's prior written consent.

8. *Confidentiality.* In the course of performing services, the parties recognize that Consultant may come into contact with or become familiar with information which the Company or its affiliates or subsidiaries may consider confidential. This information may include, but is not limited to, information pertaining to (specify), which may be of value to a competitor. Consultant agrees to keep all such information confidential and not to discuss or divulge any of it to anyone other than appropriate Company personnel or their designees.

9. *Term.* This Agreement shall commence on (specify date) and shall terminate on (specify date), unless earlier terminated for any reason by either party hereto upon Thirty (30) days prior written notice.

10. *Notice.* Any notice or communication permitted or required by this Agreement shall be deemed effective when personally delivered or deposited, postage prepaid, by first-class regular mail, addressed to the other party's last known business address.

11. *Entire Agreement.* This Agreement constitutes the entire agreement of the parties with regard to the subject matter hereof, and replaces and supersedes all other agreements or understandings, whether written or oral. No amendment, extension, or change of the Agreement shall be binding unless in writing and signed by both parties,

12. *Binding Effect.* This Agreement shall be binding upon and shall inure to the benefit of Consultant and Company and to the Company's successors and assigns. Nothing in this Agreement shall be construed to permit the assignment by Consultant of any of its rights or obligations hereunder to any third party without the Company's prior written consent.

13. *Ownership.* All ideas, plans, improvements, or inventions developed by Consultant during the term of this Agreement shall belong to (specify).

14. *Governing law.* This Agreement shall be governed by the laws of the state of (specify). The invalidity or unenforceability of any provision of the Agreement shall not affect the validity or enforceability of any other provision.

WHEREFORE, the parties have executed this Agreement as of the date first written above.

By: _____
"Consultant"

By: _____
"Company"

(**Author's Note:** Modify this agreement where applicable with the assistance and guidance of an attorney or professional advisor whenever you agree to work for someone as a consultant or independent contractor.)

CONSULTANTS

A consultant is deemed to be an independent contractor by the IRS. Thus, it is important to operate legally as an independent regardless of the kind of sales promotion, marketing, engineering, or other professional services you may provide. The first step is to utilize a written agreement whenever you contract to provide services. Among other items, always confirm:

- a description of the services to be rendered
- the amount of time to be provided for such services (e.g., "no more or less than X hours per week")
- the method of compensation, whether a per diem rate, hourly rate or fixed price for the entire job. If you are to receive a flat fee, negotiate to be paid in installments with as much up-front payment as possible and never at the end of the job.
- a commission, royalty, or incentive (such as a cost reduction or savings) from your efforts
- reimbursement for travel and incidental expenses
- manner of invoice and payment
- term of the agreement
- provisions for resolving disputes, such as binding arbitration

(Note: Information about arbitration, mediation, other forms of litigation and working with a lawyer effectively are discussed in Chapters Nine and Ten.)

STATUTORY NON-EMPLOYEES

A statutory non-employee is treated the same as an independent contractor. As such, statutory non-employees are generally excluded from the protections of most workplace laws and are treated as self-employed for federal income tax, employment tax, disability, and social security benefits purposes.

Examples of statutory non-employees include licensed real estate agents and direct sellers. The IRS defines a direct seller as a person who sells goods to an end-user consumer (such as selling cosmetics door-to-door). The IRS considers direct sellers to be statutory non-employees when their compensation is a direct result of sales output, when they use a written employment agreement that specifies that they are not employees, when they control their own work schedule and are not required to report to an employer, and when their selling is done outside an established retail store or showroom.

> **TIP:** The distinction as to whether you are legally deemed a statutory non-employee or a statutory employee is not clear-cut. For example, many delivery drivers, life insurance agents, home workers, and salespeople who might not appear to be typical employees are treated as such by state laws and the IRS. If you are a statutory employee, you are covered by wage and hour laws, overtime, and tax withholding requirements imposed on employers.

SALES REPRESENTATIVES

Sales representatives (most often called "reps," "agents," or "brokers") are persons or organizations that contract to sell the products of other organizations (called "principals" or "manufacturers"). A sales rep differs from a sales employee. A sales employee is considered an employee for all purposes; even if she is paid a commission, it is taxed at the source and a W-2 IRS form is issued at the end of the year. A sales rep, however, receives no benefits; the sole method of compensation is a commission with no taxes taken out of the payment.

Up until 16 years ago there were no federal or state laws to protect an independent salesperson. Now, more than 32 states have passed legislation ensuring the prompt payment of commissions after the working relationship ends. Some states even require written contracts that specify how commissions are earned, when they must be paid, and the penalties that ensue when these procedures are not followed.

No matter what industry you sell in, reps must be knowledgeable about the pitfalls of their business and how to protect themselves before, during, and after the relationship with a principal terminates.

The first step in reducing the chances of being exploited is to take the time to investigate the principal and the line you are considering representing. For example, it is a good idea to inquire about the principal's financial history and determine whether the firm has a low turnover of sales personnel, and that it rarely ships damaged

Sales Rep Negotiating Checklist

(Author's Note: If you are a sales employee earning a commission, many of the following negotiating points should also be considered by you before accepting any sales position.)

1. *Commissions*

   - Ask if you are entitled to a draw or an advance against commissions. If so, never agree to be personally liable to repay any money when commission earnings do not exceed the draw. In most states, you are not legally obligated to repay any unearned draw later unless you promised to do so. Courts generally consider advances to be nonrefundable salary unless salespeople sign a promissory note or agreement or acknowledge by conduct that advances were intended to be a loan. Even if you leave the company before commission earnings exceed a draw, you are probably not liable to return the excess, so never promise to do so.

   - Be sure to specify when your commissions will be earned. Many principals pay commissions only after your order is accepted, shipped, and paid for in full by the customer. Avoid this arrangement if possible. Try to get paid when the order is shipped (invoiced).

   - Understand how and when deductions from your commission are computed. Principals often deduct unfair amounts as a result of returns, freight charges, billing and advertising discounts, collection charges, and off-price goods. Avoid these deductions if possible.

   - Ask to receive credit and payment for reorders (i.e., repeats of merchandise previously purchased by the customer).

   - Discuss the amount of commissions to be paid if monies are received after a collection agency or law firm collects delinquent arrears.

   - If additional services are requested for detailed forecasting or assistance in collections, request a higher commission rate.

   - Demand a stipulation that commission rates cannot be changed suddenly without your written approval and that certain key accounts cannot be designated as non-commissionable house accounts without your consent.

   - Discuss and agree on split commission policies (i.e., sales in your territory that are shipped into another rep's territory or vice versa).

2. *Territory*
   - Specify the precise territory you will represent.
   - Try to obtain a status as the exclusive rep in your territory (i.e., that the principal cannot appoint another rep to sell goods in your territory).
   - Obtain the principal's consent to sell all its products, including those introduced in the future, if possible.
   - Specify that you will receive commissions for all sales made in your territory regardless of whether the order is procured by you or received directly by the company without your assistance.
   - Specify there will be no house accounts (i.e., non-commissionable accounts in your territory).
   - Define split commission policies in advance. For example, what commission will you receive on orders accepted by customers in your territory but shipped into another salesperson's territory?

3. *Job Security*
   - Specify the start date.
   - Try to get as much job security as possible. For example, stipulate that you can continue to represent the principal on a yearly basis or as long as your sales volume exceeds $X.
   - If you cannot get at least a one-year contract, negotiate to receive as much notice of termination as possible (i.e., that you can be fired only on six months' notice). Sometimes, reps negotiate additional notice periods as the amount of time representing the principal increases. For example, a 30-day notice period becomes 60 days after the first year and 90 days after the second year.
   - During the notice period, specify that you can continue representing the line and will be paid for all orders obtained by you or procured in your territory, even if shipped after the termination date of the contract.
   - Specify that any notices of termination must be sent by certified mail, return receipt requested, so you will be sure to have received it.

4. *Termination of Arrangement*
   - Clarify when commissions stop but avoid arrangements where they cease immediately upon termination.
   - Negotiate to receive commissions for a certain period of time after termination, i.e., through the end of the selling season

or for a specified period of time thereafter (90 days after termination is often a good figure).

- Ask for severance pay (in addition to post-termination commissions) if you significantly built up a territory's volume but
are fired through no fault of your own. Reps in many industries are successfully negotiating additional severance after
termination. This means that if you are fired without cause
you may receive your average monthly commissions during
the last year multiplied by the number of years worked.

- Specify when a final accounting will be made and commissions paid after termination.

- Discuss the handling of commissions on orders "pending" or
"in the works" for sales expected but not yet consummated
before a termination. This is a common problem that typically is not addressed when the working relationship begins.
Always negotiate the right to receive commissions for orders
that are pending or accepted prior to the termination or resignation but are shipped and paid for by the customer after
the termination date ends. If you fail to ask for these things,
the principal may only pay you commissions up to the termination date.

5. *Proper Accounting*

- Negotiate to receive accurate commission reports together
with copies of all accepted orders and invoices. Proper
accounting is vital for all people earning commissions.
Negotiate to receive this information, together with the commission check, no later than the 30th day of the month following the month of shipment.

- Avoid arrangements where the principal requires you to
protest commission statements within a certain period of time
after receipt (such as 10 days), and if no notice regarding
errors is received, they will be deemed correct.

- Request the right to inspect the company's books and records
at least annually if you detect errors.

6. *Points to Avoid*

- Never accept an arrangement where you are paid commissions on a delayed basis (such as annually).

- Resist arrangements where you must call on all accounts in
your territory a certain number of times annually, service
these accounts, and maintain accurate selling records and
lead sheets of these visits.

- Avoid being required to actively assist in collection efforts. If there is such a requirement, ask what activities will be included. For example, are you merely required to call on the account periodically to ask for payment, or must you hire and pay for a collection agency on behalf of the principal?
- Never sign contracts containing restrictive covenants prohibiting you from working for a competitor, calling on key customers, or revealing confidential information or trade secrets after termination, particularly before speaking to a knowledgeable lawyer.
- Avoid signing contracts with clauses stating that any litigation must take place in the state where the principal's main office is located.

7. *Other Negotiating Points*
   - Ask the company to provide you with proof of product liability insurance naming you as a beneficiary on its policy and indemnifying and holding you harmless in any lawsuit (including the payment of legal fees incurred in defending yourself in a lawsuit) caused by injury to a customer by a product negligently designed or manufactured by the principal, or regarding patent, trademark, or copyright matters affecting the principal or its products.
   - Be sure your contract states there can be no modifications of any terms previously agreed upon unless reduced to writing and signed by both parties. This will eliminate a flagrant abuse to reps; namely, the sudden reduction of commission rates and accounts in your territory without your approval.
   - Be sure the contract states it is binding on all successors and assigns. This way, if the company is sold, the new principal will be required to honor your contract and continue to engage you as a rep.

Once you and the company have agreed to key terms, it is essential to confirm the deal in writing. Always insist on a written contract for your protection. The sample contract beginning on page 42 is used by the author with many of his sales rep clients. This agreement should always be prepared and signed by both parties to avoid future problems. It is included for illustrative purposes only, so feel free to adapt and change some of the language, such as by adding a clause obligating the company to ship a minimum percentage of your orders (called a "guaranteed shipping clause"), or providing severance pay where applicable or when suggested by your attorney, accountant, or advisor.

goods (with low returns). If you are satisfied with the company's reputation, financial picture, and track record, you must then carefully negotiate the working arrangement. Too many reps begin working without clearly defining their contract, which often leads to future misunderstandings and disputes. The comprehensive checklist beginning on page 36 describes numerous items to request, including fall-back points, during the negotiation session, regardless of the industry you sell for.

HOW TO TURN AN ORAL CONTRACT INTO A WRITTEN AGREEMENT

An oral contract is a verbal agreement between parties defining their working relationship. Such contracts may be binding when the duties, compensation, and terms of the arrangement are agreed to by both parties. Salespeople, consultants, and other independent contractors often have oral agreements because their companies refuse to give them written contracts. Many principals use oral contracts because there is no written evidence to indicate what terms were discussed and accepted by both parties when they entered into the working arrangement. If disputes arise, it is more difficult to prove that the other party failed to abide by the terms of the agreement. For example, if a 5% commission rate was accepted verbally, a dishonest principal could deny this by stating that a lower commission rate on certain sales had been discussed and accepted. The salesperson would then have to prove that both parties had agreed to a higher commission rate.

When a legal dispute arises concerning the terms of an oral contract, a court will resolve the problem by examining all the evidence the parties offer and weighing the testimony to determine who is telling the truth. To avoid problems, all salespeople, consultants, and independent contractors should obtain written contracts to clarify their rights. However, if the company refuses to offer you a written contract or sign an agreement you prepare, there are ways to protect yourself and turn a handshake into a written agreement.

Your chief concern should be directed toward obtaining written evidence indicating the accepted terms in important areas such as your commission rate, assigned territory, job security, notice-of-termination requirements, and proper accounting. If a company refuses to sign a written agreement, write a confirming letter whenever you reach an oral understanding relating to your arrangement.

Be as specific as possible when referring to subjects that you and the company have agreed upon. Write the letter with precision, since ambiguous terms are generally resolved against the letter writer. Keep a copy of the letter for your own records and save the certified mail receipt. If at a later date the terms of the oral agreement are changed (for instance, additional territory is assigned to you), write another letter specifying the new arrangement. Keep a copy of this letter and all correspondence sent to and received from the other party.

> **TIP:** If the company fails to respond, the terms of your letter can serve as a valid contract in most instances. Thus, include language in the letter notifying the company that if there are any misunderstandings or disputes with what you have presented in the letter, it is the company's responsibility to respond back to you. The letter on page 46 serves as a good illustration of the kind of letter you may send.

STEPS TO TAKE WHILE WORKING

Follow these strategies while working to reduce the chances of being exploited:

- check your commission statements carefully
- notify the company immediately when you detect errors
- save all correspondence, records, and documents to confirm all deals and actions
- review your contract periodically to be sure all parties are complying with its terms
- document all promises made to you

Proper accounting is vital for any female salesperson who works on a commission basis. Although in most instances companies do give a proper accounting, the author has represented many clients who were cheated out of hundreds of thousands of dollars by dishonest principals who failed to record sales properly or give credit for all shipped orders.

Suggested Sales Rep/Principal Agreement

Name of Firm
Your Address
Date

Name of Principal's Officer
Title
Name of Principal
Address

Dear (Name of Officer):

This letter confirms that Name of Principal ("The Company") hereby retains Name of Representative ("The Representative") to serve as its sales representative commencing (Date) under the following terms and conditions:

1. The Representative will serve as an independent contractor and be responsible to pay for all applicable social security, withholding, and other employment taxes. The Representative will bear all expenses incurred in her sales endeavors except those which the Company agrees to pay for in writing.

2. The Representative will diligently devote its time and efforts toward the selling of the Company's products and will make no representations, warranties, or commitments binding the Company without the Company's prior consent.

3. The Representative shall act as the Company's exclusive sales representative in the following (specify: territory, states, or region) in which the Representative shall have exclusive territorial rights. There shall be no house accounts in said territory (with the exception of specify).

4. As compensation for its services, the Company agrees to pay the Representative a commission of X Percent (x %) on the (specify: gross or net) amount of sales shipped into the aforementioned Representative's exclusive territory (optional: and paid for by the customer).

5. The Representative shall receive full commission on all shipments within her exclusive territory regardless whether said orders are sent by the Representative, received directly by the Company through the mail, telephone, or fax, or taken at the Company's place of business without the Representative's assistance.

6. Commissions shall also be paid to the Representative on all orders originating from customers within the Representative's exclusive territory regardless whether the products are shipped to divisions, subsidiaries, or individual accounts or chain stores outside the Representative's exclusive territory. (Optional: In addition, full commission shall be paid to the Representative on all credit-approved orders written at trade shows and showrooms from any account outside the aforementioned exclusive territory with the Company's consent.)

7. There will be no deductions or chargebacks from the Representative's commission unless mutually agreed to by both parties in writing and the Representative shall not be responsible for payment or collection of delinquent accounts.

8. The Company shall maintain an accurate set of books and records regarding commissions due and agrees to furnish the Representative on a (specify, such as weekly) basis with copies of all accepted orders and invoices reflecting shipments into the Representative's exclusive territory. Commission statements

containing accurate purchase order numbers, shipping dates, customer's name and address, invoice numbers, and invoice dollar amounts shall be sent, together with payment, to the Representative on or about the (specify) (Xth) day of the month following the month in which the goods are shipped.

Optional. The Company shall contribute the sum of (specify) per month toward the Representative's showroom and overhead operating expenses. Said amount is to be paid in advance on the (specify) day of each and every month of this Agreement commencing (specify) and is a separate charge which will not be deducted or collected against any commissions due the Representative.

9. Either party may terminate this Agreement upon the sending of written notice sent certified mail, return receipt requested, to the other (specify, such as Sixty (60) days) prior to the effective termination date.

Optional. The Company agrees to engage the Representative for a minimum period of One (1) year from the date of the commencement of this Agreement. This Agreement cannot be shortened without the express written consent of both parties. In the event either party desires to terminate this Agreement at the end of the initial One (1) year term, written notice must be sent to the other party by certified mail, return receipt requested, no less than Sixty (60) days prior to the effective termination date. If timely notice is not given, or if no notice is given, this Agreement shall be automatically renewed, under the same terms and conditions, for additional One (1) year periods.

10. At the termination of this Agreement, a final accounting will be made between the parties. The Company shall maintain an accurate set of books and records regarding commissions due the Representative following the termination of this Agreement and the Representative will receive full commission on all accepted orders in house at the date of the termination of this Agreement which are shipped after the termination date, as well as full commission on all reorders shipped through the end of the selling season then in effect. The Company shall furnish the Representative with copies of all invoices reflecting post-termination shipments for the purpose of verifying commissions due. Notwithstanding the foregoing, the Representative shall be entitled to continue to solicit sales after receiving a notice of termination and during the notice period as more fully described in Paragraph 9.

11. The Company shall furnish the Representative with samples and sales promotion material, including catalogs, price lists, and advertising literature at no charge.

12. The Company shall provide the Representative with the names of all persons and companies within its exclusive territory requesting information on the Company's product, together with general correspondence, quotes, supply, price, and timely delivery information.

Optional. In the event the Company is late in the payment of commissions, it agrees to pay One Percent (1%) interest per month on all outstanding balances over Thirty (30) days.

13. During the period of this Agreement and for a period of One (1) year thereafter, the Company and the Representative agree that they will not hire or otherwise utilize the services of any employee or sales associate of the other. Both parties agree that the loss of such employee or sales associate would result

in irreparable harm to the other and both parties grant the other the right to seek damages and an injunction in a court of equity or other competent jurisdiction to enforce said rights.

14. The Company agrees to indemnify and hold the Representative harmless from any claims, demands, lawsuits, reasonable attorney fees, costs, and judgments arising from or in connection with the products manufactured by the Company or sold by the Representative pursuant to this Agreement. In connection thereto, the Company shall furnish the Representative with a copy of its insurance coverage presently in effect within (specify) days from the signing of this Agreement, indicating that the Representative is included as a beneficiary and is covered under such policy and shall furnish the Representative with copies of renewal endorsements naming the Representative as a beneficiary of such policy on a yearly basis thereafter.

15. Nothing in this Agreement shall be construed to constitute the Representative as a partner, affiliate, or employee of the Company.

16. If any term or provision of this Agreement shall to any extent be invalid or unenforceable, the remainder of the Agreement shall not be affected thereby, and each term and provision of this Agreement shall be valid and enforced to the fullest extent permitted by law.

17. This Agreement forms the entire understanding between the parties. It cancels and supersedes all prior agreements and understandings. There shall be no change or modification of any of the terms in the Agreement unless it is reduced to writing and signed by both parties.

18. All notices called for under this Agreement must be in writing and will be deemed given when mailed, certified mail, return receipt requested, to a party at its address written above or at such other address as a party may hereafter designate in writing to the other party.

19. This Agreement shall be binding upon each of the parties hereto, their heirs, successors, assigns, and successors in interest.

Name of Officer, I look forward to working with you for many years to come as your representative. In that regard, please sign this original Agreement in the space below where indicated and return it promptly to my office; you should keep the copy for your files.

Very truly yours,
Name of Rep Firm or
Individual Rep
("The Representative")
By: _____
Name and Title

Accepted and consented to:
Name of Principal
("The Company")
By: _____
Name of Officer and Title
Dated:

The fact you may get computer-generated commission statements does not mean you are obtaining 100% accurate accounting. Duplicate invoices are sometimes photocopied in error. In addition, some companies give each of their salespeople a different computer number. If these numbers are fed into the computer incorrectly, other salespeople will get credit for your sales.

Save all commission statements, copies of checks, letters, memos, and other documents received from the company while you are working. This information may prove useful to your lawyer later. Most important, if the company decides to reduce suddenly your commission rate or draw, or change your territory, and you have a written contract that specifically forbids it from doing this, send a letter to document your protest. The reason is that if you don't take steps to indicate your dissatisfaction, you may appear to have consented to such changes by conduct. However, since the receipt of such a letter may cause the company to consider firing you, always speak to a knowledgeable employment lawyer before considering taking such action.

STEPS TO TAKE IF YOU ARE FIRED

A principal may have the right to fire you, but you could be entitled to damages, depending on the circumstances. Implement the following strategies when you are fired or believe you are about to be fired:

1. Insist on receiving a final statement of commissions and other benefits to determine if you are owed any money.

2. Know the law regarding the prompt payment of commissions. Sales reps in 32 states are entitled to receive their final commissions shortly after being fired. These states have sales rep protection laws for independent contractors which can be used to your advantage. In many states, a company's failure to pay you earned commissions within a short period of time (say 10 days) after termination may enable you to collect damages up to three times the amount of actual money owed, plus reasonable attorney fees, costs, and interest, if the case proceeds to litigation and is not settled before a judge's or jury's verdict. Many of these state laws also require the parties to have written agreements specifying how commissions are earned and when they are due.

Sample Letter Agreement To Confirm An Oral Arrangement

Name of Firm
Your Address
Date

Name of Company Officer
Title
Company Name
Address

Dear (Name of Company Officer),

It was a pleasure meeting with you yesterday. Per our discussion, this will confirm the terms of my engagement as a sales representative (or consultant) for your Company commencing (date) under the following terms and conditions:

I agree to represent the Company in: (specify states or territory). The above territory will be covered exclusively by me and there shall be no house accounts in my territory.

I will receive a commission of (specify) percent of the gross invoice amount for all orders shipped into my exclusive territory regardless of how the order is obtained or received by you or your company.

There will be no deductions from my commission except for (specify). Commission checks together with accurate statements will be sent to me on or about the (specify) day of the month following the month of shipment and the Company agrees to send me copies of all invoices of shipments in my territory on a weekly basis.

(Optional If Applicable: In addition, the Company will contribute a showroom participation fee of ($X), payable on the first day of each month of this Agreement, which is a separate charge and not to be deducted or collected against any commission due me.)

I will be considered an independent contractor and responsible to pay all applicable social security, withholding and other employment taxes.

To cancel our Agreement, either party must send the other written notice no less than (specify) days prior to the effective termination date. Upon termination for any reason, I shall be paid a commission on all shipments made for a period of (specify) months after the effective termination date for orders in house before the effective termination date.

If any of the terms of this letter are ambiguous or incorrect, please advise me immediately in writing; otherwise, this letter shall set forth and constitute our entire understanding of this matter, which may not be modified or changed to any extent, except in writing, signed by both parties.

Very truly yours,
(Name of Rep or Rep Firm or Consultant)

Send Certified Mail, Return Receipt Requested

Speak to a knowledgeable lawyer to learn whether your state has enacted a sales rep statute where applicable.

3. Send a detailed letter demanding unpaid commissions. This should be done by certified mail, return receipt requested, to document your claim and prove delivery. Such a demand can "start the clock" for the purposes of determining the number of days that commissions remain unpaid and put the company on notice that additional damages and penalties may be owed for a continued breach.

4. Consider litigation to collect what is due for large claims. If you are owed a small amount of money (i.e., less than $3,000), consider instituting proceedings in small-claims court. Recognize, however, that since you may be permitted to bring suit only in the county where the principal resides or has its main office, the travel and incidental expenses involved may not make it worthwhile to pursue your rights when small sums are involved and the company is out-of-state.

COUNSEL COMMENTS: If you live and work in a state with a sales rep protection statute, consider litigation in a higher court since attorney fees and costs can be awarded in addition to double or triple damages.

5. Never sign a release or cash a commission check marked "payment in full" without first speaking to a lawyer. In some states, your cashing a check will preclude you from recovering anything further, despite writing protest language ("Under Protest") on the face or back of the check.

6. Seek legal advice before taking action. This is essential to receive an accurate opinion regarding your case's chances of success. The lawyer you consult should be an experienced attorney with particular knowledge of problems typically encountered by independent contractors. At the initial interview, bring all pertinent written information, including contracts, letters of intent, company memoranda, shipping lists, invoices, and commission statements. Tell the lawyer everything related to the problem since all communications are privileged and this will save time and make it easier for him or her to evaluate your case.

Once the lawyer receives all pertinent facts, he or she should then:

- Decide whether your case has a fair probability of success considering the law in the state in which the suit will be brought;

- Give you an accurate estimate as to how long the lawsuit will take; and

- Make a determination of the approximate legal fees and disbursements.

If your lawyer sees weaknesses in your case and believes that litigation will be unduly expensive, or if he desires to try to settle the matter without resorting to time-consuming litigation, he may elect to send an initial demand letter. Commission disputes are sometimes settled quickly out of court between lawyers for both sides after such a letter is sent. The letter on page 49 illustrates what a demand letter from a lawyer may state.

In any event, the chosen course of action should be instituted without delay so you will be able to receive remuneration as quickly as possible. This will also ensure that the requisite time period in which to start the action, the statute of limitations, will not have expired.

Strategies about how to hire a lawyer and work effectively with one are explained in greater detail in Chapter Ten.

TIP: Many of the concepts discussed in this section to help salespeople are also applicable for consultants and other independent contractors. Thus, review all these strategies for your protection where applicable.

Example of Lawyer's Initial Demand Letter

Law Offices of
Sack & Sack
135 East 57th Street, 12th Floor
New York, N.Y. 10022
Telephone (212) 702-9000
Facsimile (212) 702-9702

Date

Name of Officer
Title
Name of Company
Address

Dear (Name of Officer):

Please be advised that this office serves as General Counsel for the National Association of General Merchandise Representatives (NAGMR) and represents (Name and Address of Client).

Reference is made to your letter sent to my client dated (specify). Notwithstanding your offer to pay commissions on all shipments through January 15, 1999, demand is hereby made for additional commissions due for all catalogue sales and blanket orders derived from Spring 1999 programs obtained by my client as the procuring, soliciting cause for such deals. These orders and programs were negotiated by (Client's Name) and accepted by your firm prior to your company's unilateral and unjustified termination of (Client's Name). I have also been advised that orders derived from my client's efforts are continuously being received by you every day.

The timing of the firing is suspect and violates an implied covenant of good faith and fair dealing. Our request is founded on equity and to avoid unjust enrichment since these programs and the resulting orders obtained were developed by my client at great effort and expense.

In that regard, I suggest that either you or your representative contact this office immediately in the amicable attempt to resolve these and other issues to avoid expensive and protracted litigation, which, under the laws of the State of New York, will entitle my client to receive two times the commission amount due, plus reasonable attorney fees and costs, once a lawsuit is instituted. Hopefully this can be avoided and I thank you for your prompt attention and cooperation in this matter.

Very truly yours,

Steven Mitchell Sack

SMS/nc
Via Overnight Mail

CHAPTER THREE

GETTING HIRED

Smart women applicants never accept employment until they have carefully discussed and clarified all key terms, conditions, and responsibilities up front, no matter what type of job is being offered. This chapter explains how to negotiate a job properly to avoid future misunderstandings, confusion, and exploitation by dishonest employers. Since different jobs have unique concerns to be addressed at the hiring interview, a brief examination of important issues affecting part-time positions, leased and temporary employees, union workers, and statutory employees will precede discussion of the problems and concerns of full-time salaried employees.

PART-TIME POSITIONS

Part-time workers must typically comply with the same company rules, policies and procedures as full-time employees, including working regular stated hours. Most states define part-time workers as those who are employed on jobs with fewer than 40 hours per week. Most part-time workers are paid on an hourly basis and are not entitled to company benefits, such as extended vacations, company pension and profit-sharing plans, health insurance, and other benefits. Some states grant coverage to employees who work more than a stated number of hours (e.g., 25) per week. Under federal

ERISA law, employees who generally work 1,000 hours in a pension plan year must be included in all appropriate company pension-plans that are offered to other similar workers.

> **TIP:**   Contact the nearest office of your state's Department of Labor to learn about all benefits that must be offered to you as a part-time worker. In some states, part-time workers must be paid overtime, vacations, lunch breaks, and coffee breaks like regular workers. Be certain you understand what benefits are/are not available before accepting a job to be sure the company complies with all appropriate benefits laws. If, for example, you do not qualify for medical benefits, inquire how much extra it would cost to be included in such coverage. You may also learn that the company will offer prorated fringe benefits, including shorter paid vacations, sick leave and life insurance, just by asking. Point out to the prospective employer that by offering you and similar part-timers prorated benefits, the company may qualify for cheaper group HMO and medical insurance rates.

Under the federal Equal Pay Act, part-time workers and temporary employees are not subject to strict rules that men and women doing the same job must be paid equally. Also, many companies not wishing to offer benefits required to be offered to employees under the federal Family and Medical Leave Act (FMLA) are exempt from that law when they employ a sufficient number of temporary, contract employees or part-time workers (defined in the act as those who work 25 or fewer hours a week) which reduces the number of full-time employees to under 50.

However, when companies use temporaries to supplement full-time personnel, the practice has been successfully attacked by unions on the grounds that bargaining unit employees are deprived of job opportunities and overtime.

As a part-time worker, you may be terminated for poor performance and are subject to the company's work rules and requirements like other workers. Your paycheck will reflect payroll deductions and taxes. All legal obligations owed by the company to its workforce, such as complying with safety (OSHA) rules and regulations, not making promises it does not intend to keep, and avoiding discriminatory acts, apply to you as well.

TIP: Negotiate the right to convert into a full-time position if your work skills are satisfactory or if the employer's needs or your needs change. Don't forget to discuss this with management where appropriate. Additionally, inquire if the employer will allow you and someone else to share a job that requires 40 or more hours of work per week. Some companies are offering *job shares* where circumstances warrant. The advantage of a job share is that these employees often obtain prorated shares of benefits normally available only to full-time workers. They also work flexible hours and have the opportunity to take time off during the workweek to meet family obligations, such as child care, or pursue other interests. Inquire if the employer has a job-share plan in effect if appropriate.

LEASED AND TEMPORARY EMPLOYEES

Leased and temporary employees work for the service firm supplying workers to the client company. Although they report directly to an employer, they receive their paychecks and benefits from the company leasing their services. Leased employees typically do not work at one job site for more than a fixed period (i.e., one year). Once a particular job is finished, they are then assigned to work at another company.

COUNSEL COMMENTS: Although the Department of Labor reports that the use of temporary workers has surged 400% since 1982, statistics provided by *USA Today* reveal that temps earn an average 40% less per hour than full-time workers. Even though the vast majority (80%) work 35 hours a week, most do not have health benefits, pensions and life insurance and most temps are women. This has caused some commentators to point out that when you are a temp you are treated at a lower status despite the advantages of a flexible work schedule.

Although leased employees are obligated to conduct themselves in accordance with the work rules and regulations stipulated by the company for which services are being provided, they must ultimately answer to the leasing company hiring them. When a dispute arises, such as whether unemployment insurance is available after a layoff or firing, the issue may depend on the rights and remedies available against the leasing company and not the client.

Female applicants applying for work as leased employees should know the ramifications of their status before accepting employment. At a minimum, get answers to the following questions:

- Which company will pay me?
- Can I collect overtime for my efforts? If so, how do I go about this?
- To whom do I look for instructions about when, where, and how work is to be performed?
- Who controls my work schedule?
- Under what circumstances may I be dismissed?
- Who furnishes the tools and equipment used by me for the job?
- How do we resolve problems I may have with the client?
- Am I prohibited from working directly for the client company (such as being required to sign a restrictive covenant in an employment contract) if they like my skills and work performance?
- Do I have a say in my assignments?
- How often do I have to report back to the leasing company?
- What are my benefits and who pays for these benefits?

Although employee leasing is being used more these days, critics contend that employees suffer by not receiving commensurate benefits from the company leasing their services.

TIP: It is critical to negotiate a fair hourly rate or weekly salary as well as obtain equivalent benefits that would be available if you worked for a company as a regular employee.

The relationship of a leased or temporary worker to her employer has unique ramifications with respect to workers' compensation, unemployment insurance benefits, and tax matters. In some states, a person who is employed by a leasing company is also considered to be in the special employ of the client company despite the fact that the leasing employer is responsible for the payment of wages, has the power to hire and fire, has an interest in the work performed by the employee, maintains workers' compensation for the employee, and provides some of the employee's equipment. This means, for example, that if you are injured while working for the client company, you may be covered under workers' compensation and cannot institute a private negligence lawsuit.

However, if the client company approved your hiring and possessed the right of control, an employer/employee relationship might be found, making the client responsible for any discriminatory acts (including sexual harassment) perpetrated against you on

---

Jean is a skilled temporary employee who works for ABC Leasing. She is requested to apply for a full-time 40 hour/week job at XYZ Company as a computer specialist. Jean interviews several times for the position and discusses her qualifications with many senior executives. She is hired. Although Jean receives her pay from ABC, her performance is strictly controlled by XYZ. She receives daily instructions from XYZ supervisors. Although her employment with XYZ will terminate at the end of a nine-month project, Jean notices that XYZ distributes an employment manual to all of its workers. The manual states that the company cannot fire anyone suddenly, but is required to first offer a warning.

Jean learns she has breast cancer and must visit her doctor once a week (several hours per visit) for chemotherapy treatments as an outpatient. Jean is suddenly fired by XYZ before finishing her assignment.

She protests the firing and alleges a claim for wrongful firing based on the promise contained in the manual as well as asserting disability discrimination. XYZ argues that Jean cannot enjoy promises made by the company to its full-time workforce since she is a temporary, leased worker and therefore technically does not work for the company. XYZ also states that requirements of the federal Americans With Disabilities Act (ADA) do not apply to companies using temps.

A judge rules that since XYZ substantially controlled Jean's activities and had the absolute right to terminate her assignment, it is deemed to be a special employer of the temp. As such, the rights granted in the manual equally apply to her as well as protections afforded to workers under ADA. Thus, since XYZ discriminated against Jean by not providing reasonable accommodation (e.g., allowing her time off for chemotherapy treatments), it violated the law.

the job site. The same is true if you desire to take time off to care for a newborn or an adopted child, an elderly parent, or a sick spouse under the federal Family and Medical Leave Act (FMLA).

Under what conditions will companies using temporary labor be required to comply with the FMLA? Generally, where two or more businesses exercise some control over the work or working conditions of the employee, a joint relationship may be found to exist. Once this occurs, the client as the secondary employer may have the obligation to comply with the FMLA and cannot discriminate against you if you seek to exercise your rights under this law. (Note: Discussion about your rights under the FMLA is part of the next chapter.)

> **TIP:** If you are a leased or temporary employee, speak to a lawyer immediately if you believe your rights are being violated. This may include, for example, being a victim of sex, race, age, or disability discrimination, or being denied unemployment insurance benefits or workers' compensation coverage after an accident.

UNION WORKERS

A labor union is an organization of working people who collectively negotiate (or attempt to negotiate) benefits, better working conditions, grievances, and employment contracts for its members. The federal Taft-Hartley Act allows certain classes of workers to band together, form, and join unions. Supervisors, managers, executives, and some government employees cannot be union members because "blue-collar" (non-management) working-class status is often required for membership.

If you belong to a union, much of your protection as a union member derives from the powers and actions of the National Labor Relations Board (NLRB) together with the U.S. Department of Labor and state law. For example, if you believe that your union is not zealously representing your interests, or has engaged in an unfair or illegal labor practice, it may be necessary to file a grievance against your union through a local office of the NLRB.

Under the federal National Labor Relations Act and state laws, employers are forbidden from penalizing workers who decide collectively to discuss common grievances and form and participate in a labor union. Workers cannot be disciplined, demoted, reassigned, fired, threatened, or treated poorly as a result of union involvement. Neither can employers offer nonunion workers more benefits or better working conditions than union workers. Speak to a labor lawyer to protect your rights if this is the case.

In certain situations, such as when an employer has entered into a comprehensive collective bargaining agreement with a union permitting the union to act as spokesperson for all workers of the company, you may be forced to belong to a union even if you do not want to participate in union activities. This means that union dues may be automatically deducted from your paycheck and there is little you can legally do about it. However, in some right-to-work states, people are permitted to work at companies without being required to participate in union activities or be affiliated with a union.

There are several advantages and disadvantages in belonging to a union. For example, employers are bound to follow rules concerning discharge procedures in collective bargaining agreements previously negotiated and ratified by a union. In such agreements, employers are sometimes forbidden from terminating union workers except in situations involving worker misconduct or serious offenses. If a union worker is fired wrongly or under circumstances suggesting that the employer acted improperly, the union should schedule an arbitration proceeding or grievance procedure without delay so that an impartial arbitrator can hear the case and hopefully reinstate the terminated worker (and order back pay and other lost benefits in appropriate circumstances).

COUNSEL COMMENTS: If you are a union member and are treated unfairly while working, denied expected benefits, or fired from a job, speak to a lawyer hired by the union or a private lawyer immediately to discuss your rights. The specifics of your work relationship are spelled out in the collective bargaining agreement. Most agreements allow you to discuss a problem with a designated union representative, who will then communicate the matter to union officials. If the union determines that your grievance is sound, the union should guide you through the complaint process.

Most collective bargaining agreements provide little or no severance pay and other post-termination benefits for terminated union workers. This differs from nonunion employees, who may be able to receive large severance packages after having worked for an employer for many years and been discharged through no fault of their own, such as for a job elimination or company reorganization.

Also, when a union is organizing a strike, an employer may be able to keep workers off the premises legally (known as a "lockout") in an attempt to force the union to back down. Union workers may not receive any pay during a lockout, and sometimes the employer does not have to rehire workers if they were permanently replaced while on strike. Some unions provide short-term strike funds to workers who are forced to go out on strike. Under federal law, the obligation to rehire union workers who were replaced often depends on whether the employer acted properly before the strike. For example, if the employer engaged in an unfair labor practice that caused the strike (e.g., failing to provide a safe work environment), the employer may be legally required to rehire its original union workers. Rules concerning the circumstances permitting union workers to legally strike (e.g., to protest unsafe working conditions) are spelled out in the National Labor Relations Act.

STATUTORY EMPLOYEES

Many women who work at home or who are paid on a commission basis (such as life insurance agents or salespeople) are classified by the IRS as statutory employees. The fact you may work out of your home with little or no direction or control from an employer and are paid commissions for services rendered does not matter for tax purposes. If you are a statutory employee, your commissions or pay will be subject to the same tax withholding requirements as other employees. Speak to your accountant or professional advisor for more information on this subject if applicable, such as to determine if you are a statutory *non-employee* not subject to withholding requirements. (Note: Licensed real estate agents and direct sellers such as door-to-door salespeople are considered statutory non-employees.)

NEGOTIATING THE JOB PROPERLY

No matter what your job classification is, never be afraid to negotiate a job. When key terms are not discussed before the hiring, misunderstandings and confusion often follow. The more points you insist on, the more benefits and protections you will obtain. Salary, title, duties, authority, bonuses, and job advancement are fair game for negotiation. On the other hand, fringe benefits, and profit-sharing and pension plans may be fixed and not open to negotiation. Do not expect to get everything you request. However, by understanding the terms to ask for, you can receive additional benefits and protection. The following checklist is a comprehensive guide of things to consider asking for, with fall-back strategies if your initial requests are denied.

JOB SECURITY

1. Your goal is to avoid being fired suddenly at the employer's discretion.

2. Ask for a fixed contract term, such as one-year. If you can get a one-year contract in writing, the employer cannot fire you prior to the expiration of the one-year term except for a compelling reason (i.e., cause). This is often difficult for the employer to prove.

3. If the employer refuses to hire you for a definite term, ask for a guarantee that you cannot be fired except for cause or unless you fail to achieve certain goals (for example, reach a minimum sales quota if you are being hired as a salesperson). This request can give you needed protection without locking the employer into giving you job security.

4. If this request is refused, ask to be guaranteed a written warning stating a definite period of time (for example, 30 days in which to cure alleged deficient performance) before being fired.

5. If this request is refused, ask to receive written notice (say, 30 days) before any firing can be effectuated. This is called receiving notice of termination before the effective termination date so you can plan ahead and look for other employment while still collecting a paycheck.

6. If this request is refused, request pay in lieu of notice in the event you are fired without warning; for example, ask to receive two weeks' additional pay at your current salary level in the event you are fired suddenly. This notice pay is in addition to severance pay (which is discussed next).

7. Inquire if the initial probationary period is guaranteed. For example, if you are told that you will be on probation during the first three months after your hire as an evaluation period for the company to

determine if it wishes to offer you full-time employment, clarify that you cannot be fired during the first 90 days, especially if you are relocating or are resigning from a good position to accept the job.

SEVERANCE

1. Try to obtain a predetermined severance package before being hired. Does the employer have a definite stated policy regarding severance, such as one month of severance pay for every year worked?

2. Inquire whether severance is paid if you resign for a good reason as opposed to being fired. Most companies do not pay severance upon resignation or when the termination is for cause.

3. Request that notice pay (discussed above) be handled separately from severance pay.

VACATION PAY

1. How much vacation pay you get often depends on your salary grade, type of job, and how well you negotiate.

2. Be sure to understand how vacation pay is computed and other important matters regarding the granting of vacation time.

3. Ask that vacation days be carried over to the next year if they are not used, or that you will be paid for unused vacation days. Avoid allowing the company to state that vacation days are forfeited if they are not used in a given year.

4. Negotiate the amount of vacation days to increase depending on the number of years with the company (for example, three weeks of vacation pay for the first five years, increasing to four weeks of paid vacation annually from years six through ten).

5. Understand the amount of notice that is required to be given before you can take vacations.

6. Must vacation days be taken all at once, or can they be staggered? Are there times during peak seasonal demands when requests will not be granted?

7. If you leave or are terminated, what is the company's policy toward paying unused vacation time. In most states, it is illegal for employers to withhold accrued vacation days, even if you are fired for cause. Check with the Department of Labor in your state or speak to competent legal counsel where applicable.

PERSONAL DAYS

1. Negotiate for a minimum number of personal days (say 10 per year) to be paid.

2. Inquire about permitted absences due to medical and dental appointments, bereavement, maternity leave, and other leaves of absence.

3. Inquire about benefits available if you must take an extended leave, such as maternity leave or leave for child care after the birth.

SALARY AND OVERTIME PAY

1. What is your base salary and when is it payable? Understand all deductions from your paycheck.

2. When does the pay week start and end?

3. If a payday falls on a holiday, when are paychecks distributed?

4. Is overtime offered? If so, at what rate? Are more senior workers offered overtime first? How much notice will be given before you are requested to work overtime? Can you refuse to work overtime for a good reason?

BONUS PAY

1. Your goal is to make a bonus part of your compensation package and not subject to the employer's whim or discretion.

2. If possible, negotiate to receive a bonus. If so, understand how it is calculated and when it is paid.

3. Request a verifiable bonus. Specify the amount, when it is to be paid, and that there are no strings or conditions attached.

4. Request a pro rata bonus in the event you resign or are fired prior to the bonus being paid. For example, if the bonus is computed on sales volume and you work a full year but resign or are fired on December 1 of that year, you should be able to receive eleven-twelfths of the expected bonus.

5. Avoid allowing the employer the right to arbitrarily determine when and if a bonus will be paid and in what amount.

6. Resist arrangements that require you to be on the job after a bonus is earned in order to receive it. If the employer insists on this condition, negotiate the right to receive a bonus if you are fired due to a busi-

ness reorganization, layoff, or for any reason other than gross misconduct.

7. Get it in writing. Verbal promises to pay bonuses are not always enforceable.

8. Try to link the bonus to some verifiable formula (for example, gross profits or sales volume). In fact, if a bonus-enforceable-by-contract arrangement can be proved in court, you may have the right to inspect the employer's books and records in a lawsuit.

FRINGE BENEFITS

1. Your goal is to properly negotiate extra compensation in the form of fringe benefits. Many forms of fringe benefits are even more valuable than salary because they are nontaxable.

2. What fringe benefits will you receive?

3. Try to negotiate use of an automobile, free parking, car insurance or allowance reimbursement, gasoline allowance, or loans at reduced rates of interest, if applicable.

4. Are you entitled to additional compensation in the form of tax-qualified plans, including defined-benefit, profit-sharing, money purchase, and pension plans? Other benefits you should also be aware of are social security benefits, Individual Retirement Accounts (IRAs), 401(k) plans, thrift plans, stock bonus plans, and employee stock ownership plans (ESOPs).

5. Understand what benefits the employer offers in the area of additional compensation and what contributions will be made on your behalf. Key questions to ask are:

   ■ Are you required to contribute matching sums of money? If so, how much will this cost you? Can you increase or decrease matching contributions at your discretion? If so, is notice required and how much?

   ■ Does the investment accumulate tax-free?

   ■ Can the money be taken prior to your retirement? If so, is there a penalty?

   ■ What happens if you resign or are fired for cause? Is the money forfeited?

   ■ What happens if the company is sold or goes bankrupt? Is the money protected?

   ■ Who administers the plan benefits? How can you be sure that there are no funding liabilities and the monies will be set aside as promised? Are the plan benefits prudently invested in such a manner as to preclude large losses?

RELOCATION EXPENSES

1. Always negotiate to receive relocation expenses where applicable. For example, if you are moving from Cleveland to San Diego to accept a new job, request the employer to pay for all direct and incidental expenses associated with the move. This might include losses incurred in selling your house, expenses incurred to transport your personal possessions, and travel to the job site for you and your family. Points to discuss and negotiate include questions like:

   - How much relocation pay will be given?
   - When is it payable and who will pay for it?
   - Are taxes taken out of the payments?
   - What supporting documentation is required in order to receive reimbursement?

2. Do not allow the employer to unilaterally cancel relocation expenses if the job doesn't work out because you may have moved yourself and your family thousands of miles at great expense with no protection.

3. If you are planning to relocate to a distant location, ask to receive written assurances that relocation expenses will be paid regardless of how long you work for the company.

JOB ADVANCEMENT

1. Are periodic raises given? If so, what is the procedure for merit raises and job advancement?

2. Understand how raises are determined. Avoid situations where the amount of the raise or promotion is determined by one person's subjective decision. If so, do you have the right to appeal a supervisor's decision? How may this be accomplished?

JOB DUTIES

1. Understand your title.
2. What will be your job functions? Can these change?
3. Will you report to a superior? If so, who?

OTHER MATTERS

1. Are you required to protect confidential information and trade secrets acquired while working for the company? If so, understand how this will be accomplished.

2. Can you have side ventures in a noncompeting business or must you work exclusively for the company on a full-time basis?

3. Will the employer own the rights to all inventions and processes created by you during employment?

4. Are expenses reimbursable? If so, when will you receive reimbursement and what must be submitted to get paid?

5. What are the procedures for withdrawing money from retirement accounts?

6. How much advance notice is required to be given in the event you wish to resign?

7. What are the company's short-term and long-term disability policies?

8. How long must you work before qualifying for health and other covered benefits?

9. What is the company's policy toward maternity leave and unpaid leaves of absence? If you become pregnant, will the job be held open if you wish to return within a reasonable time after giving birth? How much time?

10. Will you receive a contract confirming the points discussed and agreed upon?

To perform your job better and reduce misunderstandings, ask to receive information regarding the following policies:

- Time clock regulations
- Rest periods
- Absences
- Safety and accident prevention
- Authorized use of telephones
- Reporting complaints
- Making suggestions
- Resolving disputes
- Personal appearance rules
- Conflict of interest and code of ethics rules

COUNSEL COMMENTS: The foregoing list is not all-inclusive. Rather, it describes many of the major points to be considered and negotiated prior to accepting any job, regardless of your work status, occupation, or industry.

NEXT STEP: GET IT IN WRITING

Once agreement is reached on key employment terms, ask the employer to put these terms in writing, especially if you are accepting an executive or high-paying managerial position. This can reduce potential misunderstandings and decrease your chances of being fired unfairly. With a written agreement, it is easier to prove the terms of the relationship since oral agreements are often interpreted differently by employers and employees. A handshake confirms only that you accepted employment; it does not prove what was contracted for. Some employment contracts say that terms cannot be changed without the written consent of both parties. If such a clause was included in your contract and the employer attempted to unfairly reduce your salary or other benefits, this could not be done without your written approval. You are also protected if you are fired in a manner prohibited by the contract.

Judith negotiated and received a one-year written contract to work as a fashion designer effective January 1, 1999. The contract stated it would be automatically renewed for an additional year under the same terms and conditions if notice of termination canceling the contract was not sent by either party by September 1, 1999.

Judith was suddenly fired on December 5, 1999, without notice or cause. She was told that her position was being eliminated due to a company downsizing. Judith diligently looked for similar work at approximately the same rate of pay during 2000. She was unsuccessful in obtaining another job during the year so she sued for breach-of-contract damages. The court ruled that she was entitled to one year's wages because she was terminated improperly when the employer failed to cancel her contract by September 1st of the previous year.

COUNSEL COMMENTS: A contract is an enforceable agreement that can be written, oral, or implied by the actions or intentions of the parties. The words *agreement* and *contract* legally mean the same thing. Presuming that the parties entering into the contract were of sound mind, that there was mutual acceptance of agreed-upon terms, and that consideration (something of value given or promised by one party in exchange for an act or promise of another) was given, a valid contract may be found to exist. Although many contracts can be oral and still enforceable (assuming you can prove what was agreed upon), employment contracts that cannot be fulfilled within a year (i.e., one-year contracts) must be in writing to be valid. This is to satisfy a legal requirement called the statute of frauds. For example, depending on the facts and other circumstances, if an employer has promised lifetime employment (e.g., "You have a job here with us as long as you want to work"), but the promise isn't in writing, you can probably be fired legally on a moment's notice due to the statute of frauds principle.

For important jobs, request a written contract that spells out the parties' understanding and clarifies your rights. The document should clearly confirm basic terms defining compensation, benefits, job security, notice of termination, severance pay, and other considerations. When you obtain an employment contract (or any business document), read it carefully. Question all ambiguous and confusing language. Consult an employment lawyer if you do not understand the meaning of any terms. Be sure that all changes, strikeouts, and erasures are initialed by both parties and that all blanks are filled in. Always obtain a signed copy of the executed agreement and keep it with your other valuable documents in a safe place.

The two documents beginning on the next page illustrate the kinds of employment agreements that are routinely drafted by employers. The first is a comprehensive document typically given to executives. The second document is drafted in the form of a letter; both agreements are valid provided they are written clearly and signed by all pertinent parties.

(Note: The following documents are provided for illustrative purposes only. Since they were drafted by employers, they are slanted in favor of the employer and not the employee. Do not use such documents for your own purposes without speaking to a competent lawyer for advice and guidance.)

Sample Employment Agreement
(For Executives)

The parties to this Agreement dated (specify) are (Name of Company) a (specify State and type of company) (the "Company") and (Name of Employee) (the "Executive").

The Company wishes to employ the Executive, and the Executive wishes to accept employment with the Company, on the terms and subject to the conditions set forth in this Agreement. It is therefore agreed as follows:

1. Employment. The Company shall employ the Executive, and the Executive shall serve the Company, as a (specify) of the Company, with such duties and responsibilities as may be assigned to the Executive by the President of the Company and as are normally associated with a position of that nature. The Executive shall devote her best efforts and all of her business time to the performance of her duties under this Agreement and shall perform them faithfully, diligently, and competently and in a manner consistent with the policies of the Company as determined from time to time by (specify officer) or the President of the Company. The Executive shall report to (specify). The Executive shall not engage in activities outside the scope of her employment if such activities would detract from or interfere with the fulfillment of her responsibilities or duties under this Agreement or require substantial time or services on the part of the Executive. The Executive shall not serve as a director (or the equivalent position) of any company or other entity and shall not receive fees or other remuneration for work performed either within or outside the scope of her employment without prior written consent of the President of the Company. This consent shall not be unreasonably withheld.

2. Term of Employment. The Executive's employment by the Company under this Agreement shall commence on the date of this Agreement and, subject to earlier termination pursuant to section 5 or 7, shall terminate on (specify date). This Agreement may also be extended as needed by a written amendment as discussed in section 8.

3. Compensation. As full compensation for all services rendered by the Executive to the Company under this Agreement, the Company shall pay to the Executive the compensation set forth in Schedule A attached hereto. This schedule may be amended from time to time in writing by the Company and the Executive.

4. Fringe Benefits; Expenses

A. The Executive shall be entitled to receive all health and pension benefits, if any, provided by the Company to its employees generally and shall also be entitled to participate in all benefit plans, if any, provided by the Company to its employees generally.

B. The Company shall reimburse the Executive for all reasonable and necessary expenses incurred by her in connection with the performance of her services for the Company in accordance with the Company's policies, upon submission of appropriate expense reports and documentation in accordance with the Company's policies and procedures. The Company will reimburse the Executive for the expenses involved with her acquisition and business-related use of a portable cellular telephone.

C. The Executive shall be entitled to Three (3) weeks paid vacation annually, to be taken at times selected by her, with the prior concurrence of (specify) to whom the Executive is to report.

5. Disability or Death.

A. If, as the result of any physical or mental disability, the Executive shall have failed or is unable to perform her duties for a period of Sixty (60) consecutive days, the Company may, by notice to the Executive subsequent thereto, terminate her employment under this Agreement as of the date of the notice without any further payment or the furnishing of any benefit by the Company under this Agreement (other than accrued and unpaid base salary and commissions, expenses and benefits which have accrued pursuant to any plan or by law).

B. The term of the Executive's employment under this Agreement shall terminate upon her death without any further payment or the furnishing of any benefit by the Company under this Agreement (other than accrued and unpaid base salary and commissions, expenses and benefits which have accrued pursuant to any plan or by law).

6. Non-Competition; Confidential Information; Inventions

A. During the term of the Executive's employment under this Agreement, the Executive shall not, directly or indirectly, engage or be interested (as a stockholder, director, officer, employee, salesperson, agent, broker, partner, individual proprietor, lender, consultant, or otherwise), either individually or in or through any person (whether a corporation, partnership, association, or other entity) which engages, anywhere in the United States, in a business which is conducted by the Company on the date of termination of her employment, except that she may be employed by an affiliate of the Company and hold not more than 20% of the outstanding securities of any class of any publicly held company which is competitive with the business of the Company.

B. The Executive shall not, directly or indirectly, either during the term of the Executive's employment under this Agreement or thereafter, disclose to anyone (except in the regular course of the Company's business or as required by law), or use in any manner, any information acquired by the Executive during her employment by the Company with respect to any clients or customers of the Company or any confidential or secret aspect of the Company's operations or affairs unless such information has become public knowledge other than by reason of actions (direct or indirect) of the Executive. Information subject to the provisions of this paragraph shall include, without limitation:

(i) procedures for computer access and passwords of the Company's clients and customers, program manuals, user manuals, or other documentation, run books, screen, file, or database layouts, systems flowcharts, and all documentation normally related to the design or implementation of any computer programs developed by the Company relating to computer programs or systems installed either for customers or for internal use;

(ii) lists of present clients and customers and the names of individuals at each client or customer location with whom the Company deals, the type of equipment or computer software they purchase or use, and information relating to those clients and customers which has been given to the Company by them or developed by the Company, relating to computer programs or systems installed;

(iii) lists of or information about personnel seeking employment with or who are employed by the Company;

(iv) prospect lists for actual or potential clients and customers of the Company and contact persons at such actual or potential clients and customers;

(v) any other information relating to the Company's research, development, inventions, purchasing, engineering, marketing, merchandising, and selling.

C. The Executive shall not, directly or indirectly, either during the term of the Executive's employment under this Agreement or for a period of One (1) year thereafter, solicit, directly or indirectly, the services of any person who was a full-time employee of the Company, its subsidiaries, divisions, or affiliates, or solicit the business of any person who was a client or customer of the Company, its subsidiaries, divisions, or affiliates, in each case at any time during the past years of the term of the Executive's employment under this Agreement. For purposes of this Agreement, the term "person" shall include natural persons, corporations, business trusts, associations, sole proprietorships, unincorporated organizations, partnerships, joint ventures, and governments or any agencies, instrumentalities, or political subdivisions thereof.

D. All memoranda, notes, records, or other documents made or composed by the Executive, or made available to her during the term of this Agreement concerning or in any way relating to the business or affairs of the Company, its subsidiaries, divisions, affiliates, or clients shall be the Company's property and shall be delivered to the Company on the termination of this Agreement or at any other time at the request of the Company.

E. (i) The Executive hereby assigns and agrees to assign to the Company all her rights to and title and interest to all inventions, and to applications for United States and foreign patents and United States and foreign patents granted upon such inventions and to all copyrightable material or other works related thereto.

(ii) The Executive agrees for herself and her heirs, personal representatives, successors, and assigns, upon request of the Company, to at all times do such acts, such as giving testimony in support of the Executive's inventorship, and to execute and deliver promptly to the Company such papers, instruments, and documents, without expense to her, as from time to time may be necessary or useful in the Company's opinion to apply for, secure, maintain, reissue, extend, or defend the Company's worldwide rights in the inventions or in any or all United States patents and in any or all patents in any country foreign to the United States, so as to secure to the Company the full benefits of the inventions or discoveries and otherwise to carry into full force and effect the text and the intent of the assignment set out in section 6E(i) above.

(iii) Notwithstanding any provision of this Agreement to the contrary, the Company shall have royalty-free right to use in its business, and to make, have made, use, and sell products, processes, and services derived from any inventions, discoveries, concepts, and ideas, whether or not patentable, including, but not limited to, processes, methods, formulas, and techniques, as well as improvements thereof and know-how related thereto, that are not inventions as defined herein, but which are made or conceived by the Executive during her employment by the Company or with the use or assistance of the Company's facilities, materials, or personnel. If the Company determines that it has no present or future interest in any invention or discovery made by the Executive under this paragraph, the Company shall release such invention or discovery to the Executive within Sixty (60) days after the Executive's notice in writing is received by the Company requesting such release. If the Company determines that it does or may in the future have an interest in any such invention or discovery, such information will be communicated to the Executive within the 60-day period described above.

(iv) For purposes of this Section 6E, "inventions" means inventions, discoveries, concepts, and ideas, whether patentable or not, including, but not limited to, processes, methods, formulas, and techniques, as well as improvements thereof or know-how related thereto, concerning any present or prospective activities of the Company with which the Executive becomes acquainted as a result of her employment by the Company.

F. The Executive acknowledges that the agreements provided in this Section 6 were an inducement to the Company entering into this Agreement and that the remedy at law for a breach of her covenants under this Section 6 will be inadequate and, accordingly, in the event of any breach or threatened breach by the Executive of any provision of this Section 6, the Company shall be entitled, in addition to all other remedies, to an injunction restraining any such breach.

7. Termination. The Company shall have the right to terminate this Agreement and the Executive's employment with the Company for cause. For purposes of this agreement, the term "cause" shall mean:

A. Any breach of the Executive's obligations under this Agreement;

B. Fraud, theft, or gross malfeasance on the part of the Executive, including, without limitation, conduct of a felonious or criminal nature, conduct involving moral turpitude, embezzlement, or misappropriation of assets;

C. The habitual use of drugs or intoxicants to an extent that it impairs the Executive's ability to properly perform her duties;

D. Violation by the Executive of her obligations to the Company, including, without limitation, conduct which is inconsistent with the Executive's position and which results or is reasonably likely to result (in the opinion of the President of the Company) in an adverse effect (financial or otherwise) on the business or reputation of the Company or any of its subsidiaries, divisions, or affiliates;

E. The Executive's failure, refusal, or neglect to perform her duties contemplated herein within a reasonable period under the circumstances after written notice from the President of the Company, describing the alleged breach and offering the Executive a reasonable opportunity to cure same;

F. Repeated violation by the Executive of any of the written work rules or written policies of the Company after written notice of violation from the President of the Company;

G. Breach of standards adopted by the Company governing professional independence or conflicts of interest.

If the employment of the Executive is terminated for cause, the Company shall not be obligated to make any further payment to the Executive (other than accrued and unpaid base salary, commissions and expenses to the date of termination), or continue to provide any benefit (other than benefits which have accrued pursuant to any plan or by law) to the Executive under this Agreement.

8. Miscellaneous

A. This Agreement shall be governed by and construed in accordance with the laws of the State of (specify), applicable to agreements made and performed in (specify State), and shall be construed without regard to any presumption or other rule requiring construction against the party causing the Agreement to be drafted.

B. This agreement contains a complete statement of all the arrangements between the Company and the Executive with respect to its subject matter, supersedes all previous agreements, written or oral, among them relating to its subject matter, and cannot be modified, amended, or terminated orally. Amendments may be made to this Agreement at any time if mutually agreed upon in writing.

C. Any amendment, notice, or other communication under this Agreement shall be in writing and shall be considered given when received and shall be delivered personally or mailed by Certified Mail, Return Receipt Requested, to the parties at their respective addresses set forth below (or at such other address as a party may specify by notice to the other): (specify addresses)

D. The failure of a party to insist upon strict adherence to any term of this Agreement on any occasion shall not be considered a waiver or deprive that party of the right thereafter to insist upon strict adherence to that term or any other term of this Agreement. Any waiver must be in writing.

E. Each of the parties irrevocably submits to the exclusive jurisdiction of any court of the State of (specify) sitting in (specify) County or the Federal District Court of (specify State) over any action, suit, or proceeding relating to or arising out of this Agreement and the transactions contemplated hereby. EACH OF THE PARTIES IRREVOCABLY AND UNCONDITIONALLY WAIVES THE RIGHT TO A TRIAL BY JURY IN ANY SUCH ACTION, SUIT, OR PROCEEDING. Each party hereby irrevocably waives any objection, including, without limitation, any objection to the laying of venue or based on the grounds of *forum non conveniens* which such party may now or hereafter have to the bringing of such action, suit, or proceeding may be served upon that party personally or by Certified or Registered Mail, Return Receipt Requested.

F. The invalidity or unenforceability of any term or provision of this Agreement shall not affect the validity or enforceability of the remaining terms or provisions of this Agreement which shall remain in full force and effect and any such invalid or unenforceable term or provision shall be given full effect as far as possible. If any term or provision of this Agreement is invalid or unenforceable in one jurisdiction, it shall not affect the validity or enforceability of that term or provision in any other jurisdiction.

G. This Agreement is not assignable by either party except that it shall inure to the benefit of and be binding upon any successor to the Company by merger or consolidation or the acquisition of all or substantially all of the Company's assets, provided such successor assumes all of the obligations of the Company, and shall inure to the benefit of the heirs and legal representatives of the Executive.

(Name and Title of Employer)   (Name of Employee)
(Name of Company)   ("Executive")
("The Company")

By: _____   By: _____

Sample Employment Agreement—Letter Version

Date

Name of Employee
Address

Dear (Name of Employee):

This letter confirms that (Name of Company) ("The Company") has hired you as its (specify title). In consideration thereto, you agree to be employed under the following terms and conditions:

1. You agree to work full-time and use your best efforts while rendering services for the Company. As our (specify title), you will be responsible for: (specify in detail).

2. You will make no representations, warranties, or commitments binding the Company without our prior consent nor do you have any authority to sign any documents or incur any indebtedness on the Company's behalf.

3. You shall assume responsibility for all samples, sales literature, and other materials delivered to you and you shall return same immediately upon the direction of the Company.

4. THE COMPANY EMPLOYS YOU AT WILL AND MAY TERMINATE YOUR EMPLOYMENT AT ANY TIME, WITHOUT PRIOR NOTICE, WITH OR WITHOUT CAUSE. LIKEWISE, YOU ARE FREE TO RESIGN AS OUR (SPECIFY TITLE) AT ANY TIME, WITH OR WITHOUT NOTICE.

5. The Company shall pay you a salary of (specify $X) per (specify) as consideration for all services to be rendered pursuant to this Agreement. In addition, the Company shall provide you with health insurance coverage for you and your family, and you will be eligible to participate in the Company pension plan. You will also receive Two (2) weeks paid vacation each year, provided you give the Company appropriate notice and the Company reserves the right to schedule your vacation(s) so as not to conflict with its normal business operations.

6. You shall also be paid for absences due to illness up to a maximum of Two (2) weeks per year, provided you submit a doctor's authorization indicating the reason for extended illness and the treatment received.

7. The Company shall also provide you with time off with pay for the following holidays: (specify)

8. You agree and represent that you owe the Company the highest duty of loyalty. This means that you will never make secret profits at the Company's expense, will not accept kickbacks or special favors from Customers, and will protect Company property.

9. While acting as an employee for the Company, you will not, directly or indirectly, own an interest in, operate, control, or be connected as an employee, agent, independent contractor, partner, shareholder, or principal in any company which markets products, goods, or services which directly or indirectly compete with the business of the Company.

10. All lists and other records relating to the Customers of the Company, whether prepared by you or given to you by the Company during the term of this Agreement, are the property of the Company and shall be returned immediately upon termination or resignation of your employment.

11. You further agree that for a period of Six (6) months following the termination or resignation of your employment, you shall not work for, own an interest in, or be connected with as an employee, stockholder, or partner, any company which directly or indirectly competes with the business of the Company.

12. There shall be no change, amendment, or modification of this Agreement unless it is reduced to writing and signed by both parties. This Agreement cancels and supersedes all prior agreements and understandings.

13. If any provision of this Agreement is held by a court of competent jurisdiction to be invalid or unenforceable, the remainder of the Agreement shall remain in full force and shall in no way be impaired.

Your signature in the lower left corner of this Agreement will indicate the acceptance of the terms and conditions herein stated.

Sincerely yours,

(specify Name and Title)

(NAME OF COMPANY)
("The Company")

By: _____

I, (Name of Employee), the Employee stated herein, have read the above Agreement, understand and agree with its terms, and have received a copy.

_____
(Name of Employee)

If the company fails to prepare and send you a written agreement, it is advisable to write a letter yourself confirming any oral agreements related to your job. The letter can serve as a written contract provided you can prove delivery and it is not ambiguously drafted.

> **TIP:**   The key is to state at the close of the letter that if any terms included in the letter are ambiguous or incorrect, the company must respond within a specified period of time; otherwise the letter shall be considered to confirm the parties' entire understanding. Then, if the company fails to respond within the stated time, the letter can serve as a valid contract in many instances.

> **COUNSEL COMMENTS:**   Send all such letters by certified mail, return receipt requested, or have them hand-delivered. This is how you can turn an oral handshake into a written agreement. The sample letter on the next page illustrates the kind of letter you should consider sending whenever you do not receive a written employment agreement from a company.

TIPS TO AVOID BEING HIRED BY A DECEITFUL EMPLOYER

It is important to find out all you can about a company's reputation, financial status, and credit rating and how it treats its employees before accepting an important job. Armed with this knowledge you will be in a better position for evaluating whether a particular job is for you. For example, if you are being hired to replace someone, try to learn the name of that person and the reason he or she is no longer there. If possible, speak to that person. Investigate an employer's credit rating to discover if the company is having financial difficulties. Such information can often be obtained from a credit-reporting agency or bank. This information is especially important if you expect to receive large pension benefits because a recent investigation by the U.S. Department of Labor uncovered an insidious problem involving hundreds of companies misusing and diverting money from employee 401(k) pension programs.

The following are significant items worth investigating:

- Does the employer conduct business as a corporation, Subchapter S corporation, partnership, or sole proprietorship? (Note: If you work

Sample Letter of Employment Sent by Employee

Date

Name of Corporate Officer
Title
Name of Employer
Address

Dear (Name of Officer):

I enjoyed meeting with you on (date). This letter confirms that I agree to be employed by (name of company) as a (specify job title or position) for an initial term of one (1) year commencing on February 10, 1999 and terminating on February 9, 2000.

As compensation for my services, I agree to accept an annual salary of $40,000 payable in weekly installments in the sum of (specify). Additionally, I shall be paid an annual bonus of at least $10,000 payable on or before December 1 of each year, commencing this year.

According to our agreement, the company shall also reimburse me up to a maximum of $500 per month for all business-related travel expenses, and I shall receive this reimbursement by a separate check within two (2) weeks of my presentation of appropriate vouchers and records.

This agreement cannot be shortened or modified without the express written consent of both parties. Additionally, in the event notice of termination is not received up to one (1) month prior to the expiration of the original term, this agreement shall be automatically renewed, under the same terms and conditions, for an additional one (1) year period.

Upon termination of this agreement for any reason, I shall be entitled to receive my bonus and salary for the remaining period of the quarter in which my termination occurs.

If any terms of this letter are ambiguous or incorrect, please reply within (specify) days from your receipt thereof. Otherwise this letter shall set forth our entire understanding of this matter.

I look forward to working for (name of company).

Very truly yours,

(Name of employee)

(Send certified mail, return receipt requested)

for a partnership or sole proprietorship, it is easier to sue the owners personally.)

- Who are the principal shareholders or partners?
- How many people does the business employ? Small employers (i.e., fewer than six employees) may not be subject to various state and federal discrimination laws.
- What are the locations and kinds of real property and other assets owned by the employer?
- Does the employer have a history of litigation. Are there any outstanding encumbrances or liens?
- Was the business recently sold, and did the new owners assume its liabilities or just purchase its assets. (Note: Sometimes, employees are exploited when a new owner disclaims obligations and promises concerning severance, retirement, and other benefits previously offered by a former employer.)

Investigate the status of the person hiring you. Employers sometimes argue in court that an employee was hired by someone who did not have the legal authority to offer employment, negotiate compensation, or live up to the agreed-upon terms. Only an officer (such as a vice president) or owner can bind the company. Make sure the person hiring you and signing your employment agreement has such authority.

If possible, avoid signing contracts containing restrictive covenants. Restrictive covenants (also called "covenants not to compete") can prohibit you from doing many things, most commonly forming a competing venture or working for a competitor, soliciting former customers or employees, or using the knowledge acquired on the job in future endeavors.

For years, courts have struggled to balance the conflicting considerations of restrictive covenants. Some clauses are viewed as unfair because they limit a person's ability to earn a living. However, courts also recognize the legitimate interest of employers to safeguard their business from deliberate commercial piracy. There are no set rules regarding the enforcement of restrictive covenants and each case is decided on its own particular facts and merits. When judges decide that such contracts go too far in restraining employees, they either modify the terms (making them less restrictive) or declare such covenants to be totally unenforceable and of no legal effect.

The relevant factors typically considered by a judge are:

- Any unfairness in length-of-time or geographic limitations (such as being greater than two years or restraining you from calling on customers throughout the entire United States)

- The degree of hardship on the employee if the covenant is enforced

- Any additional compensation given to the individual (such as an extra week's pay) as inducement to sign a contract containing such a clause or full pay after termination while the covenant is in effect

- The degree to which the individual has access to confidential information such as customer lists, trade secrets, specific business methods, established customers, and related information

- Special skills and training received by the employee

- The bargaining power of the parties

- The status of the individual: whether she is an employee or independent contractor. (Note: In a number of states, a company cannot legally restrain independent contractors from working for a competitor even after signing an agreement with a restrictive covenant.)

- Possible breaches by the employer of any of its own obligations under the contract (e.g., a failure to pay salary or other compensation). When employers violate agreements, this may release the individual from any liability arising from obligations contained in a restrictive covenant.

COUNSEL COMMENTS: Carefully review and resist signing contracts containing restrictive covenants. An employee who works without an employment contract and who leaves without taking any trade secrets has total freedom to work elsewhere in the same industry. This generally includes the right to solicit the ex-employer's customers. However, you may be subjecting yourself to a lawsuit (even when no valid grounds exist) by signing an agreement containing such a clause.

The agreement beginning on page 80 illustrates a sample confidentiality agreement that some employees are requested to sign before working.

COUNSEL COMMENTS: The author is often consulted by female clients asking his opinion regarding the potential enforceability of an onerous restrictive covenant clause contained in a written employment agreement. I may advise that the client not compete with the contract's terms after a resignation or termination because the expenses involved in fighting the dispute in court may be too costly. Employers typically have the money and will to fight. Thus, since such written contracts often have a "chilling effect," avoid signing contracts containing restrictive covenants if you can help it.

TIP: If you are being pressured to sign a contract with a restrictive covenant, negotiate to reduce the covenant to a reasonable period of time you can live with (such as three months only) and insist on the right to receive continued salary and other benefits while the restrictive covenant is in effect. Remember, everything is negotiable before you sign on the bottom line. Once the agreement is signed, however, you may be bound by its terms.

Sample Confidentiality and Noncompetition Agreement

In consideration of my employment or continued employment by (Name of Company) (the "Company"), and in recognition of the fact that as an employee of the Company I will have access to the Company's customer's and to confidential and valuable business information of the Company, I hereby agree as follows:

1. The Company's Business. The Company is (specify). The Company is committed to quality and service in every aspect of its business. I understand that the Company looks to and expects from its employees a high level of competence, cooperation, loyalty, integrity, initiative, and resourcefulness. I understand that as an employee of the Company, I will have substantial contact with the Company's customers and potential customers.

I further understand that all business and fees including (specify), and other services produced or transacted through my efforts shall be the sole property of the Company, and that I shall have no right to share in any commission or fee resulting from the conduct of such business other then as compensation referred to in paragraph 3 hereof. All checks or bank drafts received by me from any customer or account shall be made payable to the Company, and all premiums, commissions, or fees that I may collect shall be in the name of and on behalf of the Company.

2. Duties of Employee. I shall comply with all Company rules, procedures, and standards governing the conduct of employees and their access to and use of the Company's property, equipment, and facilities. I understand that the Company will make reasonable efforts to inform me of the rules, standards, and procedures which are in effect from time to time and which apply to me.

3. Agreement Not to Compete with the Company.

   A. As long as I am employed by the Company, I shall not participate directly or indirectly, in any capacity, in any business or activity that is in competition with the Company.

   B. In consideration of my employment rights under this Agreement and in recognition of the fact that I will have access to the confidential information of the Company and that the Company's relationships with their customers and potential customers constitute a substantial part of their good will, I agree that for One (1) year from and after termination of my employment, for any reason, unless acting with the Company's express prior written consent, I shall not, directly or indirectly, in any capacity, solicit or accept business from, provide consulting services of any kind to, or perform any of the services offered by the Company for, any of the Company's customers or prospects with whom I had business dealings in the year next preceding the termination of my employment.

4. Unauthorized Disclosure of Confidential Information. While employed by the Company and thereafter, I shall not, directly or indirectly, disclose to anyone outside of the Company any Confidential Information or use any Confidential Information (as hereinafter defined) other than pursuant to my employment by and for the benefit of the Company.

The term "Confidential Information" as used throughout this Agreement means any and all trade secrets and any and all data or information not generally known outside of the Company whether prepared or developed by or for the Company or received by the Company from any outside source. Without limiting the scope of this definition, Confidential Information includes any customer files, customer lists, any business, marketing, financial or sales record, data, plan, or survey; and any other record or information relating to the present or future business, product, or service of the Company. All Confidential Information and copies thereof are the sole property of the Company.

Notwithstanding the foregoing, the term Confidential Information shall not apply to information that the Company has voluntarily disclosed to the public without restriction, or which has otherwise lawfully entered the public domain.

5. Prior Obligations. I have informed the Company in writing of any and all continuing obligations that require me not to disclose to the Company any information or that limit my opportunity or capacity to compete with any previous employer.

6. Employee's Obligation to Cooperate. At any time upon request of the Company (and at the Company's expense) I shall execute all documents and perform all lawful acts the Company considers necessary or advisable to secure its rights hereunder and to carry out the intent of this agreement.

7. Return of Property. At any time upon request of the Company, and upon termination of my employment, I shall return promptly to the Company, including all copies of all Confidential Information or Developments, and all records, files, blanks, forms, materials, supplies, and any other materials furnished, used, or generated by me during the course of my employment, and any copies of the foregoing, all of which I recognize to be the sole property of the Company.

8. Special Remedies. I recognize that money damages alone would not adequately compensate the Company in the event of a breach by me of this Agreement, and I therefore agree that, in addition to all other remedies available to the Company at law or in equity, the Company shall be entitled to injunctive relief for the enforcement hereof. Failure of the Company to insist upon strict compliance with any of the terms, covenants, or conditions hereof shall not be deemed a waiver of such terms, covenants, or conditions.

9. Miscellaneous Provisions. This Agreement contains the entire and only agreement between me and the Company respecting the subject matter hereof and supersedes all prior agreements and understandings between us as to the subject matter hereof; and no modification shall be binding upon me or the Company unless made in writing and signed by me and an authorized officer of the Company.

My obligations under this Agreement shall survive the termination of my employment with the Company regardless of the manner or reasons for such termination, and regardless of whether such termination constitutes a breach of this Agreement or of any other agreement I may have with the Company. If any provisions of this Agreement are held or deemed unenforceable or too broad to permit enforcement of such provision to its full extent, then such provision shall be enforced to the maximum extent permitted by law. If any of the provisions of the

Agreement shall be construed to be illegal or invalid, the validity of any other provision hereof shall not be affected thereby.

This Agreement shall be governed and construed according to the laws of (specify State), and shall be deemed to be effective as of the first day of my employment by the Company.

BY SIGNING THIS AGREEMENT, I ACKNOWLEDGE THAT I HAVE READ AND UNDERSTOOD ALL OF ITS PROVISIONS AND THAT I AGREE TO BE FULLY BOUND BY THE SAME.

Employee: _____ Date: _____

Accepted by: _____ Date: _____
            (Name and Title of Officer)

CHAPTER FOUR

ON-THE-JOB BENEFITS AND POLICIES, INCLUDING PREGNANCY AND FAMILY LEAVE

This chapter examines the ways women can avoid problems regarding employee benefits. Areas of discussion include an analysis of equal pay; overtime; medical leave; rights that relate to pregnancy, maternity, and child care; and important points about health insurance, COBRA, and ERISA benefits. Helpful suggestions are offered in areas where women are subject to exploitation.

EQUAL PAY

Wage disparities unfortunately still exist in American society. It has been reported that the typical American working woman is paid 71 cents for each $1 earned by a man. The largest gap is with black and Hispanic women, who, according to U.S. Census figures, earn 64.2 percent and 53.4 percent, respectively, of what men do.

The federal Equal Pay Act (EPA) prohibits covered employers with two or more employees from paying unequal wages to male and female employees who perform substantially the same jobs. For example, a major university was ordered to pay 117 women an award of $1.3 million after a federal court judge ruled that the university paid less money to women on the faculty than to men in comparable posts.

While the EPA and the Civil Rights Act of 1964 both prohibit sex discrimination in the workplace, the EPA applies only to wage inequities between the sexes. Under the Equal Pay Act, employers are barred from paying women less than men if they are working on jobs that require equal skill, effort, and responsibility, and if those jobs are performed under similar working conditions. This includes everyone from hourly workers to salaried employees engaged in executive, administrative, and professional functions, such as teachers. The courts have held that the jobs need not be identical, only "substantially equal." Further, an employer may not retaliate against a female worker, such as by firing her, because an EPA charge was initiated.

Fringe benefits are included in the definition of wages under the law. Thus, employers may not differentiate with items such as bonuses, expense accounts, profit-sharing plans, or leave benefits. Under EPA, it is not a defense to a charge of illegality that the costs of such benefits are greater with respect to women than to men since the law is designed to ensure that women do not receive lower salaries and benefits than their male counterparts.

There are loopholes in the law however. Employers may pay different wages if there is a bona fide preestablished seniority system, a merit system, or a system that measures earnings by quantity or quality of production. Differential pay is also permitted when the jobs are different or are based on a legitimate factor other than sex.

Determining if a job is different is not always clear-cut. A major problem arises when two jobs are similar but one includes extra duties. Although it is legal to give higher pay for the job with more responsibilities, a judge will scrutinize if the greater-paying jobs are

---

ABC Manufacturing Company began operations in 1971. Initially 11 production assistants were hired, all male. Many of them are still employed by ABC. In 1994, the company expanded and hired 10 more production assistants, 6 of whom were women. Although all production assistants perform the same job, many of the older male workers receive greater hourly pay rates because of their seniority and number of years with the company. This is legal.

given only to males at a particular company. This is often the case and may be illegal depending on the facts.

A female worker may seek damages in federal or state court or through the Equal Employment Opportunity Commission (EEOC), and may obtain a trial by jury when asserting an EPA violation. Successful litigants are entitled to recover retroactive back pay, liquidated damages, reasonable attorney fees, and costs. If willful violations (defined as reckless disregard for the law) are found, double back pay may be awarded. Employers are obligated to maintain and save records documenting wages and benefits paid to all employees. Once a complainant shows that she is working in the same place, is doing equal work under similar working conditions, and is paid less than employees of the opposite sex, the burden shifts to the employer to show an affirmative defense that any wage differential is justified by a permitted exception. Practices that perpetrate past sexual discrimination are not accepted as valid affirmative defenses.

If a violation is present, you can sue the employer privately instead of filing a charge of sex discrimination with the EEOC. It is not necessary to prove motive or intent in order to recover. However, the EPA does not protect women from employers who engage in other forms of sex discrimination, such as failing to promote you or firing you. Any other form of sex discrimination must be filed under Title VII or various state discrimination laws.

COUNSEL COMMENTS: To avoid charges of EPA violations, employers are instructed to prepare precise job descriptions that demonstrate different duties and job responsibilities for different pay. When offering jobs with different salaries and benefits, companies are instructed to assign those higher-paying jobs on the basis of factors such as technical skills, additional education, work experience, and knowledge required, rather than sex.

TIP: If you believe that your company is exceeding predetermined salary ranges by offering males who are performing essentially the same job higher salaries, speak to an employment lawyer. This is a violation of EPA even if the reason is to attract minority applicants. For example, in one case, a university wanted to hire a black male assistant professor for a position with a salary ceiling of $28,000 per year. When the applicant asked for more, the university offered him the job at $40,000 per annum. A female white assistant professor who was also hired at the same time at an annual salary of $28,000 filed a lawsuit.

The university argued that the black professor was paid a higher salary because it needed to hire minorities as part of its affirmative action program. The court ruled that the university violated the law. It found that the two professors had comparable skills and were hired at the same time to do the same job. Offering the minority professor a salary that exceeded the established salary range violated the EPA, with no exceptions.

Remember, being denied equal pay because you are married, have children, or are a victim of gender-based stereotypes violates the law.

COMPARABLE WORTH

Pending cases may soon be decided to resolve the issue of comparable worth. Comparable worth is the concept of paying women equally for "comparable jobs." In the public sector, some states and localities have compared jobs and found that some fit the definition when the value of the work and the amount of effort and independent judgment involved are equal. As a result, some women's wages have been raised. Comparable-worth cases are not presently recognized under the EPA, although a few female claimants are suing private employers in this area under federal and state sex discrimination laws. (Author's Note: A recent New York lawsuit commenced by more than 100 secretaries demanding equal pay with custodians in a large suburban school district was dismissed. Although the commissioner of the Human Rights Department acknowledged the case posed very real issues of historic inequities between the genders, he rejected the case, stating that current law did not recognize the doctrine of comparative worth in New York since the law currently only focuses on the nature of the work performed [e.g., if it is the same then all people regardless of sex must be paid equally] and not on the class of people performing it. It is unknown at this time whether the decision will impact comparative worth cases filed in other states.)

TIP: If you believe you are entitled to more pay because the value of your work is similar to that of a higher-paid male at the company (e.g., that a male's assembly line job is comparable in worth to a secretarial position), speak to a competent employment lawyer for advice.

TIPS AND WAGES

Millions of women in this country work in retail sales or as waitresses or beauticians. These services are typically paid on an hourly-plus-tips basis. Rules governing hourly jobs, such as the minimum wage that can be paid, overtime, and restrictions on child labor, are primarily based on the Fair Labor Standards Act (FLSA), also known as the federal Wage and Hour Law. Some states have passed more stringent laws. For example, every state has wage and hour laws that regulate when and how employees are paid. Certain states require that employees receive a meal period a few hours after beginning work; other states require breakfast periods as well. Rules concerning the amount of paid time employers are required to extend for coffee and lunch breaks vary from state to state, and employers must typically pay accrued wages no less than twice per month.

Like the EPA, the FLSA requires that male and female workers receive equal pay for work that requires equal skill, effort, and responsibility. It also defines when employers may give compensatory time (time given off from work instead of cash payments). For part-time workers, employers may not be required to provide any benefits other than those covered under state and federal law, including social security, unemployment insurance, and workers' compensation insurance. Speak to a representative at your state's Department of Labor regional office to get the facts.

If you earn more than $30 a month in tips, your employer can pay you less than the minimum wage (up to 50 percent less in certain instances) provided the total amount of wages and tips reaches the federally guaranteed minimum wage. However, employers are generally forbidden from taking tips away from you. Rules governing the sharing of tips, withholding requirements, and deductions from your salary or tips due to cash shortages, breakage, uniforms, or use of tools and equipment are governed by state law. Check with a local Department of Labor office to determine how much minimum pay you must receive if you get additional tips in your job.

OVERTIME

If you are an hourly ("nonexempt") worker, the FLSA requires that you be paid at one and a half times your regular hourly rate if you work more than 40 hours in a five-day workweek. Several classifications of salaried employees are exempt from the minimum wage and overtime requirements of the FLSA: outside salespersons, independent contractors, employees of certain retail establishments, amusement and recreation park employees, and others who meet various statutory tests, such as persons who hold bona fide executive, administrative, or professional jobs. The rules governing whether you are considered an exempt executive, administrative, or professional worker are complex. Speak to a lawyer for more details where applicable.

In addition to claims of employee entitlement and problems regarding the computation of overtime, other disputes that sometimes arise include whether an employee can waive the right to

Susan works as a sales manager for a large company. She typically works more than 55 hours per week. She receives no overtime pay because she is paid a salary and her job is classified as an administrator, which is exempt from overtime.

Susan has already used up all 20 paid vacation and sick days. An emergency occurs toward the end of the year and she requests a day off. The company grants the request but docks her pay. Susan does not think this is fair. She contacts her state's Labor Department and the Wage and Hour Division of the U.S. Department of Labor. She learns that, according to the Labor Department, the agency responsible for enforcing the FLSA, if a company penalizes salaried persons by making them take time off without pay, or docks salaried employees for taking days off, it acted illegally and owes those exempt workers overtime for all hours over 40 that were worked in any given week.

overtime pay, what rights employers have in requiring people to work overtime, whether employers can equalize overtime on a day-to-day basis, and problems with unauthorized overtime.

In one recent case, an employer docked a worker $3,300 for taking time off. She sued and won. The court ruled that when this occurred, the worker became reclassified as an hourly worker and once any professional worker is classified as hourly, the company is liable for all overtime incurred during the past two years for that employee and similarly situated employees. The company was ordered to pay $750,000 in damages to the woman and 23 others.

> **TIP:** If you are a salaried exempt professional, question all company policies that impose partial or full-day unpaid leaves. If you are an hourly employee, recognize that most compensatory plans (also called comp plans) allowing workers time off without pay in the work period following the week they worked excessive hours, or allowing them to work more than 40 hours one week to make up for working less than 40 hours in a previous week, may be illegal. Each workweek must be considered separately in determining overtime hours, regardless of the length of the pay period, except for certain occupations (e.g., police officers or firefighters); employers giving time off must compute the value of such benefits at one and a half times the regular rate of pay.

Employers who fail to pay required overtime are liable for any unpaid overtime compensation and an equal amount as liquidated damages, plus attorney fees and costs. For willful violations, damages sometimes include earned overtime up to three years back, plus punitive damages.

> **COUNSEL COMMENTS:** Since the purpose of the FLSA is to ensure that employees are paid their full wages, employers may not make any deals to settle wage-hour claims for less than the full amount (even when a release is signed by the employee to defeat the rights of the worker). Although usually courts are pleased when prospective litigants compromise their differences, no such compromise is generally accepted under FLSA.

If you are an hourly worker, you may be entitled to overtime pay under the following conditions:

- If overtime is offered only to males and not to females

- If you arrive to work earlier than your starting time and do light work at the request of the employer

- If you typically work through lunch breaks at the employer's request

- If you take work home with the knowledge and permission of the employer

- When at home you are required to be "on call" and ready to report to work within an hour

- If you work several hours of overtime on a Friday and the employer states that you can leave work several hours earlier the following week

- If the job requires you to stay overnight for out-of-state assignments or travel extensively while on company business (but not for normal commuting travel to and from your home)

In these and other situations, speak to a knowledgeable labor attorney about your rights and options. The wage and hour law is complex, and matters are often subject to detailed investigations. However, employers are generally required to give nonexempt workers as much advance notice as possible when they are expected to stay late. They should also rotate overtime, maintain a roster recording each worker's overtime, and establish rules as to how the roster system will work. Federal law requires employers who offer overtime to post signs outlining the federal minimum wage and overtime regulations conspicuously in places where workers enter and exit.

Additional rules concerning overtime are:

1. Generally, employers cannot force workers to waive their entitlement to overtime.

2. If the company has no knowledge that an employee is working overtime and has established a rule or policy prohibiting overtime work that is conspicuously posted, an employee may not be entitled to overtime pay after making a claim.

3. The FLSA does not protect employees who deliberately over-report their overtime hours. The employer may terminate an employee who falsifies overtime hours and may not be subject to claims of retaliation or unfair treatment.

4. Generally, employees cannot refuse to work overtime unless they have a valid reason (e.g., taking care of a sick child). If the refusal to work overtime is not for good cause and the employer suffers undue

hardship, this may be grounds for a valid termination and denial of unemployment benefits, even for union workers protected by collective bargaining agreements. However, if you believe you were fired unjustifiably, speak to a lawyer immediately.

5. If you are requested to participate in a company-sponsored program after hours, such as a mercy session (e.g., a company-sponsored blood drive), and are an hourly worker, you may be entitled to overtime compensation.

COUNSEL COMMENTS: Speak to a lawyer if you are required to do extensive traveling on company business and are not paid for your time. The author recently represented a female television reporter-producer who was encouraged to spend hundreds of hours each month traveling around the world to obtain provocative news stories. The author obtained a large five-figure settlement representing overtime pay even though the reporter was paid a salary and was considered exempt by her employer.

TIP: Confer with counsel if you are unsure whether or not you are considered an exempt worker. Be sure that the company fairly rotates overtime between the sexes. Discrimination often ensues when supervisors fail to equalize overtime (e.g., they offer substantially more overtime to males than females or minority workers).

Question all attempts by your employer to dock you for time taken to attend jury duty, to vote, and to handle medical emergencies. Most states do not allow employers to do this. If you are in doubt about a company's action in this area, call your local U.S. Labor Department Wage and Hour Division office for further details.

HEALTH BENEFITS

Only a few states require employers to provide workers with health care insurance. However, when health insurance coverage is voluntarily provided, employers may not discriminate; they must offer the same coverage to all employees regardless of sex, age, or disability. For example, if health insurance benefits are provided to the spouses of male workers, the same coverage must be provided to the spouses of female workers and the extent of the coverage provided for dependents must be equal.

The law demands equality in health coverage for pregnant workers. Most state laws say that disabilities caused or contributed to by pregnancy, miscarriage, abortion, or childbirth and subsequent recovery are temporary disabilities and should be treated as such under any health or temporary disability insurance or sick leave plan available in connection with employment. This position is affirmed by federal law under the Pregnancy Discrimination Act of 1978 (PDA).

Although companies are not required to provide any health care benefits, when they do, pregnancy must be treated the same way as any other medical condition; voluntary health care benefits must include coverage for pregnancy and pregnancy-related conditions and for those who are statistically more likely to incur high medical costs. (Note: The PDA does not require employers to pay health insurance benefits for abortion except where the life of the mother would be endangered if the fetus were carried to term or where medical complications have arisen from an abortion.)

As will be discussed later in this chapter, an employer cannot base employment decisions on the fact that a worker is pregnant, since employers must treat pregnancy the same as they would treat any other employee medical condition. If company health care is provided, maternity care must be included and coverage must be the same for spouses of males and females. Limitations on maternity coverage for preexisting conditions must be similar to limits on other conditions. If extended benefits (such as paid sick leave and benefits) are given for other disabilities, so too must extended benefits be given for pregnancies occurring during a covered period of the plan.

Once health insurance is provided, the employer is bound under federal law, including the Consolidated Omnibus Budget Reconciliation Act (COBRA) and the Employee Retirement Income Security Act (ERISA), to follow through on its promises unless the company reserved the right, in company handbooks and memos distributed to its workforce, to alter or amend promises of benefits at any time, with or without notice.

Many insurance policies have preexisting condition clauses that disallow certain kinds of coverage for medical conditions that existed prior to the employee accepting employment. This is legal, as are benefits that are capped (i.e., no more than $X of reimbursement for a particular condition per year) and the requirement that you pay for all or part of the monthly premium.

> **COUNSEL COMMENTS:** The complexity of employee benefits law is well established. New cases are constantly being decided and statutory developments implemented that have an impact on particular plans and practices. It is critical for you to constantly update and evaluate the effect of these legal developments on your own health and benefit plans. One area in particular—retiree health care benefits and successor benefits (when a person leaves a company to work in a new job)—has raised numerous problems. An employer's obligation to provide post-termination or retiree health benefits largely turns on whether those benefits are actually vested at the time of leaving. Claims for employee benefits are typically covered under federal ERISA law; speak to a qualified benefits or labor attorney for more details if applicable.

Many companies are cutting back on the amount of health coverage provided, and some companies are currently offering several plans at great expense. Often, after it is too late, employees learn that their health coverage is inadequate.

To avoid this scenario, always understand the minimum coverage you are receiving and what you must pay on your own for addi-

Shannon worked at a company for 15 years. She has always been in good health and never reviewed her company-sponsored health insurance. This is a mistake. One day Shannon discovers a lump under her armpit. After a series of expensive tests, she learns that she has Hodgkin's disease, a form of lymph cancer, and must undergo radiation and extensive chemotherapy treatments for a year. Shannon learns that reimbursement for some of the expensive tests are excluded under her plan and that the maximum amount of reimbursable benefits is capped at $25,000. After that, she is required to pay 50 percent of all medical, hospital, and physician expenses out of her pocket.

tional basic protection. Answers to the following questions can help you in this area.

QUESTIONS TO ASK REGARDING EMPLOYER-PROVIDED HEALTH BENEFITS

- How much is your monthly premium? Is this taken directly out of your paycheck? Are you allowed to pay more on your own to get better coverage or shift your money to a more cost-effective plan?

- Does the company have a summary plan of benefits? If so, read the summary to get a better idea of the basic benefits offered. (Note: It may still be necessary to read the entire plan to get more specific information and check the fine print.)

- What are the plan's exclusions and limitations? What mental and physical conditions does the plan *not* cover?

- Does the plan cover preexisting conditions?

- How much is your annual deductible (the amount you must pay before your insurance kicks in)?

- What is the process for filing claims? Do you have to pay and submit proof of payment before reimbursement, or can you submit claims directly from your physician? How long must you wait before reimbursement?

- Can you appeal a negative decision not to be reimbursed? If so, what is the process for filing an appeal?

- Is your family also covered?

- Does the plan pay for second opinions and preventive tests such as mammograms and Pap smears?

- If you are close to retirement age, what impact will Medicaid and Medicare coverage have on your benefits?

- If you are close to retirement, what guarantees regarding continued retiree health benefits will you receive?

- Does medical, dental, and hospitalization coverage stop the day you are fired or resign, or is there a grace period (e.g., through the end of the month)?

- Can you extend coverage beyond the grace period?

- Can you assume any group health policy (this is sometimes referred to as a conversion policy)?

If you discover that the health benefits your employer is providing are not substantial, consider implementing coverage through your spouse's coverage or purchasing coverage from additional plans.

COBRA HEALTH BENEFITS

Federal COBRA law requires most private employers to continue to make existing group health insurance available to workers who are discharged or resign from employment. All employees who are discharged as a result of voluntary or involuntary termination, such as for poor performance, negligence, or inefficiency (with the exception of those who are fired for gross misconduct), may elect to continue plan benefits currently in effect *at their own cost* provided the employee or beneficiary makes an initial payment within 30 days of notification and is not covered under Medicare or any other group health plan. The law also applies to qualified beneficiaries who were covered by the employer's group health plan the day before the discharge. Thus, for example, if the employee chooses not to continue such coverage, her spouse and dependent children may elect continued coverage at their own expense.

The extended coverage period is 18 months upon termination of the covered employee; upon the death, divorce, or legal separation of the covered employee, the benefit coverage period is 36 months to spouses and dependents.

The law requires that employers or plan administrators separately notify all employees and covered spouses and dependents of their rights to continued coverage. After receiving such notification, the individual has 60 days to elect to continue coverage. Additionally, employees and dependents whose insurance is protected under COBRA must be provided with any conversion privilege otherwise available in the plan (if such coverage exists) within a six-month period preceding the date on which coverage would terminate at the end of the continuation period.

Some employers run afoul of the law in failing to follow rules regarding notification requirements, conversion privileges, excluded individuals, and time restrictions. In the event the employer fails to offer such coverage, the law imposes penalties ranging from $100 to

An employer offered its two health care plan options to a laid-off employee, Maureen. When the plan chosen by the ex-employee went bankrupt, only the second plan, an HMO, remained. All current employees of the company were in the plan's geographic area, and they signed up with the HMO. Since Maureen lived outside the area, she was left without any health continuation coverage.

Maureen sued her former employer for health care coverage that she claimed was her right under COBRA. She prevailed. Although federal regulations require only that COBRA coverage be the same as insurance offered "similarly situated beneficiaries" as the employer argued, a U.S. District Court ruled that the employer had not satisfied its obligations.

$200 per day for each day the employee is not covered and other damages.

COUNSEL COMMENTS: Cases typically pit a former employee or an employee's dependent with substantial medical expenses against the employer or an insurance company. Courts are sometimes willing to interpret and apply COBRA with a view toward extending coverage wherever possible. For example, in one case, an employee incapacitated by a series of strokes was maintained on her employer's group insurance policy. After about a year, the employee was taken off the company's rolls. At that time she was in a coma, and the COBRA continuation notice was sent to her husband. Misunderstanding the intent of the offer and thinking that his wife was still covered under the employer's group plan without premium payments, he waived his wife's insurance continuation rights. Later, as legal guardian, the ex-employee's husband tried to regain the option of COBRA coverage, but the insurance company refused. The husband sued and won; the court ruled that the employer should have included the Summary Plan Description with the COBRA notice sent to the husband and that without the summary he was unable to make an informed decision.

TIP: Know your COBRA rights before accepting any job and in the event you resign or are fired. This is especially true if you or a spouse or dependent is sick and needs the insurance benefits to pay necessary medical bills. You are entitled to such protection even if you have worked for the employer for a short period of time. Most short-term employees can generally enjoy COBRA protection for periods exceeding the length of their employment. The only requirement is that you must have been included in the employer's group plan at the time of the firing and that the employer was large enough (i.e., employed 20 or more workers, including part-timers, independent contractors, and agents, during the preceding year) under federal law to qualify.

You cannot obtain benefits if you are fired for gross misconduct. This term is relatively ambiguous; the burden of proof is on the employer to prove that the discharge was for a compelling reason (such as starting a fight or stealing).

If an employer reduces your working hours to a point that makes you ineligible for group health coverage, refuses to negotiate continued health benefits as part of a severance package, or fails to notify you of the existence of such benefits, contact the personnel office immediately to protect your rights. If the employer refuses to offer continued COBRA benefits after a discharge for any reason, consult an experienced employment lawyer immediately.

Other points to remember are:

1. A company's hands may not be tied in the event that a group health plan is modified or eliminated; an employer may be permitted to change or eliminate a current plan provided all qualifying beneficiaries and covered employees are allowed to participate similarly under new plans, if any.

2. Coverage for adopted children, children born out of wedlock, and other dependents has been expanded under the Omnibus Budget Reconciliation Act of 1993 and recent court decisions.

3. Speak to a lawyer if you or a dependent is excluded from COBRA protection because of the existence of a secondary health plan or other factors, such as because of an alleged discharge for gross misconduct.

4. Never waive your COBRA rights when accepting severance payments or signing a release after a discharge.

5. Be sure the company notifies you in a timely fashion so you can make the election properly before the short period of employer-provided coverage expires.

BENEFITS DURING PREGNANCY

Employers cannot treat pregnancy-related disability or maternity leave differently from the way they treat other forms of disability or leaves of absence. To do so violates both federal and state discrimination laws. The Pregnancy Discrimination Act of 1978, an amendment to Title VII of the federal Civil Rights Act of 1964, prohibits discrimination on the basis of pregnancy, childbirth, and related medical conditions. The law requires employers to review their health, disability, insurance, sick leave, benefit, job reinstatement, and seniority policies to ensure that they treat pregnancy-related disability and maternity leaves of absence the same as other temporary absences for physical disabilities.

The following general rules illustrate what employers may and may not do in this area:

■ Employees who are on maternity leave (defined as the child-care period commencing after disability from the pregnancy and birth has ended) are entitled to accrue seniority, automatic pay increases, and vacation time on the same basis as other employees on medical leave.

■ Employers may not require pregnant workers to exhaust vacation benefits unless all temporarily disabled workers are required to do the same.

■ Employers may require a physical examination and doctor's certification of ability to return to work only if such is required of all temporarily disabled workers.

■ Although employers may require workers to give notice of a pregnancy, such requirement must serve a legitimate business purpose and must not be used to restrict the employee's job opportunities.

■ Employers are prohibited from discriminating in hiring, promotion, and firing decisions on the basis of pregnancy or because of an abortion.

■ After a birth, an employer cannot prohibit a woman from returning to work sooner than company policy dictates.

■ Employers are barred from forcing pregnant workers to take mandatory maternity leaves (i.e., forcing a woman to leave work against her

Employees at one company were granted basic hospital, surgical, and major medical benefits under the company's health insurance plan. Employees and their dependents were reimbursed 100 percent of the charges for basic medical care with the exception that wives of male employees were reimbursed for pregnancy-related charges at the rate of only 80 percent of the actual charges. Benefits for dependents terminated at the same time as those for employees, except for pregnancy benefits for dependent spouses. A spouse of a male employee was covered for maternity expenses throughout her pregnancy, even if it extended for more than three months after her husband's termination.

Marsha, terminated because of a business slowdown, learns she is pregnant a few weeks after her dismissal. She participates in the three-month continuation of the medical plan and then requests medical benefits for her pregnancy equal to those provided to wives of male employees under the company's health insurance plan. The company rejects her claim.

Marsha hires a lawyer and commences a lawsuit charging sex discrimination. In court, the company argues that benefits to a female employee could be different from those granted to the spouse of a male employee, and that her claim confused discrimination between employees (which the law forbids) with discrimination between an employee and a non-employee spouse (which the law allows).

The court rules in Marsha's favor. It states that it is an unlawful employment practice for an employer to make available benefits for the wives and families of male employees where the same benefits are not made available for the husbands and families of female employees, or to make available benefits for the wives of male employees which are not made available for female employees.

wishes in anticipation of giving birth) as long as the employee is able to do her job.

■ The decision as to whether payment for pregnancy disability leave will be given must be in accord with policies governing other forms of disability leave; if paid leave is provided for workers with other disabilities, the employer must provide pregnant workers with paid leave for their actual disability due to pregnancy and related childbirth.

- Time restrictions based on pregnancy-related leaves (e.g., that pregnancy leaves not exceed four months) must be reasonable and job-related; if not, they may be illegal. Also, employers are generally required to provide disability benefits for as long as a pregnant woman is unable to work for medical reasons.

- It is illegal to place pregnant workers on involuntary sick leave if the company has no policy of placing workers with other forms of disabilities on involuntary leave; if a worker is physically able to work, the company cannot force her to leave merely because she is pregnant.

- An employer cannot refuse to hire a pregnant worker because it does not want to find a replacement when the employee takes a leave to give birth if her skills and qualifications meet or exceed those of other applicants.

- Women who take maternity leave must be reinstated under the same conditions as employees who return from leaves for other disabilities. For example, if an employer reinstates a worker who was absent from work due to a case of chronic bronchitis, the employer must reinstate a worker after childbirth to avoid violating Title VII.

- If an employer accommodates partially disabled workers who cannot perform certain job assignments (such as lifting heavy objects because of a strained back), the employer is obligated to make similar arrangements for a pregnant worker.

- Employers cannot limit pregnancy disability benefits to married employees. Federal law states it is illegal to fire female workers who get married if the employer does not fire male workers who get married. Many state laws have gone even further to protect women; statutes have been enacted that prohibit employers from making any adverse decisions on the basis of a person's marital status even if the employer applies its policies equally to males and females.

- At the hiring interview, you cannot be asked questions about childbearing plans or pregnancy.

- Employers are not allowed to ask a pregnant employee to choose between a lower-level job and resignation.

(Author's Note: The above rules may not apply, depending on the law and the particular facts and circumstances of your case.

Always consult an experienced employment lawyer for advice and guidance where applicable.)

Thousands of pregnancy-related discrimination lawsuits are filed each year; the kind of mistreatment varies. For example, in one recent reported case, six workers who said they were laid off after asking for lighter duties because of pregnancy sued their employer in Federal District Court. One of the plaintiffs, a train operator, asked for light-duty assignment when she announced her pregnancy. According to the court papers, she was then placed on involuntary unpaid leave despite the fact that she was ready, willing, and able to continue working and that appropriate work was available. The suit also charged that the women who were laid off were unable to collect unemployment insurance because the employer advised the Unemployment Insurance Department that they had gone on voluntary leaves. The employer argued that no employee is allowed to remain on light duty longer than 14 days, whether pregnant or disabled by any other condition. The case has yet to be decided by a judge.

Although pregnant workers were subject to poor treatment from employers in the past, the laws are now attempting to put pregnant women on an equal footing with other employees. The number of pregnancy discrimination claims filed with the EEOC increased by more than 33 percent between 1991 and 1995. While an estimated 84 percent of women expecting children work into the final month of pregnancy, and about one-third return to work within eight weeks and half return within three months of giving birth, millions of women have lost their jobs after giving birth. Fortunately, with the passage of the Family and Medical Leave Act (discussed in the next section), pregnant women who work for employers with more than 50 full-time employees are guaranteed equivalent jobs when they return.

COUNSEL COMMENTS: In some cases, however, pregnant women lose their claims because they fail to prove their case or ask for accommodations beyond the minimum provided by law. The following two cases illustrate the problems often associated with winning pregnancy discrimination lawsuits.

In one case, a woman 19 weeks pregnant asked for reassignment to a job that did not require heavy lifting. She was given a job at the service desk, which required evening and weekend work. She was unable to work those hours because of family conflicts and declined the assignment. The company fired her and she sued for pregnancy discrimination. She lost her case because she failed to prove a *disparate impact* (i.e., that other employees who were reassigned for medical reasons and objected were not terminated). The judge commented that the law does not *guarantee* that pregnant workers not suffer any adverse employment decisions. He wrote that "the law only protects against employment decisions which, for discriminatory reasons, are different from decisions relating to persons who are not pregnant."

In another case, a female salesperson suffered severe morning sickness during her first trimester. As a result, she was often late in reporting to work. The woman was placed on part-time status but continued to report to work late. After several warnings and being placed on probation, the company fired her. Although she was fired one day before taking maternity leave, the court ruled that that fact did not warrant a finding of liability because the company was free to fire anyone who could not work due to a medical condition, whether pregnant or otherwise.

> **TIP:** The second case is significant as a teaching model for several reasons. The woman salesperson's case might have been strengthened if she had found other, nonpregnant workers who had not been fired due to excessive absences or right before taking a leave of absence. And although the company was guilty of poor timing, the woman failed to introduce significant evidence at the trial, such as damaging statements made to her indicating that the reason given for the firing (i.e., excessive lateness) was really pretextual (i.e., unfounded) and offered just as an excuse to terminate because she was pregnant. Apparently, given the absence of important comparisons and other evidence, she lost her case. This illustrates the kind of evidence you must be able to offer if your lawyer is to be successful in proving a pregnancy discrimination case.

Speak to a competent employment lawyer if you feel you have been discriminated against on the basis of pregnancy. Women who are fired while pregnant should naturally suspect that pregnancy was the reason for the discharge. Consider filing a claim alleging pregnancy discrimination with the EEOC or appropriate state antidiscrimination agency. The filing is free, and you do not need a lawyer to assist you in the process. Information on how to file a discrimination charge is given in Chapter Six.

Employers are often advised that even when a decision to fire has nothing to do with a woman's pregnancy, it may be wise to continue her employment until she voluntarily leaves to give birth, rather than fire her several months before the birth, to avoid the added costs and burdens of contesting a charge of pregnancy discrimination. Employers are also advised by their attorneys that if they must fire a pregnant worker, they should be sure that her file supports the decision (i.e., that unfavorable job performance appraisals and repeated written warnings are present in the file and the worker was repeatedly warned about her performance before the company was notified of her pregnancy).

STRATEGIES TO STRENGTHEN A CLAIM

1. Tell your supervisor and other bosses immediately after you learn that you are pregnant. Once you become pregnant you enter a protected class under the law, and the company may have to reevaluate any decision to fire you if that was being considered before your notification. Thus, in marginal performance cases, becoming pregnant could give you added job security. Some litigants lose their cases, however, because they cannot prove the company knew they were pregnant before taking adverse action. Do not be afraid to tell key people at the job site that you are pregnant, since this may work to your legal benefit.

2. Understand your options to take paid short-term and long-term disability leaves and unpaid leaves.

3. Be aware of how the company treated pregnant workers in the past for comparison purposes.

4. Remember that the payment of costs for pregnancy-related conditions may be limited to a specific dollar amount stipulated in an insurance policy, collective bargaining agreement, or other statement of employee benefits provided limits are imposed for other health conditions.

5. Always read and understand your employer's health insurance policies and coverage before incurring medical treatment.

6. If you are offered a choice between enrolling in one of two health insurance plans, be sure to choose the one that covers pregnancy-

related conditions so that you will be reimbursed on the same basis as for other medical conditions.

7. Employers are not generally responsible to provide health insurance covering abortions. However, they may be required to offer sick leave and other fringe benefits as a result of an abortion. Additionally, while some health plans do not pay for abortions, they do cover complications resulting from the procedure, such as treatment due to excessive bleeding. Always read the fine print of your policy to determine your options where applicable.

PREGNANCY AS A DISABILITY

The ability of pregnant workers to succeed in demanding special accommodations has been strengthened by the passage of state and local laws. Although the federal Americans with Disabilities Act (ADA) does *not* consider pregnancy a covered disability (since it is classified as a temporary nonchronic impairment with no long-term impact), some state laws have ruled it is a per se disability requiring a company to make reasonable accommodation when requested by an employee. Under these state laws, the physical demands of pregnancy may require companies to allow pregnant workers to work at home or rearrange their work schedules. When a woman seeks reasonable accommodation during pregnancy, an employer should be responsive to the particular physical limitations that the employee brings forward on a case-by-case basis. Employers unwilling to comply with such a request are required to justify their decisions by demonstrating that compliance would create an undue hardship.

A recent case illustrates these issues. When a New York employee filed a lawsuit claiming she was fired for taking too many days off because of her pregnancy, a judge ruled that she could continue with her case. The judge held that while pregnancy itself may not be a disability under federal law, physical complications resulting from pregnancy can qualify for statutory protection under both federal and state guidelines.

The woman suffered severe physical symptoms resulting from pregnancy complications, forcing her to call in sick on numerous occasions. She also missed work because her doctor could see her only during normal working hours. Although she conscientiously called in sick and gave adequate advance warning, she was fired.

The employer asked the judge to dismiss the case since pregnancy is not a covered disability under the ADA. However, the judge ruled that while a normal pregnancy is not considered an impairment, physical complications resulting from the pregnancy, such as severe back pain, nausea, and bleeding, may constitute a physiological impairment substantially limiting a major life activity (i.e., working). The judge also ruled that an employee qualifies for ADA protection even if she does not have an actual disability, if the employer treats her as if the disability existed and makes adverse decisions as a result.

Finally, the employee argued that she was able to reasonably perform her job duties despite her absence and that the company had not fired other workers with significant absences caused by other disabilities.

The case is now proceeding to a jury trial.

TIP: Check your state's law on this issue to understand the extent of protection available to you. If you find the law is favorable, consider requesting reasonable accommodation (such as reporting to work an hour later each day or being allowed to work from bed if you risk losing a baby without extensive bed rest). Speak to a lawyer for more details when applicable.

In another case, when an employee discovered she was pregnant, she was warned by a co-worker that her manager would not be happy to hear the news. After she told her manager, he asked personal questions about birth control and how her parents felt about her being unmarried and pregnant. He later noted in a performance appraisal that she was an unwed expectant mother.

After giving birth, the woman suffered complications and requested an extended leave. Her doctor submitted a request for additional time off. The company refused and sent her a letter accepting her "voluntary termination."

The woman sued, claiming that the company violated the federal Pregnancy Discrimination Act (PDA). Based on the company's refusal to honor the doctor's written request and the manager's actions, the court awarded her more than $90,000 in back pay, punitive damages, and damages for emotional distress.

COUNSEL COMMENTS: Recognize, however, that the law might be decided differently, depending on the facts. For example, in another case, a supervisor noted that a female employee had trouble meeting deadlines, handling her workload, and dealing with others. When the employee went on maternity leave, a backlog of her work was discovered. Management decided to demote her to a job with less independence, discretion, and pay. The employee refused to take the job and sued the company under the PDA. She claimed that her status as a new mother prompted the demotion, especially since she had been told by her supervisor that the job "was good for a new mother."

The company defended the case on the basis of solid documentation of her shortcomings and deficiencies in performance reviews. Based on this evidence, the judge sided with the company.

In conclusion, speak to a lawyer whenever you believe that your pregnancy is being used as an excuse for downgrading your performance rating or removing you from the fast track for promotions. Employers must demonstrate legitimate business reasons for all decisions impacting you. This includes a scrutiny of your performance. When the company promotes a nonpregnant employee over you but cannot demonstrate the other person's superior qualifications, educational background, or accomplishments, speak to employment lawyer immediately. This is also true when you experience insensitive remarks, are not given the opportunity to make your own decisions regarding hazardous jobs, or believe that you have not been dealt with in a consistent even-handed way compared to nonpregnant workers at the company.

(Final Note: A court recently ruled that a company medical benefit plan that specifically excluded infertility treatment for both men and women did not violate the ADA, PDA, and Title VII. The court held that infertility is strikingly different from pregnancy and childbirth. Furthermore, the court stated that there is no evidence that the infertility exclusion impacted female more than male employees.)

PREGNANCY LEAVE AND REEMPLOYMENT

Even before the enactment of the Family and Medical Leave Act (FMLA) in 1993, the rights of pregnant workers to have their jobs back within a certain period of time after giving birth and the ability to enforce the right to take paid maternity leave were being recognized in a number of states. Passage of the FMLA now guarantees that pregnant workers who work for companies with 50 or more employees will get their jobs back after giving birth. The act affects private and nonprofit employers as well as federal, state, and local government employees, public agencies, and private elementary and secondary schools. It applies to companies that employ 50 or more employees within a 75-mile radius for each working day for each of 20 or more calendar workweeks in the current or preceding calendar year. This is about half of the nation's workforce. Part-time employees and employees on leaves of absence are counted in this calculation provided they are on the employer's payroll for each day of the workweek. Conversely, employees who began employment after the beginning of a workweek, were terminated prior to the end of a workweek, or who worked part-time on weekends are not included in the equation.

Since companies with fewer than 50 employees are exempt, analyzing the number of employees who must be counted becomes an important consideration for organizations close to the "magic" 50 number. If a company hires temporary, contract employees or part-time workers who work 25 or fewer hours a week to get under the number, they will not be subject to the law's provisions.

An eligible employee, defined as someone who has been employed for at least 12 months and worked for the employer at least 1,250 hours during the 12-month period immediately preceding the commencement of the leave, is allowed to take up to 12 weeks of unpaid leave in any 12-month period for:

- The birth of a child (commencing from the date of the birth of the child);
- The adoption of a child (commencing from the date of the adoption);
- To care for a child, dependent son or daughter over the age of 13, spouse, or parent with a serious health condition; or
- To convalesce from a serious condition that makes it impossible for the employee to work.

(Note: The 12 months of employment need not have been consecutive.)

Under the law, a "serious health condition" is defined as an illness, injury, impairment, or physical or mental condition requiring either inpatient care at a hospital, hospice, or residential medical care facility, or continuing treatment by a health care provider. Thus, an overnight stay in a hospital, any condition requiring absence from work of more than three consecutive calendar days, or a health condition that demands continued treatment by a health care provider may qualify. This includes voluntary or cosmetic treatments if inpatient hospital care is required, restorative dental surgery after an accident, and continued treatment for serious allergies or stress or for substance abuse.

Thus, some employees who require continuing medical supervision (i.e., workers with early-stage cancer or who have major heart surgery) and must undergo frequent medical examinations or treatment but are nonetheless capable of working part-time still fit into the category of suffering from a "serious health condition" and qualify for leave time.

For those workers claiming serious health situations, the law permits an employer to obtain medical opinions and certifications regarding the need for a leave. The certification must state the date on which the serious health condition began, its probable duration, the appropriate medical facts within the knowledge of the health care provider regarding the condition, and an estimate of the amount of time the employee needs to care for a family member or herself. If an employer has doubts about the certification, it may require a second opinion from a different health care provider chosen by the employer. If the two opinions differ, a third opinion from a provider jointly designated or approved by the employer and the employee will be final and binding.

The law applies equally to both female and male employees. Thus, a father, as well as a mother, can take family leave, at the same time or sequentially, depending on the family's preferences and economic considerations. (Note: If both spouses work for the same company, the law limits the total amount of leave to 12 weeks for both in some situations, but not to care for themselves, their spouse, or a child.)

Although written notice is not generally required, women who qualify for unpaid leave are required to give 30 days advance notice unless this is not practicable or foreseeable, such as in a premature birth or sudden, unexpected illness. If 30 days notice cannot be given, notice must be given as soon as practicable. This is because you are required to make a reasonable effort to schedule the leave so as not to unduly disrupt the employer's operations.

TIP: It is not necessary to state that you require FMLA leave. Rather, it is sufficient only to indicate that time is needed and provide some details why. After your notice is received, the employer has an immediate obligation to provide you with a written statement concerning your rights, duties, and obligations within two business days. The written notice must provide you with answers to the following:

- Whether the leave will be counted against your annual FMLA entitlement

- Whether you are required to submit medical certification

- Your right to paid leave and if this will be substituted by the employer for FMLA purposes

- Any requirements for you to make premium payments to maintain health benefits

- Your liability for medical premiums paid by the employer during your absence if you do not return to work after the leave

- Your right to receive the same or an equivalent job upon your return

- Any requirement that you must present a certification stating your fitness before returning

- Whether you are considered a key employee under the FMLA and therefore not entitled to coverage

If such a timely notice is not received, the law presumes that you are qualified to take FMLA leave as soon as practicable. Also, if you receive answers that you do not agree with, consult an employment lawyer immediately.

The key element of the law allows a person taking leave to be given her old job back or assigned an equivalent position, with equivalent benefits, pay, and other terms and conditions of employment, when she returns. The burden is on the employer to give the worker back her same or an equivalent job (not a comparable job) wherever possible.

An equivalent position is one that is virtually identical to the employee's former position in terms of pay, benefits, and working conditions, including privileges, prerequisites, and status. It must involve the same or substantially similar duties, equivalent skill, effort, responsibility, and authority. The job must be in the same geographic proximity and offer the same opportunities for bonuses, profit sharing, salary increases, promotions, additional health insurance, sick leave, and educational benefits.

Also, no employer may deprive an employee of benefits accrued before the date on which the leave commenced. During the time the worker is on leave, an employer is not required to pay her but is required to maintain health insurance benefits, as well as life and disability insurance, pensions, educational benefits, and any annual sick leave that has accrued prior to the commencement of the family leave, at the level and under the conditions coverage would have been maintained if the employee had continued in employment. However, if the employer was legitimately about to lay off the worker just before being notified of the leave, the employee's right of reinstatement is no greater than what it was when the discharge occurred.

> **COUNSEL COMMENTS:**   Nothing requires an employer to provide health benefits if it does not do so at the time the employee commences leave. However, if the employer was considering establishing a health plan during the employee's leave, the worker on leave is entitled to receive the same benefits other workers still on the job receive. Also, an employer has the right to demand repayment for the group health care premiums paid by the employer during the leave if the employee fails to return after the period of leave to which she is entitled has expired and the reason was not caused by a recurrence or onset of a serious health condition or other circumstances beyond her control.

> **TIP:**   An employee may refuse to make the contributions during the leave period but still must be offered health insurance on the same terms and conditions when returning to work. If that occurs, the employer cannot require you to undergo a new health insurance qualifying period or a physical, or impose other restrictions that did not exist prior to your leave. Finally, if the health insurance plan benefits improved during your absence, you are entitled to those improved benefits upon your return.

There are numerous exceptions to be aware of. First, the FMLA prohibits a worker on leave from collecting unemployment or other government compensation. Part-time workers and those who have not worked for at least a year do not qualify for FMLA leave. Also, an eligible employee may elect, or an employer is permitted, to substitute any accrued paid vacation leave, personal leave, or family leave of the employee under preestablished policies in handbooks or employee manuals for any part of the 12-week period of family leave. As a result, companies are required to provide both paid and unpaid leave only up to a total of 12 weeks, and employers may count time off against paid vacation days or other accrued personal leave.

The leave request may not generally be intermittent or on a reduced schedule without the employer's permission or except when medically necessary; employers are permitted to require an employee taking intermittent leave as a result of planned medical treatments to prove the medical necessity of the leave and to transfer temporarily to an equivalent alternative position. Thus, for example, employers may have the right to demand that pregnant workers take the time off in a continuous period and then return. This provision gives employers greater staffing flexibility by enabling them to transfer employees who need intermittent leave or leave on a reduced schedule to positions that are more suitable for recurring periods of leave.

If you are a top executive (defined as being in the highest 10 percent of the company's payroll), the company may refuse your request to take leave when it would cause substantial economic harm. If you nonetheless take the leave, you are still eligible for continuation of medical benefits but the company is not obligated to take you back or guarantee that an appropriate job will be available upon your return. However, in such situations, no recovery of premiums may be made by the employer if the employee has chosen to take or continue leave after being denied her request for leave because she is ill or needs to continue the care of a relative or child. (Note: If the employee refuses to come back because she took a better-paying job, the company can lawfully demand repayment.)

Also, while you are on leave, economic benefits such as employer-contributed pension and profit-sharing payments and vacation pay do not continue to accrue unless you are receiving full pay with benefits. When in doubt, ask your employer about your entitlement to such continued benefits before you go out on FMLA leave.

Although many situations may qualify as important or as emergencies (such as having to accompany your child to an out-of-state college or take care of a sick grandparent for several weeks), these may not be covered under the law. While you are out you must report regularly to your employer and advise when you think you will be returning.

> **TIP:**   Speak to a knowledgeable lawyer if you return from pregnancy leave and/or unpaid child care leave to a different position. This is because receiving a job of equal pay and grade may still violate the law if it is a different job.

The Secretary of Labor has the authority to investigate alleged violations of the FMLA. This includes requesting employers to submit their books and records for inspection. Violations are punishable by injunctive and monetary relief. For employers who violate the law, monetary damages include an amount equal to the wages, salary, employment benefits, or other compensation denied or lost to an employee. In cases where no compensation or wages are lost, the law imposes other forms of damages, such as the actual amount of out-of-pocket money paid to someone else to provide care. In the event a willful violation is proved, employers are liable for additional damages equal to the amount of the award. The law also imposes

---

Joan works for a large company as a supervisor. She takes unpaid leave to care for her sick husband. When she returns 10 weeks later, she is given a new job at the same rate of pay. But the new job has fewer duties (she supervises only two people instead of five) and she is required to perform clerical functions not present in her prior position. Joan advises management that she is dissatisfied with her new position and that the company has violated the FMLA by not giving her back her old job or an equivalent position. The company states that it reorganized her department while she was on leave.

Joan consults a lawyer for advice. Rather than sue her employer, she is told first to try to negotiate better benefits. Joan listens to her lawyer. She receives another week of paid vacation, an office with a window, a prime parking spot, and the employer's promise not to terminate her for at least two years. She is also promised her old job back if it becomes available. Joan is pleased with her negotiation efforts.

reasonable compensation for attorney fees, expert witness fees, and other costs and disbursements. Employers are forbidden from discriminating against workers who attempt to utilize the act or who protest alleged violations. Similarly, it is unlawful to retaliate against any worker by discharge or reduced benefits because the employee has filed a charge or instituted a proceeding concerning the law or is about to give (or has given) testimony regarding the FMLA.

COUNSEL COMMENTS: In the event your state law is more comprehensive or offers greater benefits than federal law, state law will control. State or local laws that provide greater protection, longer leave periods, or paid leave are enforceable, so check the law in your state where applicable. You may discover, for example, that state law applies to smaller-size employers (i.e., those with 20 or more full-time employees).

TIP: The FMLA cannot rescind rights granted to employees in collective bargaining agreements, pension plans, ERISA rights, or rights granted as a result of the ADA and other discrimination laws. If you believe you have been discriminated or retaliated against by asserting your rights, speak to a lawyer. You have the option of commencing a private lawsuit and seeking money to pay for a caregiver's bills (up to 12 weeks) if you were denied leave provided you bring the action within two years of the date of the violation or three years if the violation is willful. You can also sue for job reinstatement and resulting damages if you are illegally denied a leave, take it anyway, and are not given your old job back when you want to return. An employer may appeal negative results of an investigation by the Department of Labor. Have your lawyer explain all your options and rights to you and then map out an effective action plan.

HAZARDOUS JOBS

The Supreme Court has ruled that employers cannot ban women from certain hazardous jobs, even if the motive is preventing birth defects in fetuses those female workers may be carrying. In an important ruling, the Supreme Court decided that a manufacturer acted illegally by prohibiting women capable of bearing children from holding jobs involving exposure to lead during the manufacture of batteries. The court determined that such a policy forces some women to choose between having a child and keeping a job, and this violated federal laws against sex discrimination.

> **TIP:** Despite the ruling in this case, women who insist on remaining in such jobs still have the right to sue their employers for damages on behalf of a child born with prenatal injuries caused by workplace conditions, even years after being exposed to such hazardous conditions. To reduce the chance of injury, consider asking for reassignment from a hazardous job when you become pregnant. However, if any reassignment is not voluntary but forced, and there is a reduction in workers' compensation benefits or seniority rights, or you are asked to sign a release waiving your right to sue in the future, consult a lawyer immediately.

ERISA BENEFITS

Employer-sponsored health, pension, and profit-sharing plans are governed by the federal Employee Retirement Income Security Act of 1974 (ERISA). ERISA sets minimum standards for benefit plans, the vesting of benefits, and communication to plan participants and their beneficiaries. This includes all plans, funds, or programs that provide medical, surgical, or hospital care benefits; retirement income or the deferral of income after retirement or termination (such as severance); or deferred compensation plans such as stock bonus and money purchase pension plans. The act covers six basic areas, including:

- Communications: what must be disclosed to employees, how it must be disclosed, and what reports must be filed with the federal government
- Eligibility: which employees may participate in a benefit plan
- Vesting: rules regarding when and to what extent benefits must be paid
- Funding: what employers must pay into a plan to meet its normal costs and to amortize past service liabilities
- Fiduciary responsibilities: how the investment of funds must be handled and the responsibilities of the plan administrators to oversee the plan and plan benefits

■ Plan termination insurance: the availability of insurance to protect the payment of vested benefits

The law does not require employers to establish pension or profit-sharing plans. Once they do, however, virtually all private employers are regulated by ERISA in one form or another.

The first step to understanding and enforcing your ERISA rights is to ask for details regarding the nature of your benefits when you are hired. You are entitled to an accurate, written description of all benefits under federal law. Be aware of all plans, funds, and programs that will be established on your behalf. These may include the following:

■ *Defined contribution plans* (e.g., profit-sharing plans, thrift plans, money purchase pension plans, and cash or deferred profit-sharing plans). All these plans are characterized by the fact that each participant has an individual bookkeeping account under the plan which records the participant's total interest in the plan assets. Monies are contributed or credited in accordance with the rules of the plan contained in the plan document.

■ *Defined benefit plans.* These are characterized as pension plans that base the benefits payable to participants on a formula contained in the plan. Such plans are not funded individually as are defined contribution plans. Rather, they are typically funded on a group basis.

■ *Employee welfare benefit plans.* These are often funded through insurance and typically provide participants with medical, health, accident, disability, death, unemployment, or vacation benefits.

■ *ERISA plans.* These may not be as definite as the plans above. Rather, if the employer communicates that certain benefits are available, who the intended beneficiaries are, and how the plan is funded, the employer may be liable to pay such benefits even in the absence of a formal, written plan.

COUNSEL COMMENTS: An investigation by the U.S. Department of Labor uncovered hundreds of companies misusing and diverting 401(k) employee pension programs. In 401(k) plans, workers save and invest their own money for retirement through automatic savings programs set up by their employers. When the plans are operated correctly, workers determine how much they contribute, the employer withholds the stipulated amount from employee paychecks, and the company forwards the money to a plan administrator, who invests worker contributions in a manner selected by the worker. The Department of Labor discovered that many small and midsize companies violated plan rules and federal law by delaying payment to plan administrators, diverted funds to pay other corporate expenses, or stole the money outright and never reported the contributions. In a recent 401(k) amnesty plan, the Department of Labor reported that 170 companies admitted they failed to deposit $4.8 million in the retirement accounts of 16,800 workers. The money came from technology firms, law firms, doctors' offices, credit unions, and manufacturers in 38 states and payments ranged from $43 to $200,000. Some companies admitted using the money to cover business expenses. (Note: Money withheld from workers' paychecks must be deposited to 401(k) accounts within 15 business days after the end of the month the money is withheld. For more information, call 202-219-9247 to get a copy of the free publication "Protect Your Pension" published by the Labor Department.)

TIP: The best way to avoid such problems is to monitor and regularly scrutinize reports given to you by the employer concerning your current benefits. If your returns show constant losses, plan officials may not be investing your money properly. Speak to management about how you want your money invested. If your statements are coming late or at odd intervals, check with your benefits department to find out why. Demand such reports if they are not periodically forthcoming. If your retired friends say they can't get the pension plan to pay them what's due, start checking further. Always request such reports when you believe the company is having financial difficulties, such as when paychecks are not being distributed on time. Most important, keep track of how much you're contributing to the pension and then match your records to the reports you receive from the plan. These statements should indicate the amount you and your employer have contributed, plus the rate of return you've earned on your investments. If the numbers don't match, it is possible (especially with small companies) that the employer is illegally holding or diverting your contributions.

To safeguard benefits, ERISA mandates that assets in a beneficiary's pension be virtually "untouchable." This is accomplished by requiring that plan administrators file numerous reports with the U.S.

Department of Labor, the Internal Revenue Service, and the Pension Benefit Guaranty Corporation (a federal agency located in Washington, D.C.), including plan descriptions, summary plan descriptions, material changes in the plan, description of modifications of the terms of the plan, an annual report (Form 5500), an annual registration statement listing employees separated from services during the plan year, and numerous other reports for defined benefit plans covered by the termination insurance provisions with the Pension Benefit Guaranty Corporation.

Demand a copy of the employer's pension and/or profit-sharing plans from the plan administrator if the employer refuses to furnish you with accurate details. (Note: You may have to pay for the cost of photocopying said plans when requesting them.) ERISA provides that plan participants are entitled to examine without charge all plan documents filed with the U.S. Department of Labor, including detailed annual reports and plan descriptions. If you request materials and do not receive them within 30 days, you may file suit in federal court. In such a case, the court may require the plan administrator to provide the materials and pay up to $100 a day until you receive the materials, unless the materials are not sent for reasons beyond the control of the administrator.

> **TIP:** If you are fired just before the vesting of a pension (e.g., two months before the vesting date), argue that the timing of the firing is suspect and that public policy requires the employer to grant your pension. If the employer refuses, consult an experienced employment lawyer immediately.

Contact the plan administrator immediately to protect your rights if your claim is denied or if you suspect there are problems with your plan. Under federal law, every employee, participant, or beneficiary covered under a benefit plan covered by ERISA has the right to receive written notification stating specific reasons for the denial of a claim. You have the right to a full and fair review by the plan administrator if you are denied benefits.

If you suspect the company has not acted properly with respect to your benefits, inquire about your account with the plan administrator. Determine whether the amount of each payment corresponds with the amount that was deducted from your paycheck and reflects any promised matching contributions. If you are not satisfied with the answers, contact your nearest Department of Labor office to discuss the matter with a representative. Request an investigation on behalf of you and your coworkers where warranted.

If you have a claim for benefits that is denied or ignored in whole or in part after making a request to a plan administrator, speak to a lawyer and consider filing a lawsuit in either state or federal court. If it should happen that plan fiduciaries misuse a plan's money, or if you are retaliated against for asserting your rights (such as being demoted, reassigned, or fired), seek assistance from the U.S. Department of Labor, or file suit in federal court. The court will decide who should pay court costs and legal fees. If you are successful, the court may order the employer or person you have sued to pay these costs and fees.

> **TIP:** If your company goes out of business, files for bankruptcy, or has no assets, many states require the owners (i.e., stockholders) and officers to be personally liable to repay pension and other retirement benefits. Thus, all may not be lost if you discover your benefits were diverted and the company goes out of business. Speak to a lawyer about this point where applicable.

The Pension Benefit Guaranty Corporation has created an office to help workers trace their pensions. By law, a pension plan that terminates is required to make only one attempt to get in touch with workers. The Pension Benefit Guaranty Corporation can assist you by making repeated attempts to find the plans of employers that have gone out of business. Contact this agency in Washington, D.C. and supply it with copies of any plan summaries and plan identification numbers, which are often printed on such papers. Permanently save all plan documents and summaries because you never know when the information will come in handy to document and enforce a claim.

Speak to a benefits lawyer if your company orally modifies any plan benefits, if a summary description does not accurately depict essential elements of the plan, or if a division of the company you are working for is sold and the new company offers far less severance and other benefits than previously promised. When companies merge and workers are laid off or denied promised benefits they previously enjoyed, issues of severance and other post-termination and on-the-job benefits should be scrutinized by a competent lawyer to determine whether ERISA violations have occurred.

CHAPTER FIVE

ON-THE-JOB RIGHTS AND CONDUCT

Women employees possess many on-the-job rights, including rights of privacy. These privacy rights are sometimes violated by executives, security personnel, private investigators, and fellow workers. The law allows employees to recover damages under a variety of legal theories for unlawful interference into a woman's personal relationships and off-duty conduct, including suits for invasion of privacy, intentional infliction of emotional distress, and wrongful discharge, among other causes of action. Areas such as personal appearance rules, romantic relationships with co-workers, and related subjects are typically protected by the U.S. Constitution. This chapter will discuss a variety of areas impacting female workers and will suggest strategies to overcome such problems.

LIE DETECTOR TESTS

The federal Polygraph Protection Act of 1988 bans virtually all employers from requiring workers to submit to lie detector tests. If you are pressured to take such a test, speak to a lawyer immediately because such a request is probably illegal. If you refuse to take a test and are fired, you may have grounds to sue.

SEARCHES AND INTERROGATIONS

Employers faced with growing security problems are resorting to stricter measures to protect company facilities, property, and employees. Although such measures may accomplish their objectives, too often employees' rights are violated in the process. Employers use a variety of techniques when they suspect someone of misconduct, including searching a person's office or locker without your knowledge or consent, requesting you to open a briefcase or package when leaving a company facility, and conducting a "pat-down" search of your person.

Although each case is decided on its own merits, the law generally states that office searches are permitted if an employer has a reasonable basis for suspecting the employee of wrongdoing and the search is confined to nonpersonal areas of the employee's office. Although the office and documents relevant to company business are the property of the employer, clearly visible personal items cannot be searched and employers cannot conduct a search if there is no reasonable ground for suspicion. Also, employers cannot conduct nonconsensual searches of your home; doing so leaves them liable for trespass.

> **COUNSEL COMMENTS:** Suppose your employer decides to search your desk or locker. Do you have the right to sue for invasion of privacy? The answer depends on how much privacy you legitimately expected to have. If the employer announced that the company had a policy of searching desks, lockers, and other areas in the workplace, you can't expect much privacy and probably won't get a favorable decision in court from a judge if those areas are searched. But if no policy existed, you kept your locker or desk locked, and only you had the key or the combination, you might reasonably expect those areas to be protected and be able to prevail in a lawsuit, especially if the employer searched and retrieved personal contents in your handbag that were kept in a locked desk.

Searches of your briefcase, locker, or packages can be legitimate provided the employer posts signs reminding employees that personal property is subject to search and there is probable cause to single you out for the search. But such practices must be imposed on all employees in a nondiscriminatory manner. For example, searching the lockers only of women or a particular ethnic group may be illegal.

TIP: If you believe you were the victim of an employer's search, ask yourself the following questions:

- Were similar searches conducted before?
- Were you notified that the employer reserved the right to search? If so, how?
- What was the object of the search? Was it reasonable?
- Was personal or company property confiscated?
- What did you do during the search? Who conducted the search?
- Did you refuse to cooperate?
- Did the search have an offensive impact? Were you grabbed, jostled, or held? Were you coerced, physically threatened, or verbally abused to force you to cooperate?
- Was a pat-down search done with probable cause, out of view of other employees, with no aggressive behavior used? (Note: If so, this may be legal.)
- Were you held against your will? Were you so intimidated by the experience that you were afraid to leave or told that you could not leave until you answered all questions?
- Were you chosen at random with others, or were you the only one singled out and searched in front of others? If so, were you stigmatized by the suspicion of wrongdoing?

If you answered yes to some of the preceding questions, speak to an employment lawyer immediately. You may have a strong case for reinstatement or compensation if you were fired, placed on probation, suspended, or given an official reprimand after the search. If you were grabbed, jostled, held, or physically threatened during a search, or instructed not to leave a room while being questioned, the employer could be liable for damages as a result of various legal causes of action, including assault, battery, and/or false imprisonment.

TIP: In any interrogation, you generally have the right to know whether you are a suspect, the purpose of the interview, why questions are being asked, the ability to leave the room at any time, and the right to refuse to sign anything and speak to a lawyer. You may also have the right to refuse that a tape recording be made of the interview or request that a tape be made of the conversation for future reference.

However, by asserting your rights, you could be providing the company a basis to fire you on the spot for insubordination. This sometimes occurs so be aware of it.

PERSONAL APPEARANCE RULES

Some companies prescribe standards in dress and personal appearance. Although such codes have been attacked at times, they are legal provided the policies do not unfairly impact a group of workers such as females. If a different rule is imposed for female employees than for male employees (such as requiring women waitresses to wear skimpy clothes while male counterparts wear whatever they wish), the policy may be discriminatory and a violation of Title VII for an adverse (disparate) impact based on sex. Also, a grooming code that severely impacts women (e.g., requiring all female employees to have short haircuts), thus having an adverse impact under Title VII, may also violate the law unless the employer can demonstrate a legitimate business necessity (such as safety considerations) to enforce the rule.

When employers prove that a dress code is reasonable and job-related, it will probably be enforceable and employers may terminate workers who refuse to follow reasonable rules. In many situations, arbitrators and judges will uphold a company's personal appearance policy when it is justifiable. Good grooming regulations are often imposed in an attempt to reflect a company's image in a highly competitive business environment. Reasonable requirements in furtherance of that policy may be legal if challenged, particularly if the company disseminated written rules advising workers of the consequences flowing from violations of such policies.

However, the law varies by state and depends on each set of facts. In one case, for example, a worker dyed her hair purple. She was given one week to change her hair color. When she rejected the boss's order, she was fired. The company was so incensed that it opposed her claim for unemployment compensation. It stated at a hearing that her job involved dealing with customers, many of whom were revolted by her unconventional hair coloring, and keeping her aboard would have resulted in loss of business. The company also believed it was misconduct and insubordination for the worker to refuse a reasonable request to change her eccentric hair style.

The worker defended her position by stating that the company had no right to dictate her personal appearance and that there was no evidence that customers complained about her purple hair. She stated that since several customers had complimented her new appearance, she was unjustifiably terminated in a manner that should not have precluded her from receiving unemployment benefits.

The court found there was no evidence that the color of the worker's hair significantly affected the employer's business or caused customer complaints. Although it stated that the company had the right to fire her as an at-will employee, it was unlawful to deny her unemployment benefits for her actions. It wrote: "We do not question the employer's right to establish a grooming code for its employees, to revise its rules in response to unanticipated situations, and to make its hiring and firing decisions in conformity with this policy. However, it is possible for an employee to have been properly discharged without having acted in a manner as would justify a denial of unemployment benefits."

> **COUNSEL COMMENTS:** While rules requiring employees to wear uniforms may be legal, such rules can violate your rights if the cost of purchasing mandatory uniforms is deducted from your pay. This may be a violation of the FLSA if your wages then drop below the minimum wage. It may also be a violation of federal and state discrimination laws if female employees are required to purchase uniforms while males are not.

OFFICE ROMANCES

Does management have the right to actively enforce a nonfraternization rule aimed at curbing interoffice romances? This varies depending on the facts. One supervisor who was fired commenced a lawsuit against a former employer. The supervisor had allegedly given his live-in lover a promotion that placed her above several employees with more seniority, even though the company had an unwritten, traditional rule forbidding social relationships between management and lower-echelon employees. When questioned by the home office, the supervisor admitted that he and the co-worker were lovers; citing the nonfraternization rule, the company abruptly terminated him.

The supervisor took the company to court and argued that his employment contract brought with it the company's implied covenant of good faith and fair dealing, which the company violated when he was fired. He also stated that the nonfraternization rule was unfair, unreasonable, and selectively enforced.

The company responded that its nonfraternization rule became reasonable and necessary after the company discovered that attachments between supervisory employees and their subordinates led to accusations of favoritism, which had a negative impact on morale. The company also argued that since the employee had no written contract guaranteeing job security, he could be fired at any time for any or no reason.

The court found that the company was legitimately concerned with appearances of favoritism and employee dissension caused by romantic relationships. Given his actions, the terminated supervisor did not make a strong case that the company failed to act in good faith toward him.

COUNSEL COMMENTS: Other courts have similarly upheld the dismissal of employees romantically involved with co-workers. A Wisconsin court ruled that there were no constitutional or statutory rights barring such a dismissal. In another case, termination because of marriage to the employee of a competitor was found not to violate public policy and the worker's lawsuit for unfair discharge was rejected. Other employees have been fired for violating company fraternization rules by having extramarital affairs or taking a girlfriend to an out-of-state convention. However, since the law is unsettled in this area and each case is decided on its own set of facts and circumstances, never assume that a company's actions are legal in this area. Consult an employment lawyer for advice.

TIP: Although it may be legal to forbid employees from fraternizing, all employees must be treated similarly to avoid violations. For example, if an employer reprimands a male employee for dating a co-worker but fires a female employee for a similar infraction, the employer may be committing illegal sex discrimination.

For off-the-job illegal conduct, a company typically has the right to fire a worker if the illegal conduct harms the employer's reputation or has a negative impact on job performance. The law is not so clear regarding attempts to regulate *legal* off-the-job behavior. Some cases have given employers the right to bar employees from cohabiting with persons who work for a competitor. In one such case, a court upheld a company's written policy that stated: "The Company will not continue the employment of any person who lives in the immediate household of a person employed by a competitor." But in another case in a different state, an employer's rule prohibiting workers from dating employees of a competitor was found to be illegal.

LEGAL ACTIVITIES OFF-PREMISES

Beginning in the late 1960s, the United States Supreme Court ruled that government employees could not be fired in retaliation for the exercise of free speech. The notion of free speech, privacy, and related constitutional protections has now been expanded to private employees in certain instances, particularly in states that have enacted broad civil rights laws.

For example, in some states, a private employer cannot discipline, fail to promote, or fire an employee because the company does not agree with the employee's comments on matters of public concern. A majority of states have laws that prohibit employers from influencing how their employees vote. Attempts to regulate off-duty legal conduct is also sanctioned.

Most states have laws making it illegal for companies to fire workers who participate in legally permissible political activities, recreational activities, or the legal use of consumable products before or after working hours. Political activities include running for public office, campaigning for a candidate, and participating in fundraising activities for a candidate or political party. Those activities may be protected if they are legal and occur on the employee's own time, off company premises and without the use of employer property or equipment.

Recreational activities are defined as any lawful leisure-time activities for which the employee receives no compensation. The definition of consumable products even protects the rights of people who smoke cigarettes or drink alcohol before and after working hours and off the company's premises.

The right not to be demoted, retaliated against, or fired for engaging in these legally permitted activities generally depends on state law. To date, many states have passed laws making it illegal to be fired from a job because you are a smoker and smoke off premises; the trend is for more states to follow. In New York, employers cannot discriminate in hiring, promotion, and other terms of employment due to off-duty activities in four specific categories: political activities, use of a consumable product, recreational activities, and union membership or exercise of any rights granted under federal or state law (such as voting). However, a female employee was recently fired by a New York company for dating a co-worker after hours. She sued the employer and argued that her discharge violated this law. The judge, however, ruled that having a sexual relationship was not included in the definition of a "recreational activity" as defined by the statute (sky diving, scuba diving, bungee jumping, and overeating were included) and ruled against her.

> **COUNSEL COMMENTS:** In the vast majority of states with such laws, it is illegal to refuse to hire smokers. It may also be illegal to discriminate against smokers by charging higher insurance premiums unless the company can demonstrate a valid business reason, such as higher costs. However, women who smoke off-duty must still comply with existing laws and ordinances prohibiting smoking on-premises, such as only in designated areas. And just because it may be legal to drink alcohol off-premises late into the night does not give you the right to stagger into work drunk the next morning.

Employers who violate state law in this area are generally subject to a lawsuit by their state's Attorney General seeking to restrain or enjoin the continuance of the alleged unlawful conduct. Significant penalties are provided in most of these laws. Additionally, individuals may commence their own lawsuits and recover monetary damages and other forms of relief, including attorney fees, under the laws of many states.

> **TIP:** Contact a representative at the American Civil Liberties Union (ACLU) in New York City for advice and guidance if you are being pressured to stop asserting legal political activities, affiliations, or political action. This includes organizing together with other workers to protest poor working conditions. In one recent California

case, a group of individuals organized to promote equal rights of homosexuals at a large company via a class action lawsuit. The court ruled that such activity was protected by state law.

Since some states do not have specific laws protecting employees who engage in political activity and other activities, and the laws vary so, always consult with counsel and review applicable state law before engaging in questionable activities or taking action to protect such activities.

ACCESS TO RECORDS

Some states have passed laws allowing employees access to their personnel records to correct incomplete or inaccurate information at a reasonable time and place. In such states, you usually are not allowed to copy any of the documents in the file except for those you previously signed (such as an employment application or performance review). Such states usually allow you to make notes however. In other states, you generally do not have the right to review your records, so check the law in your state where applicable. (Note: The Federal Privacy Act deals mainly with access to employee records. This law forbids federal government employers from disclosing any information contained in employee files without the written consent of the employee in question. Discuss the ramifications of this federal law with your lawyer where applicable.)

Even in states where access to records is not permitted, employers are prohibited from distributing confidential information, such as medical records, to nonessential third parties and prospective employers, and you generally are permitted to inspect all your files containing confidential medical and credit information. Also, some union employees covered under collective bargaining agreements have the right to examine their own records and to be informed of what information is used in making decisions relevant to their employment.

> **TIP:** Since it is often difficult to review the contents of your personnel file, make and save copies of all documents the minute you receive them so you don't have to retrieve them later. Also, in some arbitrations and lawsuits, employers are prohibited from introducing "memos in the file" that were never read or signed by you. Advise your lawyer about this where applicable.

COUNSEL COMMENTS: Some states grant workers the automatic right to include a rebuttal statement in their personnel file if incorrect information is discovered. Other states allow employees to do this when the employer will not delete such comments. A few states (notably Connecticut) have laws that require employers to send copies of rebuttal statements to prospective employers or other parties when information pertaining to a worker or her employment history is conveyed. Since each state treats the subject differently, review your state's law if relevant.

Some states require employers to seek workers' approval before employee records can be collected, distributed, or destroyed, and it may be illegal to distribute personal information without your consent. The circulation of confidential memoranda within a company has given rise to lawsuits, particularly where the employer did not take adequate precautions to determine whether derogatory information was accurate.

With respect to medical records and investigations, the law generally recognizes that a duty of confidentiality can arise to protect this information and avoid dissemination to nonessential third parties. Under emerging state laws and case decisions, employers who request medical information may be liable for the tort of intrusion and for the tort of public disclosure of private data. Several states have recognized a claim for negligent maintenance of personnel files when files containing inaccurate medical information are made available to third parties. For example, Connecticut has enacted a statute requiring employers to maintain medical records separately from personnel files and permitting employees to review all medical and insurance information in their individual files.

Roberta, a terminated employee, sued her boss on the basis of defamation. Letters describing her poor job performance were distributed and read by several executives. It was later determined that the letters were leaked by a former boss who had a known crush on Roberta. She was awarded $90,000 after proving company officials knew the letters were false but did not stop their dissemination.

WIRETAPPING AND EAVESDROPPING

In most states you have the right to be told at the start that your phone conversation, interrogation, or interview is being taped. Wiretapping and eavesdropping policies are generally regulated and to some degree prohibited by federal and state law. Title III of the Omnibus Crime Control and Safe Streets Act of 1968 prohibits the deliberate interception of oral communications, including telephone conversations.

Conversations between employees uttered with the expectation that such communications are private (for example, in a ladies' bathroom) are typically confidential, and employers are forbidden from eavesdropping. Employers who violate the law may be liable for actual and punitive damages and criminal liability for willful violations.

TIP: If you discover that your employer has wiretapped your business or home telephone with electronic devices and is eavesdropping on your business or private conversations, you can bring a civil lawsuit and possibly file criminal charges. Speak to a lawyer to determine whether your state permits the employer to listen in on an extension telephone used in the ordinary course of business. This is sometimes allowed (depending on state law) provided you were notified in advance that your business calls would be monitored. However, once you talk about private matters, it is generally

While in her office, Erica received a phone call from a friend advising her about a job opening in another organization. Erica's employer, who had a well-known policy of monitoring business calls in the office, overheard this conversation and fired Erica the next day.

Erica contacted a lawyer and commenced a lawsuit for invasion of privacy, unfair discharge, and other legal causes of action. Her lawyer should seek to have the court reject the employer's probable argument that Erica's knowledge of its monitoring policy constituted consent; arguably, Erica consented only to monitoring of outgoing business calls, not incoming personal calls.

illegal for the employer to continue to listen to calls of a private nature. (Note: You may be legally fired though for discussing personal matters while on company time.)

Does an employer have the right to monitor electronic E-mail messages or intercept your private mail? Probably not, but this often depends on the facts of each case and the law in your state.

In most states, it is illegal for employers to set up cameras in a non-work area, take photographs, or use video cameras to monitor workers, especially in places where female employees have expectations of privacy (i.e., in restrooms, locker rooms, bathrooms, and lounges). It is also illegal for employers or their workers to observe you disrobe or change without your knowledge. (Author's Note: Workers generally do not have rights of privacy to stay in restrooms for extended, unreasonable periods of time, particularly after being warned of such excessive respites and when the restroom visits are not medically related.) Also, the National Labor Relations Act (NLRA) prohibits employer surveillance of employee union activity, discussions about unions, or union meetings. Speak to a lawyer immediately if you think your privacy rights have been violated.

Many states prohibit employers from using an employee's photograph for commercial purposes (such as in an advertisement or in a company brochure) without your written consent. Cases have been won by female employees who discovered their likeness on such materials but did not authorize their employers to use them.

Regarding off-duty surveillance, a few states prohibit employers from gathering and maintaining information regarding an employee's political, religious, and other nonbusiness activities. In these states, employees and former employees can inspect their personnel file for the purpose of discovering whether any such information exists. If their file contains such prohibited information, the employer may be liable for damages, court costs, attorney's fees, and fines.

Finally, as discussed in Chapter Four, the National Labor Relations Act allows employees to unionize and bargain collectively. Employers are prohibited from interfering with the exercise of these rights; they cannot fire, lay off, or demote workers who participate in such activities. Contact your union, regional labor relations board, state department of labor, or a lawyer if you believe your rights have been violated.

RIGHT TO WORK IN A SAFE ENVIRONMENT

The 1970 Occupational Safety and Health Act requires employers to provide a safe and healthful workplace. The Occupational Safety and Health Administration (OSHA) is the federal agency created to enforce the law in this area. The law protects employees who band together to protest wages, hours, or working conditions. Under this law, workers are allowed to refuse to perform in a dangerous environment (e.g., in the presence of toxic substances, fumes, or radioactive materials) and to strike to protest unsafe conditions. Employees may also initiate an OSHA inspection of alleged dangerous working conditions by filing a safety complaint and cannot be retaliated against by taking such action when justified. While it may not necessarily be a good idea to walk off the job suddenly when you believe you are working in a dangerous or unhealthy environment unless it is likely that the work is placing you in imminent danger of serious injury, always discuss such conditions with a supervisor, union delegate, management, or OSHA representative. This will make your demands seem more reasonable and minimize potential conflict.

> **TIP:** Employers cannot fire, demote, or transfer workers who assert their health and safety rights to any federal, state, or local agency empowered to investigate or regulate such conditions. Contact your union, regional labor relations board, OSHA representative, lawyer, or state department of labor if you believe your rights have been violated.

In one case, for example, seven machine-shop workers walked off their jobs, claiming it was too cold to work. The company fired them, stating they violated company rules by stopping work without notifying the supervisor. The workers filed a complaint alleging this was an unfair labor practice, The U.S. Supreme Court ruled that the employees had a constitutional right to strike over health and safety conditions, and that the firing violated the law. The workers were awarded back pay and job reinstatement as a result.

RIGHT TO WORK IN A SMOKE-FREE ENVIRONMENT

Most states have passed laws recognizing the rights of nonsmokers to work in a smoke-free environment. Various federal agencies, including the Merit Board and the Equal Employment Opportunity Commission, have ruled that employers must take reasonable steps to keep smoke away from workers who are sensitive to it, and OSHA has issued similar requirements to enhance safety in the workplace. If you have any trouble in this area, gather the facts and speak to management. Confirm all grievances in writing to document your claim (as the letter on the following page illustrates).

If you receive a negative response, send a follow-up letter (like the one on page 134) and speak to a lawyer to protect your rights. Contact an appropriate agency for further advice. A regional Department of Labor, Department of Health, or OSHA office will provide you with more information. Finally, speak to a doctor about workers' compensation. If you incur medical expenses due to a smoke-related on-the-job illness, discuss filing a workers' compensation claim with your doctor.

RIGHT TO BE WARNED BEFORE A MASSIVE LAYOFF

Employees are entitled to be warned of large layoffs under the federal Worker Adjustment and Retraining Notification Act (WARN). Employers with more than 100 workers are required to give employees and their communities at least 60 days notice or comparable financial benefits (60 days notice pay) of plant closings and large layoffs that affect 50 or more workers at a job site. Speak to an experienced employment lawyer or contact your nearest regional office of the Department of Labor for more information. Companies must be careful when contemplating a substantial reduction of their workforce, and a representative from the Department of Labor can advise you if your rights are being violated.

> **TIP:**   Consider filing a lawsuit alleging WARN violations if you are terminated due to a large reorganization or downsizing (e.g., your whole department is suddenly axed) and are not given a reasonable warning or decent severance package. Speak to a lawyer for more details if applicable.

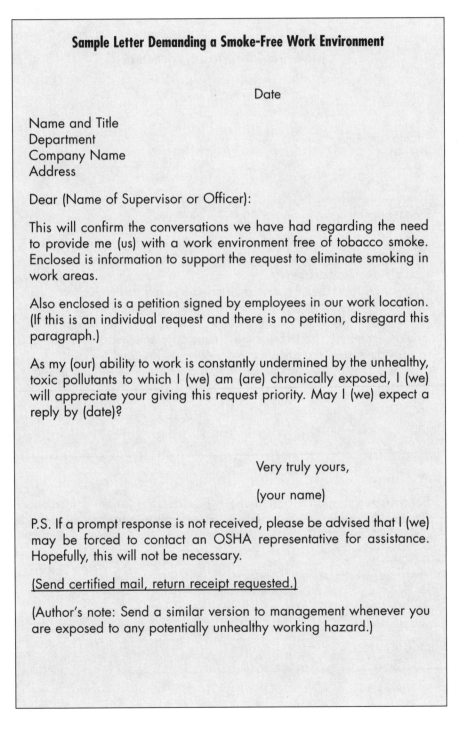

Sample Letter Demanding a Smoke-Free Work Environment

Date

Name and Title
Department
Company Name
Address

Dear (Name of Supervisor or Officer):

This will confirm the conversations we have had regarding the need to provide me (us) with a work environment free of tobacco smoke. Enclosed is information to support the request to eliminate smoking in work areas.

Also enclosed is a petition signed by employees in our work location. (If this is an individual request and there is no petition, disregard this paragraph.)

As my (our) ability to work is constantly undermined by the unhealthy, toxic pollutants to which I (we) am (are) chronically exposed, I (we) will appreciate your giving this request priority. May I (we) expect a reply by (date)?

Very truly yours,

(your name)

P.S. If a prompt response is not received, please be advised that I (we) may be forced to contact an OSHA representative for assistance. Hopefully, this will not be necessary.

(Send certified mail, return receipt requested.)

(Author's note: Send a similar version to management whenever you are exposed to any potentially unhealthy working hazard.)

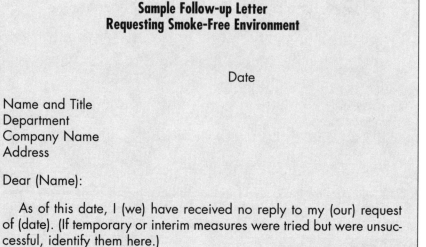

**Sample Follow-up Letter
Requesting Smoke-Free Environment**

Date

Name and Title
Department
Company Name
Address

Dear (Name):

As of this date, I (we) have received no reply to my (our) request of (date). (If temporary or interim measures were tried but were unsuccessful, identify them here.)

To protect my (our) health while in your employ, it is vital that the company provide me (us) with a smoke-free work area so as to comply with the laws of this state (specify applicable statute). I (we) have asked organizations that are expert in the area of occupational health to provide you with additional information on my (our) behalf.

I (we) will appreciate your immediate response to this urgent matter.

Sincerely,

(your name)

Send copies to middle management, president of company, medical director of company, union representative, and personal physician.

DRUGS AND ALCOHOL TESTING

All forms of employee testing raise significant issues of potential violations of an employee's privacy rights. Additionally, due to the enactment of the Americans With Disabilities Act, all such tests are closely scrutinized. With respect to AIDS testing, such tests are permitted only in certain states in limited circumstances where the job involves the public health and safety, such as for food handlers, hospital workers, and people in the military. Most genetic testing is prohibited.

With respect to drug and alcohol testing, some states prohibit such tests but state law varies dramatically. For example, some states permit employee testing with required procedural safeguards to ensure the testing is done in a reasonable and reliable manner with concern for an employee's rights of privacy. Thus, intrusive monitoring of blood and urine testing through the use of closed-circuit cameras is not permitted. Other states permit individual tests where a particular employee is suspected of being under the influence of drugs or alcohol and her impaired state adversely affects job performance. However, in other states, employees who test positive may not be fired if they consent to participate in and successfully complete a rehabilitation program.

Since the law varies so from state to state, is constantly changing, and may even be more stringent as a result of the ADA, speak to a lawyer or representative from the Department of Labor or the EEOC for advice in this area to determine relevant state law. In approximately two-thirds of the states in this country, private employers may implement and conduct drug and alcohol tests provided certain procedural safeguards are followed that minimize potential offensiveness. This typically includes adopting a comprehensive testing policy and putting it in writing, periodically reminding employees of the stated drug or alcohol testing policy, reducing the incidence of errors, treating test results carefully (i.e., confidentially) to avoid improper dissemination, and following local, state, and federal laws and decisions.

Perhaps the most important change to occur legitimizing such tests results from the federal Drug Free Workplace Act. This law requires certain employers who do business with the federal government to publish strict statements prohibiting drugs in the workplace and educating employees on substance abuse. It also requires employers to report any workers convicted of workplace-related drug activities and to certify that they will not condone unlawful drug activity during the performance of a contract with a government agency. Companies that fail to follow such rules will be subject to suspension of payments due under their contracts with the federal agency or termination of the contract. Thus, there is a great incentive for companies dealing with the government to comply with the requirements of this law. However, although the law creates a heightened drug-awareness policy, it does not mandate drug testing for employees. Nor does the law explicitly sanction testing.

COUNSEL COMMENTS: Generally the decision to test is basically an individual choice for private employers.

TIP: If you work for a private employer and are not a member of a union, what concerns should you have when advised that the employer intends to test you for drugs and alcohol? First, it is preferred that you receive advance notice in work rules and policy manuals. For example, the manual should outline the steps management would take when it suspected that an employee was impaired on the job, such as immediate testing, with a description of how the test will be administered and the consequences flowing from a positive result (such as a suspension without pay or discharge for cause). If no such notice was received before the test was administered, you could have a valid claim that your privacy rights were violated, especially when there was no rational reason for asking you to submit to the test (e.g., you were randomly selected) and you were told to take the test without warning.

Even if your privacy rights are not violated, all tests must be administered in a consistent, evenhanded manner. For example, if female employees are being tested and fired as a result of such tests in far greater numbers than male employees, a charge of sex discrimination might be valid under certain circumstances.

How the employer handles the test results is another important consideration. Results must be treated in the same manner as other confidential personnel information. Unwarranted disclosure of this information (even within your company) when made with reckless disregard for the truthfulness of the disclosure, or excessive publication, can allow you to sue for damages. One employee was awarded $200,000 for defamation after her employer internally and externally published written statements regarding drug screening results incorrectly showing a trace of methadone.

Additionally, a firing based on a positive test finding that later proves inaccurate could lead to a multitude of legal causes of action, including wrongful discharge, slander, and invasion of privacy. If the employer fails to hire a reputable testing company or the test results are inaccurate, you can challenge the test on this basis. Thus, recognize that there may be ways to challenge the test results in the event you are fired or treated unfairly. Speak to an experienced lawyer immediately when:

- The test was not administered fairly; i.e., no advance warnings were given or there was inconsistent enforcement;
- The penalty for violations was too severe (e.g., an employee was fired for possessing a small amount of marijuana in her locker but proved she did not smoke the drug on company time);
- The reliability of test procedures and/or results is suspect;
- The employer cannot prove the identity of the illegal drug allegedly found in the test;
- The specimen was not properly identified as belonging to the accused worker;
- No confirmatory tests were made following positive preliminary screening; and
- The company engaged in discriminatory practices relating to its testing procedures.

Recognize that federal workers, employees engaged in security-conscious industries (e.g., those who are required to carry firearms), and employees who handle money or engage in transporting members of the public (bus drivers and train engineers) have fewer legal rights to oppose drug and alcohol tests because of the nature of their jobs. However, even when testing is legal, employers must follow proper procedures to be sure that results are accurate and are not disseminated carelessly. Results should be handled on a strict need-to-know basis, employees should be given an opportunity to explain any result, and the test results should be reconfirmed if possible.

Finally, since former drug users (and current alcoholics) may be characterized as individuals with a former or current disability that does not prevent them from performing the duties of their job, any adverse action (such as discharge) taken may be fought under federal and state discrimination laws, possibly even in the presence of positive test results.

The checklist beginning on page 139 was written by the author to explain employers' rights in this area and is a helpful summary.

RIGHT TO APPLY FOR AND RECEIVE WORKERS' COMPENSATION

Each state has enacted its own peculiar rules with respect to workers' compensation, which provides aid for employees who suffer job-related injuries. Under state compensation laws, the amount of money paid in benefits is linked to the worker's rate of pay prior to the injury and the kind and extent of injuries suffered. Workers' compensation is a substitute for other remedies you may have against the employer, such as bringing a private lawsuit for negligence. In many cases, the issue becomes one of determining whether the injuries suffered were job-related and whether you are legally considered an independent contractor (not subject to workers' compensation laws) or an employee. The reason is that people typically prefer to sue the employer privately and obtain greater damages than are awarded under workers' compensation statutes.

> **TIP:** Since the outcome of each workers' compensation case varies depending on the particular facts and unique state law, always seek the advice of a lawyer specializing in workers' compensation law. Issues such as how long you may delay before filing a claim, whether coverage is available for stress-related injuries, and what kinds of injuries are covered, together with strategies to help maximize the benefits received, can become complicated and typically require a lawyer's assistance and advice.

Always notify your employer when you are injured while working. This is your right and you cannot be retaliated against in any way for taking such action. Fill out all necessary forms. If no forms are available, contact your nearest workers' compensation office for details. Speak to a lawyer immediately if a claim is contested. Visit

Comprehensive Checklist Regarding Drugs and Alcohol in the Workplace

A. *General Overview*

1. Illegal drug and alcohol use in the workplace is a major problem these days for employers.

2. At least 20 million workers use marijuana/hashish; 6 million are cocaine users; and 100 million are alcohol users.

3. Studies suggest that the typical recreational drug user in the workplace is three times as late as fellow employees, has 2.5 as many absences of eight or more days, is five times more likely to file a workers' compensation claim, and is involved in accidents 3.6 times more frequently than other workers.

4. More companies, especially those in high-tech and security-conscious industries, are resorting to drug testing to identify drug users and reduce on-the-job accidents.

B. *Preliminary Considerations Concerning Applicant Drug and Alcohol Testing Programs*

1. Many state and local governments have passed laws permitting applicant drug and alcohol tests.

2. Such tests generally are not viewed as violating an individual's privacy rights if applicants are told in advance they must take and pass the test to get the job and all applicants must submit to such tests after a job offer and as a condition of employment.

3. Check the law in your state and local municipal laws regarding the legality of such tests, because some states (e.g., New York) still prohibit preemployment drug testing in certain situations.

4. Drug and alcohol tests of job applicants are neither encouraged nor prohibited by the Americans with Disabilities Act (ADA).

5. Former drug users or alcoholics who have been rehabilitated or who are participating in a supervised rehabilitation program are protected under the ADA and generally must be considered for the job.

6. An applicant who is currently engaging in illegal drug use is not protected under federal ADA law.

7. An employer may prohibit the use of illegal drugs and alcohol at the workplace and require that employees not be under the influence of illegal drugs or alcohol while at work.

C. *Strategies to Protect Employers When Testing Applicants*

1. Know the law.

2. Adopt a plan and record it in work rules, policy manuals, employment contracts, and/or collective bargaining agreements.

3. Prepare employment applications to incorporate this right.

4. Make sure that the applicant authorizes drug and alcohol tests and agrees that a positive result will mean forfeiture of a job offer; make the applicant sign such a statement in the employment application.

5. To avoid discrimination lawsuits, be sure all applicants are tested, not just a particular class of applicant, and that each applicant is tested in the same way.

6. Handle the results of drug/alcohol tests as you would any other confidential information.

7. Unwarranted disclosure of this information may result in breach of privacy and defamation lawsuits.

8. Hire a reliable testing company.

9. Before you hire a testing company, get references and be sure the company is bonded and licensed and will provide proof of current insurance and indemnification coverage.

10. If an applicant tests positive for drugs, be careful not to automatically disqualify that applicant should that person reapply after a certain period of time (e.g., one year later).

11. Avoid inflexible drug policies with a fixed waiting period for future employment.

12. Obtain legal advice before implementing any testing policy.

13. Companies whose employees are represented by unions cannot unilaterally implement a testing program.

14. Review the requirements and conditions imposed by the Drug-Free Workplace Act if your company has federal government contracts.

15. Treat alcoholics differently than drug users since they may be considered to have a disability under the ADA and cannot be fired if a "reasonable accommodation" can assist the employee perform the job.

16. Outline the steps, in work rules, policy manuals, employment agreements, and other materials, that management will take if the company suspects an employee is impaired on the job.

17. Inform employees that immediate testing will be conducted if drug use is suspected.

18. Describe how the test will be administered and the consequences flowing from a positive result.

19. Apply stated rules consistently for drug or alcohol involvement.

20. Determine the scope of the testing program's coverage, how employees will be tested, under what conditions, and the selection of testing facilities.

21. Inform employees that testing for substance abuse is required under OSHA guidelines.

22. Avoid conducting random drug testing unless you receive clearance from counsel.

23. Treat the test results carefully.

24. Establish a separate employee file for testing information and results to minimize disclosure and safeguard employee privacy.

25. Choose correct specimen collection procedures that balance privacy with authenticity.

26. If possible, avoid direct observations of employee urination to reduce emotional distress lawsuits.

27. Take the temperature of the specimen immediately after it is provided since this makes substitution difficult.

28. Outline specimen identification procedures and establish a specific chain of custody to ensure accuracy.

29. Understand the scientific ways in which a test could produce an inaccurate result and minimize the risk of such a possibility.

D. *Special Concerns About Alcohol Use*

1. Be especially careful before making any adverse decision affecting an alcoholic worker and analyze each case on its particular facts.

2. Offer counseling before discharge.

3. If the employee refuses counseling, offer a first choice of treatment or discipline; do not take any adverse action during the period of the rehabilitation program.

4. In case of relapse, do not automatically terminate, but impose some discipline short of discharge.

5. Before termination, determine if retention of the worker would create an undue hardship on your company.

6. If removal is the only solution, consider leave without pay before termination.

7. Treat alcoholism in a professional but sympathetic way since it is considered a disability and protected under the ADA.

8. Always proceed with caution in this area to avoid substantial statutory potential damages.

(Author's Note: Since this summary was written for employers, discuss any applicable points with your lawyer where warranted.)

several doctors to obtain accurate evaluations of your condition. Be sure you understand your rights if you are a part-time worker or are injured during work-related travel. The following list summarizes the kinds of injuries that are typically compensable:

- Preexisting conditions that the workplace accelerates or aggravates, such as a bad back, even if pain from the injury is delayed until a later time.

- Injuries caused during breaks, lunch hours, and work-sponsored recreational activities, such as a company-paid party, and on-the-job injuries caused by company facilities, such as a shower located on the premises.

- Ordinary diseases such as lung cancer, if contracted by asbestos exposure at work as a result of the usual conditions to which the worker was exposed by her employment.

■ Injuries resulting from mental and physical strain brought on by increased work duties or the stress caused by a requirement that the employee make decisions on other employee dismissals. In some states, this includes employees who develop a disabling psychosis because they cannot keep up with the demands of the job and a supervisor's constant harassment.

An employer may not inquire whether you have ever filed for workers' compensation when you apply for a job. You also have the right to select your own physician for treatment, provided that physician is authorized by the state's workers' compensation board.

SUMMARY OF IMPORTANT STEPS TO TAKE WHILE WORKING

In addition to the many rights discussed in this chapter, it is important to develop strategies to reduce exploitation while working. For example, knowing how to properly respond to inaccurate or subjective evaluations, performance reviews, and progressive discipline policies may prove helpful later if you are fired. The following tips can help you protect and enhance your job rights. Thus:

1. Save all correspondence, copies of records, and other documents.

2. Notify your employer immediately if you discover errors in your salary, bonus, commissions, compensation, or benefits.

3. Do not accept reductions in your salary or other benefits, particularly if you have a written contract that prohibits oral modifications of important terms.

4. Write letters to protest illegal actions, such as to complain about sex harassment or health and safety violations in the workplace. This is important so that you will not be deemed to have consented to such treatment by your lack of action.

5. Write a rebuttal to any subjective or incorrect performance review or evaluation you receive. Explain why you perceive the review to be inaccurate.

6. Recognize your rights to privacy, to unionize, and to health and safety in the workplace, and seek competent legal counsel at once if your rights are violated.

As the above summary illustrates, there are many steps to take while working to reduce the chances of being exploited. These include checking your compensation arrangement and notifying the company immediately when you are not being paid properly per your understanding or if you detect errors. You should also get in the habit of saving all correspondence, records, and documents to confirm all deals and actions and document all promises made to you (e.g., being told, "You are doing a great job here so we would never fire you without adequate notice except for cause"). By taking proper steps while working, you can help your case in the event you are fired unfairly and decide to take legal action down the road.

> **TIP:** If you don't take steps to indicate your dissatisfaction with unfair company actions you may be viewed by a court as having accepted such actions by your conduct. For example, many employees refuse to sign unfair and subjective employee evaluations. This is not recommended. Rather, it is best to sign the review with a notation that you are attaching a rebuttal as part of the evaluation. This is the way to properly document your dissatisfaction, and the rebuttal can protect you against subsequent illegal action by the company.

> **COUNSEL COMMENTS:** Firing and/or disciplining a female worker is not as simple as it used to be. Because the terminated individual may consult a lawyer, companies are now being instructed to "set you up" (i.e., document problems in your personnel file). The reason is that when employers fail to note performance problems on appraisals and lack sufficient documentation to prove inadequate job performance, they may not have a legal basis for firing an employee (since a poor performance excuse may be viewed as a pretext) and may be subjecting the company to a ready-made claim of sex discrimination.

Thus, always protest (in writing preferably) company actions you do not agree with.

If you believe that a future lawsuit with your employer is inevitable, get the edge by planning ahead. It is easier to obtain pertinent documents, including a copy of your employment contract, employee handbook, performance reviews, and favorable recommendations contained in your file from co-workers and management, while you are still working at the company. It is also a good idea to consider meeting with a lawyer *before* you resign or are fired. If you perceive problems that are valid, your lawyer may be able to

Arlene is an executive who has worked 10 years for a company. She previously received excellent performance reviews, merit raises and promotions. Her performance was never criticized until a new supervisor with less experience replaced her boss, who retired.

The new supervisor and Arlene clash on petty matters. Soon they disagree on what is expected and demanded of Arlene. Although she tries her best, it is apparent that their personalities are not suited for one another and her work is not appreciated. Arlene then receives a neutral-to-negative annual review which she believes is subjective, biased, and unfair. She senses the company is setting her up to be fired. She is so unhappy that she is considering resigning just to get away from the stress her supervisor is causing.

Arlene consults a skilled lawyer for advice and guidance. The lawyer recommends that she not, under any circumstances, resign from her job because she will forfeit valuable stock options, retirement benefits, and severance pay. He drafts a respectful but accurate rebuttal on her behalf, which Arlene retypes and submits. The lawyer reviews her employee manual and notices that the company maintains an informal internal grievance procedure to handle employee complaints. He recommends that she discreetly contact the president of the company (whom Arlene likes and has known for many years) for a private informal meeting.

Arlene meets with the president and explains her dissatisfaction and problems. She shows the president her review and rebuttal. The president was unaware of the problems she was having. He advises her that she is an important part of the company and that her work and dedication have always been appreciated. Arlene's next review is excellent. Her job is saved and the supervisor is eventually reassigned.

(Author's Note: The above example illustrates various tactics to be considered before final action is taken. Always discuss your problem with a competent lawyer so you don't make a foolish decision you may later regret.)

recommend additional strategies, such as sending a final letter of protest or requesting a meeting to discuss and attempt to resolve any difficulties. These options may not be available after the firing and can enhance your case if litigation proves necessary.

The lawyer can give you a better evaluation of the possibility of success with your case when he or she views all pertinent records and documents. That is why it is important to collect and acquire all key evidence for presentation to your lawyer before a case is litigated. Be aware of this and act accordingly.

CHAPTER SIX

SEX DISCRIMINATION, SEX HARASSMENT, AND OTHER FORMS OF DISCRIMINATION

Sex discrimination law encompasses many facets. The law mandates equal pay for equal work. It requires equal treatment, policies, standards, and practices for males and females in all phases of the employment relationship, including hiring, placement, job promotion, working conditions, wages and benefits, layoffs, and discharges. For example, it is generally discriminatory in all states and under federal law to:

■ Refuse to hire women with preschool-age children while hiring men with such children

■ Require females to resign from jobs upon marriage when there is no similar requirement for males

■ Include spouses of male employees in benefit plans while denying the same benefits to spouses of female employees

■ Restrict certain jobs to men without offering women a reasonable opportunity to demonstrate their ability to perform the same job adequately

■ Refuse to hire, train, assign, or promote pregnant or married women, or women of childbearing age on the basis of sex

■ Deny unemployment or seniority benefits to pregnant women, or deny granting a leave of absence for pregnancy if similar leaves of absence are granted for illness

■ Institute compulsory retirement plans with lower retirement ages for women than men

Numerous cases of women winning large verdicts for sex discrimination have been reported recently. For example, Chevron reportedly agreed to pay more than $8 million to settle a class action filed by 777 female employees who claimed they were discriminated against in terms of pay, promotions and assignments. A New Jersey judge upheld a $7.1 million sex discrimination jury verdict against a company after the plaintiff successfully alleged that senior managers removed her from accounts she had helped build and gave them to male brokers. After 12 years with the company, the woman was accused of poor productivity and fired. The verdict included a $5 million punitive damages award.

Publix reportedly agreed to pay $81.5 million to settle a class action lawsuit by 150,000 women who accused the big grocery chain of relegating them to dead-end, low paying jobs. The settlement applies to all women who worked at any of the 535 Publix stores in Florida, Georgia, South Carolina and Alabama since 1981. The suit was brought in 1995 by eight women who accused Publix of passing them over for raises and repeatedly denying them management jobs. They and four others who quickly joined the case said they watched as men with less experience and less seniority got promotions. Some said their requests were met with unwanted sexual advances from managers. The EEOC later joined the suit, and it was expanded to a class action covering past and current employees.

Although the Publix settlement is the largest involving supermarket chains, Lucky Stores allegedly paid $107 million to 14,000 women to settle similar allegations, and Albertson's allegedly paid a $29.4 million settlement to women and Hispanic workers. It was also reported that Safeway Stores settled for $7.5 million in a 1994 sex discrimination suit covering 20,000 employees in California.

$250 million was reportedly paid in 1992 in a suit against State Farm for a class of women who said they were denied or deterred from positions as insurance agents. And Home Depot faces a similar challenge from more than 200,000 current and former female employees who filed a class action lawsuit claiming the company's personnel structure is set up to limit their access to sales jobs, supervisor and manager positions. The lawsuit claims women are placed in positions with fewer opportunities while men are given jobs with greater advancement potential. The suit also alleges a pattern of sexual harassment and unequal pay. The case is currently proceeding to a jury trial.

This chapter will tell you about sex discrimination and other forms of discrimination. You will learn what practices are illegal, when you have been victimized, and how to take proper steps to protect and file a valid claim. For example, if you are being forced to work in a hostile and offensive environment, you will learn why it is best to send letters to the company to document the offensive conduct.

When a recently fired female employee consults the author in his New York City office, one of the first points to be considered is whether she has a valid claim of illegal treatment. For example, assuming equal work, did the company pay the same salary and benefits to her as it did for similarly-situated men? Was the female employee fired suddenly because of excessive absences and lateness while a male employee was not? Was an elderly female sales employee the first to go because of a slipping sales quota?

Recognizing and fighting back against job discrimination is not always easy. For instance, suppose a company fired a 60-year-old salesperson because she wasn't meeting quota. That sounds like a legitimate reason, right? Maybe, but what if the company's sales were down in many of its territories? Were the younger, male sales-people fired as well, or were they merely given a warning and placed on probation?

Suppose a female worker was fired for lateness. Were male workers with the same record of absences and lateness merely warned and not fired? Was the female employee fired in retaliation for complaining that she did not receive the same benefits as her male counterparts? In these examples, illegal discrimination may have occurred and should be redressed. (Author's Note: Although this chapter stresses gender-based discrimination problems, other forms of discrimination, including age, race, national origin, disability, and religious discrimination are also discussed, since many women who assert sex discrimination claims also allege other forms of discrimination in their complaint. Often the discrimination asserted by female workers is not based on sex at all but falls into one of these other categories.)

THE LAW

The Civil Rights Act of 1991 implemented a series of sweeping changes in federal antidiscrimination laws. The legislation expanded procedural options and remedies available to women and overruled a series of important U.S. Supreme Court decisions that limited employees' legal recourse. In doing so, Congress amended six different statutes that together prohibit discrimination based on race, color, religion, sex, national origin, disability, and age. Those statutes are Title VII of the Civil Rights Act of 1964, the Americans With Disabilities Act of 1990, the Vocational Rehabilitation Act of 1973, the Age Discrimination in Employment Act of 1967, the Civil Rights Act of 1866 and the Civil Rights Attorney's Fees Awards Act of 1976. Virtually all employers are covered by these laws.

The 1991 Act prohibits discrimination in all aspects of the employment process, including compensation, assignment, classification of employees, demotions, transfers, promotions, wages and working conditions, recruitment, testing, use of company facilities, training programs, fringe benefits, retirement plans, disability leave, hiring, and discharges. An illegal act can be committed by any member of an employer's staff, from the president down to the supervisor and receptionist.

Retaliation and on-the-job harassment are also prohibited. This means that if you file a charge of discrimination in good faith you cannot be fired, demoted, or reassigned while the case is pending. However, if you knew the claim had no merit and filed it in bad faith, you could be fired legally.

Many states have enacted even stronger discrimination laws with greater coverage and penalties. For example, although federal law does not recognize discrimination on the basis of a person's marital status or sexual preference, some state laws do. Thus, it is illegal in some states to fire a female who is a known lesbian. Also, many small employers (defined as companies employing more than 15 persons) not covered by Title VII fall within the jurisdiction of state law. Some local laws offer even greater protection; for example, age discrimination protection may apply to the young as well as those who are over 40, and homosexuals may be protected under local sex discrimination laws.

COUNSEL COMMENTS: A question frequently asked is: Which law takes precedence? The answer essentially is *the law that is the strictest*. Thus, to ensure proper protection of your rights, try to be familiar with federal and state laws as well as those governing employment in your local business community or municipality. If there is a difference in coverage on the same subject, seek to enforce the law that is the most favorable to your situation. To learn whether you have greater protection and how it applies, contact an appropriate state or city agency for further details, or speak to a knowledgeable employment lawyer.

Prior to the Civil Rights Act of 1991, claimants typically could only receive their jobs back, together with retroactive job pay and restoration of seniority benefits. Now, in cases where intentional race, sex (including pregnancy), national origin, skin color, religion, or handicap discrimination can be proved, the act also authorizes jury trials, reasonable witness and attorney fees to be paid to the individual harmed, punitive damages, and compensatory damages up to $300,000 depending on the size of the employer. Compensatory damages are defined as money paid to compensate individuals for future pecuniary losses, emotional pain and suffering, inconvenience and mental anguish, loss of enjoyment, and physical pain and suffering. Compensatory damages typically are available only for intentional discrimination and unlawful harassment, and do not apply where a job practice is not intended to be discriminatory but nonetheless has an unlawful disparate impact on women or persons within another protected class, such as workers over 40.

Before we begin an analysis of various forms of discrimination, the following are general rules employers must follow. These rules are recommended by Eric J. Wallach, a New York employment lawyer.

1. All employers must review hiring, promotion, and compensation criteria to ascertain whether they are validly job-related and consistent with business necessity. For example, are there statistical imbalances in the workforce that are directly or indirectly traceable to such standards?

2. Proper documentation, including employment forms, job descriptions, and performance evaluations, must be prepared to adequately support any personnel decisions regarding hiring, promotion, and compensation.

3. Appropriate procedures must be consistently applied in every case, and such decisions must never be made on the basis of a person's sex, race, or religion.

4. Employers with overseas operations must be attentive to whether their managers abroad are enforcing the antidiscrimination laws for all employees who are U.S. nationals.

5. All employment strategies must take into account the demographics of the workplace. Companies must avoid statistical personnel imbalances with regard to women and minorities.

6. Management should consider hiring additional qualified minorities such as females or nonwhites to avoid charges of discrimination.

SEX DISCRIMINATION

Sex discrimination, also called gender discrimination, is legislated by Title VII of the Civil Rights Act of 1964 as well as the revised Civil Rights Act of 1991. Gender discrimination covers a variety of subjects and is protected by many laws, including the Equal Pay Act of 1963, which makes it illegal to discriminate against women concerning salary or wages, and the Pregnancy Discrimination Act of 1978, which prohibits discrimination on the basis of pregnancy, childbirth, and related medical conditions and health benefits. For more information on these subjects, please consult Chapter Four.

You may be the victim of sex discrimination when you:

■ are receiving disparate treatment (i.e., being treated differently from other employees);

■ are being denied employment opportunities primarily because you are a woman; or

■ the effect of a company policy or rule has a disproportionally negative effect on women in your company, causing an adverse impact.

The various acts described in the first page of this chapter identify common areas of sex discrimination. It is also illegal for companies to use advertising that denies women a chance to apply for a job or screening procedures that eliminate female applicants because the requirements are too demanding (i.e., requiring a college degree for secretarial work.). No longer can women not be considered for physical jobs, nor is it lawful for employers to refuse jobs to women because they think that their turnover rate is higher, they take more sick leave, or they may become pregnant. As mentioned in Chapter One, any questions to women regarding their families or childbearing plans are also illegal. In certain cases the law is also making it easier for women to claim the reason they were passed over for a promotion, such as not being made a partner in an accounting firm, was their sex and not their work performance (which is sometimes offered by employers as a pretext). Speak to a lawyer for more details where applicable.

SEX HARASSMENT

Another prohibited form of sex discrimination is sex harassment. In 1986 the Supreme Court ruled that sexual harassment was actionable under Title VII of the Civil Rights Act of 1964. Many thousands of cases are filed yearly with the EEOC and state agencies. In fact, studies indicate that the vast majority of working women (more than 85 percent) believe they have been sexually harassed on the job at one time or another.

The newspapers are full of large verdicts women are receiving in this area. In one case, a former airline employee was awarded $7.1 million in punitive and compensatory damages for a sex-discrimination-harassment charge. In another recent case, the EEOC obtained a $1.85 million settlement in a sexual harassment case on behalf of a group of 10 women who had worked for a company as secretaries or executive assistants. The women complained that the company's chairman sought sexual favors in exchange for job benefits and had engaged in a pattern and practice of harassment against them by forcing them to discuss sex acts, touching them in their private parts, and other harmful acts. The money is to be divided among the women based primarily on their seniority. Additionally, as part of the settlement, the employer must provide individualized counseling and training for all its employees nationwide, hire an outside consultant and several new employees to respond to sexual harassment complaints, and institute a toll-free number for reporting sexual harassment.

Sexual harassment cases are on the rise in a variety of nontraditional areas. For example, sexual harassment was found in one case when female employees were required to wear revealing uniforms and suffer derogatory comments from passersby. In another case, a jury awarded $196,500 in damages to a man who claimed his supervisor demoted him because he refused her sexual advances. According to court testimony, the employee and his supervisor met one night in a hotel room, but the man refused to continue the relationship. The man proved he was demoted and passed over for a promotion as a result. In another case, the termination of a male employee for rejecting the advances of his homosexual male supervisor proved costly to a company.

The Supreme Judicial Court in Massachusetts recently heard arguments in a case about same-sex sexual harassment. The employer appealed a lower court decision awarding three gay men $75,000 each for same-gender sexual harassment. The company argued that while it did not condone such behavior, it should only be liable if gay men harassed heterosexual men or vice versa. The court's decision has not been reported as of this writing.

Imaginative lawyers representing claimants in sexual harassment suits are also asserting other nontraditional causes of action in federal and state courts. These include wrongful discharge, fraud, intentional infliction of emotional distress for outrageous conduct, invasion of privacy, and assault and civil battery. Additionally, the Supreme Court in *Harris v. Forklift Systems, Inc.*, in 1993 made it easier for plaintiffs asserting such actions by ruling that they were not required to prove that any abusive conduct actually caused an injury or affected the person's psychological well-being. Lawyers representing claimants now only have to show that a "reasonable person" would have found the conduct to be offensive to prevail.

DEFINITION OF SEXUAL HARASSMENT

Unwelcome sexual advances, requests for sexual favors, and verbal or physical conduct of a sexual nature all constitute sexual harassment when:

- The person must submit to such activity in order to be hired;
- The person's consent or refusal is used in making an employment decision (e.g., to offer a raise or promotion); or
- Such conduct unreasonably interferes with the person's work performance or creates an intimidating, hostile, or offensive working environment (e.g., humiliating comments are repeatedly addressed to the complainant).

Defining what constitutes sexual harassment depends on the facts of each particular case. In "quid pro quo" cases (instances when employees of either sex are propositioned for sexual favors in order to receive a job, raise, or promotion), the issue may be clear-cut. If a person is passed over for a promotion or denied benefits in favor of an individual who submitted to sexual advances, the passed-over person is considered to be a victim of sexual harassment under federal and state guidelines.

Additionally, if a worker initially participates in social or sexual contact, but then rejects continued unwelcome advances, that constitutes sexual harassment in most instances. The fact that the person does not regularly communicate her negative reaction often may not exculpate the company from liability.

Sandra has a consensual sexual relationship with her boss, the company president. Sandra voluntarily continues the relationship for two years, knowing the president is married. She decides to call off the affair after he refuses to obtain a divorce and marry her.

The boss treats Sandra differently after her decision. He runs after and propositions her in front of co-workers at the company Christmas party. During the year, he regularly makes demeaning comments about her physical appearance at the office. Twice at a luncheon, he touches her backside in front of customers.

Sandra files a sexual harassment charge against her boss and her employer. The company argues that since the couple were lovers, no liability should ensue. It also argues that the boss was drunk at the Christmas party and didn't know what he was doing. Most important, since Sandra discussed her problems with a supervisor only once, and never followed up her complaints or alerted management to more recent acts immediately after they ensued, the company defended its position by stating she contributed to such treatment.

A judge ruled the company failed to investigate her charges and take immediate action (probably because others were afraid to offend the president). All the company's defenses were rejected and the judge decided the case in Sandra's favor. The company fired the president as a result of his harmful, illegal acts and was required to pay Sandra a substantial amount of money and reimburse her for her lawyer's fees and costs. The company also agreed not to retaliate against Sandra for winning the case.

In hostile, intimidating, and unprofessional work environment cases, the issues are not always clear-cut. Typically, to establish a prima facie case, the employee must prove that:

a. she was subjected to unwelcome sexual conduct;

b. the unwelcome sexual conduct was based on her gender;

c. the unwelcome sexual conduct was sufficiently pervasive or severe to alter the terms and conditions of the person's employment and create an abusive or hostile working environment; and

d. the employer knew or should have known of the harassment and failed to take prompt and reasonable remedial action.

Courts have ruled the following to constitute sexual harassment with respect to hostile, intimidating work environment cases:

■ Extremely vulgar and sexually related epithets, jokes, or crusty language, provided the language is not isolated and is continuously stated to the complainant

■ Sexually suggestive comments about an employee's attire or body

■ Sexually degrading words describing an employee

■ Repeated touching of the employee's body, provided the touching is unsolicited and unwelcome

■ Showing lewd photographs or objects of a sexual nature to employees at the workplace

■ Offensive or repeated requests for dates, even if the calls are made to the complainant after work

■ Continued advances of a sexual nature which the employee rejects, even after the parties break off a consensual sexual relationship

■ Requiring females to wear revealing uniforms and suffer derogatory comments from nonemployees

How the company investigates and acts on complaints is a major factor in determining whether it will end up in court and incur substantial damages. For example, in one case, after a company investigated a sexual harassment charge and found that it had merit, the employer did nothing further but warn the supervisor only once. When the supervisor continued his unlawful conduct (by showing lewd pictures to the complainant), the female worker quit her job and filed a complaint with the EEOC. She was awarded $48,000 when the court ruled that the company had failed to act on its investigation.

> **COUNSEL COMMENTS:**   EEOC guidelines specify preventive affirmative steps that sometimes shield employers from liability. In determining whether an employer is liable, courts look to see if a comprehensive policy against sexual harassment was in place at the time the incidents occurred and whether the employer acted promptly and properly. When policies are vague or the incident is not immediately and adequately investigated, or if the complainant is punished for coming forward, the company will probably be found liable if the facts are true.

Sexual harassment cases are dangerous to employers because some courts have ruled that companies are responsible for the acts of their supervisory employees regardless of whether the company knew or should have known of the occurrence. In quid pro quo cases involving supervisors, there is a good chance that an employer will be held strictly responsible for the actions of its supervisors, whether or not it knew the acts were occurring. In hostile environment cases, companies are often liable for incidents they should have known about, but didn't, when no effective action is taken to end the harassment, even if the company's official policies prohibit sexual harassment.

To avoid these and other potential legal hazards pertaining to sex harassment cases, many employers have begun disseminating periodic reminders in policy manuals, journals, and letters distributed to employees that the company does not tolerate sexual harassment of any kind on the job, that anyone who experiences or observes such treatment should report this to management or their immediate supervisor (but not to the one doing the harassing) immediately, and that all communications will be held in strict confidence with no direct or indirect reprisals to the informant or complainant. In addition, companies are taking steps to instruct supervisors about sexual harassment and other forms of discrimination, what the adverse effects on the company could be, and ways to handle problems if they arise.

(Author's Note: The checklist for sexual harassment investigations on page 158 is a guideline that employers are advised to follow to properly investigate charges.)

Checklist for Sexual Harassment Investigations for Employers

I. Preliminary Considerations

    A. Use two investigators if possible.

    B. Create a confidential file.

    C. Conduct interviews in a private room.

II. Gathering the Facts

    A. Review relevant personnel files and company policies.

    B. Interview the victim.

        1. Take her complaint seriously.

        2. Explain the investigation but don't promise complete confidentiality.

        3. Find out what happened: Get specifics.

        4. Find out the effect of the harassment on the victim.

        5. Find out names of witnesses.

        6. Ask the victim what she wants.

        7. Assess her credibility.

        8. Take a statement if warranted.

        9. Type the notes of the interview.

    C. Interview the perpetrator.

        1. Explain the purpose of the interview but state that no decision has been made on the truthfulness of the allegations.

        2. Identify the victim and the specific basis of the sexual harassment complaint.

        3. Ask him to respond to the charges.

        4. Find out names of witnesses.

        5. Assess his credibility.

        6. Take a statement if warranted.

        7. Type the notes of the interview.

    D. Interview corroboration witnesses.

        1. Try to elicit the identity of the victim and perpetrator from the witness, as opposed to identifying the victim and perpetrator to the witness at the beginning of the interview.

2. Find out what he or she knows: Get specifics.

3. Distinguish between firsthand and secondhand knowledge.

4. Assess the credibility of the witness.

5. Take a statement if warranted.

6. Type the notes of the interview.

III. Evaluating the Facts and Making the Decision

    A. Evaluate the facts from a reasonable woman's perspective.

    B. Distinguish between "unwelcome" and "voluntary" sexual conduct.

    C. Draft a thorough, even-handed report.

        1. Make the report chronological.

        2. Describe when first learned of the complaint.

        3. Provide exact details of the complaint.

        4. Note the documents reviewed.

        5. Describe the interviews.

        6. For all witnesses, distinguish between firsthand knowledge and rumor.

        7. State conclusion as to whether sexual harassment occurred and provide specific justification.

        8. Recommend corrective action if sexual harassment occurred. The corrective action should:

            a. be reasonably calculated to prevent further harassment.

            b. not punish the victim.

            c. be consistent with the discipline imposed in the past in similar situations.

    D. Submit the report to the decision-making official. That official should:

        1. not be a rubber stamp.

        2. point out deficiencies in the report.

        3. ask follow-up questions.

        4. conduct interviews him or herself if necessary.

        5. document his or her actions.

Checklist (continued)

E. Follow up with the victim and the perpetrator after the decision has been made.

Reprinted with permission from *Employee Relations Law Journal*, vol. 18, no. 2 (Autumn 1992) by Executive Enterprises Inc., 22 West 21st Street, New York, NY 10010-6990. All Rights Reserved.

(Author's note: If your employer does not conduct an investigation properly, it may be violating the law. This checklist will inform you of the proper steps employers should take when conducting sexual harassment investigations. Speak to a lawyer if you experience any harmful deviations.)

How to Prove Sex Harassment

Courts consider the nature and frequency of the acts, the conditions under which the conduct occurred, whether the company was promptly notified by the complainant, and what steps, if any, the company took after being notified. To prove a case of sex harassment, it is crucial to take prompt steps to document your claim. For example, if you are being teased on the job, it is wise to complain to a supervisor or manager *in writing* immediately after the incident occurred. Judges, arbitrators, and EEOC hearing officers are more willing to award damages for sex harassment when a formal complaint was made requesting that the offensive conduct stop and *the request was ignored.*

The following case illustrates this point. A woman was the only female traffic controller stationed at an air traffic center. While working there she was subjected to substantial sexual slur, insult, and innuendo by other employees, including various supervisory personnel. When the woman alerted her supervisors of this in a letter, several suggested that her problem might be solved if she "submitted to one of the controllers." The court held that the woman proved that sexually harassing actions took place, that such acts were offensive and severe, and that the employer did little to stop them after receiving a warning through her letter; she was awarded substantial damages as a result. Thus, by sending a letter similar to the one on page 163, you may be able to prove a repetitive pattern of conduct and demonstrate that the offensive acts were not condoned.

> **TIP:** By sending a letter you notify the company of the allegations. When an employer does not properly investigate a claim, it can further compound the problem and be legally exposed. Most important, you have proof that a formal complaint was made. If the company then takes any negative action against you in retaliation, you may be able to prove the retaliation occurred after and because the letter was sent.

Send a copy of this letter to the president or other high officer of the company. Always keep a copy for your files. Save the receipt to prove delivery. If you feel you are the victim of harassment, discuss the incident with other employees you trust to discover if they have suffered similar abuse. By doing so, you may strengthen a claim and be less at risk for making a complaint since there is always safety in numbers. For example, it was recently reported that a sexual harassment and discrimination lawsuit against a well-known investment firm was amended to include 20 more women in a total of 11 states. The newest plaintiffs joined the action (which was started by one woman only) and alleged being subjected to lewd language, unwelcome touching, and being denied opportunities and privileges afforded men. The suit seeks class-action status on behalf of all women employed by the firm, in part for the company's alleged explicit descriptions and sexual talk in the basement of one of its offices.

If possible, collect and save evidence (e.g., the pornographic pictures shown to you). Maintain a diary of all incidents of harassment recalling the location, events, time, persons involved, and name of any witnesses who may have observed the illegal conduct. Recall whether supervisors participated in creating or tolerating a sexually poisoned atmosphere.

Speak to an experienced employment lawyer immediately if:

- the matter is not resolved satisfactorily
- you are retaliated against for making a complaint, such as being demoted, reassigned, denied benefits or a promotion, receive an unfavorable job evaluation, or are fired

- you feel uncomfortable while being questioned about the events (i.e., the company is not conducting a fair and unbiased investigation and is accusing you of contributing to or causing the harassment by your dress, behavior, or language)

- the employer fails to take speedy action to investigate your complaints

- you wish to pursue money damages for stress, mental suffering, and physical injuries caused or induced by the harassment

- the company mistakenly determines that no harassment occurred, that the acts do not constitute harassment, that it had no knowledge of the incident and thus is not responsible, or fails to make a decision in an objective manner

- the employer disparages your character, job performance, or family life

- the employer refuses to allow you to grieve the incident through its complaint procedures

An experienced lawyer can tell you whether it makes sense to confront the harasser, use a company complaint procedure, immediately file a claim in court or with an appropriate federal agency (such as the EEOC) or a state agency, or if more desirable and/or advantageous, to contact the employer and try to settle the matter out of court.

> **COUNSEL COMMENTS:** Most states have laws that expressly prohibit sexual harassment; there are occasions when it might be advantageous to apply state law and file charges with a state agency instead of the EEOC. Talk to your lawyer about this. Consider filing a private tort lawsuit for assault and battery if you are touched, kissed, or rubbed without your consent. The advantage of being able to file a private lawsuit is that you may receive greater damages for your injuries and may be able to file a charge more than 300 days after the acts occurred. Claimants who are not able to file a discrimination charge because the statute of limitations has expired may still be able to commence a private lawsuit in some cases. (Note: By law, you are required to file a charge of discrimination with the EEOC within 300 days of the incident.)

In any event, do not be afraid to assert your rights when you are subjected to conduct you find uncomfortable. A course of strategy should be implemented immediately so you don't suffer more

Sample Letter Protesting Sexual Harassment

Your Name
Address
Telephone Number
Date

Name of Supervisor or Officer
Title
Name of Employer
Address

Dear (name):

While working for the company, I have been the victim of a series of offensive acts that I believe constitute sexual harassment.

On (date), I (describe what occurred and with whom). I immediately (describe your reaction) and ordered that such conduct stop. However, on (date), another incident occurred when (describe what occurred and with whom).

I find such behavior intimidating and repugnant. In fact, (describe the physical and emotional impact on you), causing me to be less efficient on the job. Please treat this letter as a formal protest of such conduct. Unless such conduct ceases immediately, or in the event the company illegally retaliates against me for writing this letter, I will contact the Equal Employment Opportunity Commission to enforce my rights.

I do not wish to take such a drastic measure. All I want to do is perform my job in a professional environment.

Thank you for your cooperation in this matter.

Very truly yours,

(your name)

CONFIDENTIAL

(Send certified mail, return receipt requested.)

abuse and to protect your rights in this area. If you delay contacting an appropriate agency or lawyer, your inactivity may be viewed as a waiver of your rights or an acceptance of such illegal acts, which can jeopardize a claim.

SEXUAL BIAS DISCRIMINATION

Although not recognized by federal law, some states and municipalities have passed laws that forbid employers from discriminating in all phases of the job on the basis of an individual's sexual preferences. A lesbian or homosexual faced with hostile conduct or denied employment opportunities should seek legal advice about relevant state and local ordinances and rulings. Lawyers representing gays and lesbians who practice in states where sexual bias discrimination statutes do not exist are suing employers and supervisors for invasion of privacy and other causes of action.

NONSEXUAL HARASSMENT

All employers must take adequate steps so that no harassment, even if it is not sexual in nature, occurs within the company. Can an employee charge her psychiatric injuries to a supervisor's harassment? This depends. In one case, for example, an employee experienced constant "run-ins" with her supervisor. Matters between them took a bad turn one day when the worker, having completed all her work, was chatting with her co-workers. When the supervisor ordered her back to work, she told him she had nothing to do because the computer that generated assignments was not operating. The supervisor nevertheless demanded she begin working. When the employee insisted there was no work, the supervisor suspended her for the remainder of the working day and the following day.

When the employee returned to work, the supervisor began giving her work orders despite the fact that other co-workers received their work orders from a dispatcher. When she questioned this procedure, she was again suspended. The worker became hysterical and was rushed to a hospital, where she was given a tranquilizer. She remained under a doctor's care for over two months.

Shortly after she returned to work, she was warned about munching on some food while working. When she told the supervisor not to interrupt her work, she was again suspended.

This time, the employee did not return for three months, during which time she was treated by a psychiatrist. She filed a claim for workers' compensation, seeking benefits for the two periods she was away from work. The company opposed her claim. During a hearing, the company stated that her case for benefits was built on malingering and exaggeration and that her job experiences involved only the normal give-and-take between employees and supervisors; a bit of criticism about not working was insufficient to produce the reaction the employee claimed she endured. The company also argued that the worker was blaming it for mental difficulties having nothing to do with the job.

The employee stated that even before the day the supervisor accused her of not working he had repeatedly singled her out for criticism and had taken an intense, irrational hatred to her. She argued that she was treated by a psychiatrist for anxiety and depression caused by the supervisor's harassment.

A Pennsylvania Court ruled that the employee's mental injuries were job-related and ordered that she receive workers' compensation. It stated that the employee's testimony was not limited to her belief that she was being harassed; she also *described actual events* such as being singled out by her supervisor and told to go back to work when her duties had been completed to the same extent as those of co-workers in the same vicinity. These events constituted abnormal working conditions as a matter of law. With the addition of medical evidence establishing that the abnormal working conditions caused the psychiatric injuries, the court found that the employee had established her case for benefits.

COUNSEL COMMENTS: In some cases, work-related stress caused by on-the-job nonsexual harassment resulting in documented physical and mental injuries can give rise to a valid legal claim. Similarly, some claimants have successfully asserted that such conduct is a form of sex discrimination when the acts complained of were directed to them because of their gender. When the same treatment is not directed to males, a charge of disparate sex discrimination can be asserted.

TIP: It is often easier to win *sex-related* harassment cases since the law specifically authorizes claimants to collect damages for illegal acts and proof of physical or mental injuries is not necessary. For nonsexual harassing acts, you must prove the acts were so severe that they caused you harm. This is often difficult to do. In fact, the author is consulted by numerous female clients each year who request legal assistance as a result of nonsexual harassment (such as for verbal abuse from a supervisor). Sometimes, the author declines representation because the law does not ordinarily provide protection. In most situations, perhaps the best strategy is to discuss the problem with someone from personnel and request that the harassment stop. Many supervisors are cognizant of the potential causes of action arising from physical and mental distress claims and are instructed to avoid contributing to these problems where possible. You can also write the company a letter protesting such activity. If you do, however, you could be retaliated against (i.e., fired) for making a complaint because the law may not protect you in this area.

Confer with a lawyer if you are the victim of extensive nonsexual harassment to explore your options. The lawyer may advise you to consult a physician, take prescribed medication, or institute other steps without delay to prove the extent of your injuries and enforce a claim. For example, in another case, a workers' compensation claim was awarded to a female employee whose mental troubles arose because she was repeatedly singled out for public criticism; co-workers were not subjected to this treatment. The employee eventually developed a fear of going to work, which led to a disabling "panic disorder."

FINAL POINTS ABOUT SEX DISCRIMINATION

Sex discrimination in the workplace exists in many forms. In case after case, courts and antidiscrimination agencies have hacked away at the long-time stereotype of the "weak female" who must be barred from strenuous "men's work" and restricted to gentler employment. For example, a federal court judge ordered a public utility to consider women for switchmen's jobs; another employer was forbidden to impose a 35-pound weight-lifting limit on women employees. As a result of management steps being taken to train supervisors to act properly in all areas potentially affecting women, these stereotypes are beginning to vanish.

Retirement, pension plans, and fringe benefits must be equally applied, since any program that favors one sex over another violates federal and state discrimination laws. Be aware that the following practices have been declared illegal in the application of fringe benefits pertaining to vacations, insurance coverage, pensions, profit-sharing plans, bonuses, holidays, and disability leaves:

- Conditioning benefits available to employees and their spouses and families on a particular status (e.g., "head of household" or "principal wage earner")
- Making certain benefits available to wives of male employees but denying them to husbands of female employees
- Basing provisions of a pension plan on norms applied differently according to sex
- Denying a job or benefit to pregnant employees or applicants

These are just some of the ways employers commit violations concerning benefits. If you have doubts about any current practices, seek competent legal advice.

Although common illegal practices regarding preemployment screening were discussed in Chapter One, it is worthwhile to mention this subject again. Unfortunately, many employers ask illegal questions of females at job interviews, particularly with respect to their marital status. EEOC guidelines and most state regulations declare that the only lawful question that may be asked of a female applicant is "What is your marital status?"

Familiarize yourself with the kinds of questions that are illegal at job interviews. If you refuse to answer such questions and are denied a job, you may wish to consider filing charges with the EEOC or appropriate state rights organization or agency alleging sex discrimination on the basis of such illegal inquiries.

Know your rights regarding pregnancy. For example, it was recently reported that just before closing arguments, a lawyer who worked for a large law firm accepted a substantial sum from her former employer in an out-of-court settlement. The woman was fired from her position two months after her return from maternity leave. The firm said she had a poor attitude, economic times were tough, and alleged declining work quality to support its claims. But the woman's lawyer pointed to excellent work reviews and suggested the firm not only had invented the criticisms but also may have included them in personnel files after she announced her pregnancy.

Understand the difference between maternity leave, child leave, unpaid child leave, and paternity leave for a spouse and what benefits are available to you.

Recognize that female independent contractors (such as insurance agents) cannot sue for sex discrimination under the laws of many states. Speak to a lawyer to discuss this where applicable.

Finally, understand that there is a trend in extending a company's benefits package to the same-sex partners of its homosexual and lesbian employees. In a growing number of companies, for example, same-sex domestic partners are being given the same access to health insurance and family and medical leave as married couples. Most employers that offer such benefits require employees who want to participate to certify that they've been living together at least six months and are committed to mutual emotional and financial support. When a relationship ends, employees can terminate their former partner's benefits. (Note: The Internal Revenue Service may tax you for receiving extra taxable income if your partner received benefits, so speak to your accountant where applicable.)

AGE DISCRIMINATION

Federal and state discrimination laws are designed to promote employment of older persons based on their abilities, irrespective of age. The most important federal law, the Age Discrimination in Employment Act (ADEA), protects workers over 40 from being arbitrarily fired, refused a job, forced to retire, or treated unfairly with respect to pay, promotions, benefits, health care coverage, retirement plans, and other employment opportunities because of age. The ADEA governs all private employers with 15 or more workers. It also protects employees of labor organizations, unions, and local, state, and federal government employees. Many states have enacted even tougher laws protecting workers by reducing the number of employees an employer must have to be subject to the law or reducing the cut-off age for inclusion into a protected class (i.e., age 30 in a few states).

The following thumbnail sketch outlines what employers can generally do under the ADEA and state discrimination laws pertaining to age:

- Fire older workers for documented, inadequate job performance or good cause (e.g., excessive tardiness or absences)

- Entice older workers into early retirement by offering additional benefits, such as bigger pensions, extended health insurance, or substantial severance packages, that are *voluntarily* accepted

- Force employees to retire if the worker is 65 or older, has worked as an executive for the past two years and is entitled to a pension exceeding $44,000, or if the job calls for physical fitness (e.g., airline pilots or police officers) and age is recognized as a bona fide occupational qualification (BFOQ) factor in fitness and job performance

- Lay off older workers when younger employees are similarly treated

- Refuse to hire older applicants when successful job performance absolutely requires that a younger person be hired for the job (e.g., in the case of flight controllers)

- Make adverse decisions provided the acts are taken as a result of a demonstrated good-faith business decision that does not have a discriminatory impact on all older workers at the company

TIP: Some employers may legally discriminate against older workers when they hire independent contractors (which the law doesn't generally protect) or employ fewer than 15 workers and there is no state antidiscrimination law to protect the rights of older workers. Always check the law of your state to see what protection is available if you work for a small employer or are an independent contractor. Additionally, since some state agencies process discrimination cases more quickly than the EEOC and provide greater damages and remedies under applicable state law, consider pursuing your rights with a state agency or in state court after discussing your options with a labor lawyer.

The following actions are generally prohibited by federal and state law:

- Denying an older applicant a job on the basis of age
- Imposing compulsory retirement before age 70

- Forcing older employees into retirement by threatening them with termination or loss of benefits, unless the company has instituted a valid seniority system or retirement plan
- Firing older workers because of age
- Denying promotions, transfers, or assignments because of age
- Penalizing older employees with reduced privileges, employment opportunities, or compensation because of age

Significant damages are recoverable when a woman receives unfair treatment because of age. These may include job reinstatement in the event of a firing, wage adjustments, back pay and double back pay, future pay, promotions, recovery of legal fees, witness fees and filing costs, compensatory damages up to $300,000 depending on the size of the employer, and punitive damages. Recourse can also include the institution of an affirmative action program on behalf of fellow employees, counseling, and enhanced outplacement assistance.

> **COUNSEL COMMENTS:** Whenever an older employee (over 40) is fired and that individual is claiming discrimination, the issue is basically whether the company's decision was made because of age or was the result of a reasonable, nondiscriminatory rational business reason. Typically the older worker must use circumstantial evidence to prove an employer's motive was improper. This is sometimes done by demonstrating she was between 40 and 70 years of age, was doing satisfactory work, was fired, and the position was then filled by a substantially younger employee under 40. If a younger male employee replaces her, the female employee may also have a claim for sex discrimination. However, when employers support firing decisions with documentation of poor work performance or other factors, an older female worker's chances of proving age discrimination diminish.

> **TIP:** It is easier to prove age discrimination when age-related statements are made to or about the claimant (e.g., "you are too old"; "Why don't you retire?") or by using statistics (i.e., that the company fired 10 older workers in the past six months and replaced them all with employees under 40).

However, when staff did not make liability-sensitive statements, remarks, or threats with respect to age and the employee is unable to demonstrate statistical proof that the company had a practice of firing older workers and replacing them with younger ones, the chances of success with a claim are reduced. A Supreme Court ruling that an employer's decision to lay off mostly older workers close to receiving vested retirement benefits did not, in and of itself, constitute age discrimination (even though the older workers were more severely affected by the discharge than younger workers) has not helped the cause of older workers asserting age claims. In that case, the court found that since the employer proffered a rational business justification for firing a large number of older workers (i.e., to save the company money since older workers with the most seniority had the highest salaries), no illegality occurred. (Note: The Supreme Court did say that the individuals might consider filing ERISA claims to protect forfeited retirement and severance benefits as a result of the company's actions.)

The following is a discussion of areas where age discrimination often occurs.

PREEMPLOYMENT SCREENING

Employers sometimes set requirements that are too high or commit violations through illegal ads. Many make statements or ask questions during the hiring interview that are illegal. For example, discrimination against older applicants occurs when they are told by an interviewer that:

- They are "overqualified"
- They lack formal education credits even though they are highly qualified by previous work experience and a college degree is not necessary for successful job performance
- They must take a preemployment physical that is either unnecessary, not job-related, or not requested of all other applicants
- They are required to answer questions such as "How old are you?", "What is the date of your birth?", or "Why did you decide to seek employment at your age?"

With respect to preemployment questions concerning age, be aware that under federal and state guidelines, employers can only ask the applicant if she is between 18 and 65, and if not, to state her age. Any other type of question concerning age is illegal. If you refuse to answer such a question and believe you were denied a job as a result, consider contacting the EEOC, a local Human Rights Commission office, or your state's attorney general's office to pursue your rights.

PHYSICALS

Companies sometimes require potential employees to take preemployment physicals. This is not legal as a result of the passage of the Americans With Disabilities Act (ADA). Physicals can be given only if they are directly related to successful job performance (e.g., a firefighter's job) and are required by all employees after a job has been offered, not before. Thus, employers are allowed to offer a job that is conditioned on passage of a successful physical exam.

ADVERTISING

Pay special attention to language in advertisements used to attract job candidates. The ADEA prohibits companies from publishing advertisements indicating any preference, limitation, specification, or discrimination based on age. Thus, targeted advertisements containing language such as "Industrial management trainee, recent college degree," "Sales trainee, any recent degree," "Prefer recent college grad," or "Corporate attorney, 2-4 years out of law school" are illegal. However, help wanted notices or advertisements that include a term or phrase such as "college graduate" or other education criterion, or specify a minimum age less than 40, such as "not under 21," are not prohibited by federal statute.

JOB REQUIREMENTS

When preparing criteria for a particular job, companies sometimes set a higher requirement than is necessary to attract higher-caliber applicants. This may discriminate between classes of applicants. If you are an older applicant and believe a potential employer has established unwarranted requirements (such as a college degree) that are not job-related, be aware that you may have a valid case of age discrimination.

> **COUNSEL COMMENTS:** Simply showing that a younger individual was hired over a qualified older applicant does not prove

age discrimination if the employer can show its decision was based on an honest evaluation of the candidate's qualifications (e.g., the rejected applicant would be bored or likely to leave upon finding a better job, or both). Furthermore, an employer is under no obligation to provide a laid-off employee with a job for which that person is overqualified. And, when eliminating a position, an employer does not assume an obligation to retain or create a position for the displaced employee simply because the employee is within a protected class, such as being a female or over 40.

PROGRESSIVE DISCIPLINE AND WARNINGS

The practice of progressive discipline (in which notice is given to the employee of a company's dissatisfaction with her work performance) is used to reduce the risk of wrongful termination lawsuits. By documenting the incidence of employee disciplinary measures through precise records of conferences, warnings, probationary notices, remedial efforts and other steps, employers sometimes demonstrate that an eventual termination was not due to a discriminatory motive but stemmed from a good-faith business decision.

Many companies, however, apply their system of discipline and warnings in a haphazard fashion and fail to use the same punishment for similar infractions. This often invites a discrimination lawsuit if there are several employees with a chronic problem (such as absenteeism) and the older worker (or the female) is the first to be fired for that reason while workers under 40 (or males) are only given a warning.

> **TIP:** If you are an older worker who believes that an employer is treating you more harshly than younger workers for identical infractions, or you are receiving dissimilar, unfair on-the-job treatment with respect to benefits, promotions, or other matters, speak to an employment lawyer for advice.

SENIORITY RIGHTS AND VACATION TIME

Nothing in the federal laws barring age discrimination prohibits employers from altering the terms of a benefit seniority system provided the new system is not a subterfuge for engaging in arbitrary age discrimination. For example, when companies change vacation pay policies by putting a cap on the amount of annual paid vacation a person can take (this penalizes older workers when all employees regardless of seniority must take the same number of days off) or reduce medical insurance and retiree benefit plans, such acts are legal where justified by significant cost considerations. However, the burden falls on the employer to justify that its actions are lawful.

RETIREMENT PLANS AND FORCED RETIREMENT

This is an area where older female executives are often exploited. It occurs when companies exert pressure on older workers to opt for early retirement or face firing, demotion, a cut in pay, or poor recommendations. Companies contemplating a large layoff or seeking to reduce payroll through early retirement incentives must do so carefully to avoid charges of age discrimination. Under the ADEA and in most states, it is illegal to impose compulsory retirement before age 70 unless the employee is a "bona fide executive" receiving an annual company-paid retirement benefit of at least $44,000 per year after reaching 65, or is in a "high policy-making position" during a two year-period prior to reaching age 65.

Some states have passed similar laws to protect older employees from being victimized by forced retirement and mandatory retirement plans. For example, New York has a law that prohibits most public employees from being forced to retire, no matter how old they get (except for firefighters, police officers and other law enforcement positions). Private sector employees (with limited exceptions for some executives and tenured college faculty members) are also protected.

> **COUNSEL COMMENTS:** If the employer can show that a retirement plan is "bona fide" (e.g., plan benefits are based on an employee's length of service), that the employee's decision to accept early retirement is voluntary, and that the reasons for the plan are nondiscriminatory (i.e., not based on age), a plan may not violate the ADEA. Also, if an employee can no longer perform her job duties, the employer may be allowed to discharge her or, alternatively, force her to retire (depending on the circumstances).

Ask yourself the following questions if you believe you were fired because of age:

- Did you request a transfer to another position before you were fired? Was it refused? If so, were similar requests granted to younger workers?

- How were you terminated? Were you given false reasons for the termination? Did you consent to the action or did you protest (such as by sending a certified letter to the company refuting the discharge)?

- Were you replaced by a younger worker under 40 (or between 40 and 45 if you are between 60 and 65)? Were younger workers merely laid off and not fired (i.e., rehired several months later)?

Positive answers to these questions may prove you were fired as a result of age discrimination. Your case will be strengthened when fellow employees are also victimized. In one case, for example, 143 persons were forced to retire prematurely from an insurance company at the age of 62. The large number of older employees all the same age made it difficult for the company to claim it was a valid reduction in force (called a RIF), and the workers collectively received more than $6 million in back wages.

TIP: Before implementing a RIF, companies must take steps to ensure they have acted properly. For example, if they have a practice of permitting bumping or transfers before a discharge, not extending such opportunities to older workers during a RIF may give rise to a claim of disparate treatment. Also, selection of individuals for layoff based on their current cost of retention may be unlawful where wage and benefit rates are found to be a function of length of service and, as such, an arguable product of age.

One federal court jury found a well-known bank guilty of age discrimination in dismissing five female customer service representatives. The employer was ordered to pay more than $700,000 to the women who were allegedly dismissed as a result of corporate restructuring. Their ages and seniority were:

Plaintiff #1: age 45, years of service 18
Plaintiff #2: age 43, years of service 25
Plaintiff #3: age 59, years of service 19
Plaintiff #4: age 62, years of service 14
Plaintiff #5: age 42, years of service 12

The lawyer representing the women said there were other positions they could have been offered (but weren't) and that shortly after the dismissals the bank advertised for replacements. The five were awarded $141,000 for back pay (doubled as a result of the jury's finding of "willful" discrimination); $408,750 for lost future wages and benefits and $25,000 for emotional distress.

> **COUNSEL COMMENTS:** The employer has appealed the decision. However, the case is instructive in several respects. It demonstrates that you don't have to be in your late 60's to win an age claim when you are fired. Also, a case may be strengthened when despite having greater seniority, you and other senior workers are terminated (instead of junior employees) for an alleged downsizing, but your job is filled by new inexperienced workers soon thereafter.

WAIVERS

To avoid charges that a person was not given sufficient time to reflect and weigh the options of an early retirement offer and thus was constructively discharged, employers are now required to prepare written releases that give retirees and older workers time to consider the offer, seek advice from a lawyer, and even repudiate the decision within seven days after signing the document. Historically, Congress did not recognize the ability of employers to enforce the waiver of age discrimination claims. As a result, some lucky workers who signed releases prior to 1990 were able to cash their settlement checks and still sue an employer thereafter.

The enactment of the federal Older Workers Benefit Protection Act (OWBPA) has eliminated confusion provided its provisions are properly followed. The act makes clear that in relation to a firing or resignation of a worker over 40, a company can protect itself from potential violations of ADEA claims by utilizing waivers, provided:

1. The waiver is part of an agreement that specifically states the worker is waiving her ADEA rights and is not merely a general release;
2. The agreement containing the waiver does not disclaim any rights or claims arising after the date of its execution;
3. The worker receives value (such as an extra month of severance) in exchange for signing the agreement;
4. The worker is advised in writing of the right to consult an attorney of her choosing before signing the agreement;

5. The worker is advised in writing of her right to consider the agreement for a period of 21 days before it is effective; and

6. The worker is given at least seven days following the execution of the agreement to revoke it.

When employers request the signing of releases or waivers in connection with mass termination programs and large-scale voluntary retirement programs, the act is even more strict. All individuals in the program must be given at least 45 days to consider the agreement and each employee must also be provided with numerous facts, such as the class, unit, or group of individuals covered by the program, any eligibility factors for the program, time limits applicable to the program, the job titles and ages of all individuals selected for the program, and the ages of all individuals not eligible for the program.

The release beginning on page 178 illustrates the kind of document that is often prepared by employers to comply with the OWBPA,

A benefit of the OWBPA is that all voluntary early retirement programs are now scrutinized closely to determine there is no chance of threat, intimidation, or coercion to the worker to whom the benefit is offered. Older employees must now be given sufficient time to consider the offer and receive accurate and complete information regarding benefits.

> **TIP:** If you are an older worker being terminated after working
> years for an employer, *always* try to negotiate a better severance
> package. Information on how to do this successfully is included in
> Chapter Seven. When companies agree to pay more money in sev-
> erance and/or benefits, they typically prepare releases for individu-
> als to sign. Carefully review such a document. Question all ambigu-
> ous or confusing language. Consult an experienced employment
> lawyer for advice and guidance where necessary. Do not be afraid
> to do this, since the release, to be valid, must specifically allow the
> right to consult an attorney of your choosing. Take advantage of
> this provision. The lawyer you consult may advise that the company
> has violated the ADEA and you are entitled to a greater settlement
> before signing away your rights. Some workers hire employment
> lawyers to negotiate a better severance package or sue the employ-
> er in court after an evaluation has been made.

Cover Letter and Release
(Specifically Waiving an Age Discrimination Claim)

To: Severed Employee

From: The Company ("The Employer")

Re: Older Workers Benefit Protection Act

This communication apprises you of your rights under the Older Workers Benefit Protection Act ("OWBPA") which amends the Age Discrimination in Employment Act ("ADEA"), that Congress passed. The OWBPA establishes certain standards as regards waivers that the Employer obtains from its Employees.

The OWBPA amends the ADEA by adding a new section which establishes standards for a "knowing and voluntary" waiver:

(1) The waiver has to be part of an agreement between the Employee and the Employer and it has to be written in understandable English;

(2) The waiver must refer specifically to rights or claims arising under the ADEA;

(3) The waiver cannot cover rights or claims that may arise after the date on which it is signed;

(4) The waiver must be exchanged for consideration, and the consideration must be in addition to anything of value to which the Employee is already entitled;

(5) The Employee must be advised in writing to consult with an attorney before signing the agreement;

(6) The Employee has to be given a period of at least 21 days to decide whether to sign the waiver; and

(7) The Employee is entitled to revoke the waiver within seven days after signing it, and the waiver does not become effective or enforceable until the revocation period has expired.

FINAL COMMENTS

If you sign an employment contract containing an arbitration clause, a claim made by a fired employee under the ADEA may fall within the scope of the clause and you may be forced to litigate an age discrimination dispute in arbitration, rather than in court before a jury. This could work to your disadvantage because arbitrators are not empowered to award punitive damages, injunctions stopping further harassment, and legal fees in most instances.

Furthermore, arbitrators are usually business people or lawyers, and their philosophical orientation is often not as closely aligned to an individual's rights, as a jury is. Arbitration awards tend to be smaller for discriminatory harms committed. Thus, it is important to understand the ramifications of any arbitration clause in an employment agreement before signing. Consider seeking legal advice when presented with a comprehensive employment contract for an important job.

Recognize that waivers signed by a departing worker may not protect the employer if the worker later applies for a job. One 55-year-old executive was dismissed in a downsizing move. He accepted an enhanced severance package (twice the usual severance) and signed a waiver relinquishing his right to sue the company. A year later, still unemployed, he saw his old job advertised in the newspaper. With the encouragement of a former superior, he applied for the position. He lost out to a much younger worker under 40 with little experience.

The man sued, claiming that he was a victim of age discrimination. The trial court dismissed the case as a result of the waiver he had signed. But the appeals court noted that the ADEA disapproves people waiving age discrimination claims. It ruled that although the waiver would normally preclude the worker from suing the company, it did not cover discriminatory events that occurred after the waiver was signed and thus was ineffectual!

HANDICAP DISCRIMINATION

The federal Americans With Disabilities Act (ADA) was enacted in 1990 to widen the scope of protection available to disabled workers. Employers with more than 15 workers must avoid disability dis-

GENERAL RELEASE

FOR GOOD AND VALUABLE CONSIDERATION, the adequacy of which is hereby acknowledged, in the form of payment to Employee of a severance benefit in the amount of ($XX)_____ salary less withholding for federal and state taxes, FICA, and any other amounts required to be withheld, Employee agrees that he/she, or any person acting by, through, or under Employee, RELEASES AND FOREVER DISCHARGES (Name of Employer), and its parent company and subsidiaries, affiliates, successors, and assigns, as well as the officers, employees, representatives, agents and fiduciaries, *de facto or de jure* (hereinafter collectively referred to as "Released Parties"), and covenants and agrees not to institute any action or actions, causes or causes of action (in law unknown) in state or federal court, based upon or arising by reason of any damage, loss, or in any way related to Employee's employment with any of the Released Parties or the termination of said employment. The foregoing includes, but not by way of limitation, all claims which could have been raised under common law, including retaliatory discharge and breach of contract, or statute, including, without limitation, the Age Discrimination in Employment Act of 1967, 42 U.S.C. Sections 621-634, as amended by the Older Workers Benefit Protection Act of 1990, Title VII of the Civil Rights Act of 1964, 42 U.S.C. Sections 2000e *et seq.* and the Employee Retirement Income Security Act of 1974, 29 U.S.C. Sections 1001 *et seq.* or any other Federal or State Law; except that this General Release is not intended to cover any claim arising from computational or clerical errors in the calculation of the severance benefit provided to Employee, or retirement benefit to which Employee may be entitled from any plan or other benefits to which Employee may be entitled under any plan maintained by any of the Released Parties.

Employee covenants and agrees to forever refrain from instituting, pursuing, or in any way whatsoever aiding any claim, demand, action, or cause of action or other matter released and discharged herein by Employee arising out of or in any way related to Employee's employment with any of the Released Parties and the rights to recovery for any damages or compensation awarded as a result of a lawsuit brought by any third party or governmental agency on Employee's behalf.

Employee further agrees to indemnify all Released Parties from any and all loss, liability, damages, claims, suits, judgments, attorneys' fees and other costs and expenses of whatsoever kind or individually Employee may sustain or incur as a result of or in connection with matters hereinabove released and discharged by Employee. Employee warrants that he/she has not filed any lawsuits, charges, complaints, petitions, or accusatory pleadings against any of the Released Parties with any governmental agency or in any court, based upon, arising out of, or related in any way to any event or events occurring prior to the signing of this General Release, including, without limitation, his/her employment with any of the Released Parties or the termination thereof.

Employee acknowledges, understands and affirms that: (a) This General Release is a binding legal document; (b) (i) Released Parties advised him/her to consult with an attorney before signing this General Release, (ii) he/she had the right to consult with an attorney about and before signing this General Release, (iii) he/she was given a period of at least 21 calendar days in which to consider this General Release prior to signing, and (iv) he/she voluntarily signs and enters into this General Release without reservation after having given the matter full and careful consideration; and (c) (i) Employee has a period of seven days after signing this General Release in which he/she may revoke this General Release, (ii) this General Release does not become effective or enforceable and no payment shall be made hereunder until this seven-day-revocation period has elapsed, and (iii) any revocation must be in writing by Employee and delivered to (specify), Human Resources, within the seven-day-revocation period.

IN WITNESS WHEREOF, the Employee signs this General Release this day of _____ (specify day and year).

Employee's Name (please print)

WITNESS:

Signature: _____ Date: _____

ACKNOWLEDGMENT

I HEREBY ACKNOWLEDGE that (Name of Employer) in accordance with the Age Discrimination in Employment Act, as amended by the Older Workers Benefit Protection Act, informed me in writing: (1) to consult with an attorney before signing this General Release; (2) to review this General Release for a period of 21 days prior to signing; (3) that for a period of seven days following the signing of this General Release, I may revoke this General Release, and this General Release will not become effective or enforceable until the seven-day-revocation period has elapsed; and (4) that no payment shall be made until the seven-day-revocation period has elapsed.

I HEREBY FURTHER ACKNOWLEDGE receipt of this General release for my review on the (specify day and year).

Employee:
(Print or Type)

Signature of Employee

Witness:

crimination in all phases of the job. Employers are required to eliminate any inquiries on medical examinations and forms designed to
identify an applicant's disabilities. Persons with disabilities cannot be
disqualified from applying for a job because of the inability to perform nonessential or marginal functions of the job. Employers must
scrutinize all job requirements so they do not inadvertently screen
out qualified disabled applicants. Under the ADA, it is unlawful to
refuse to hire people with disabilities who have equal skills after the
employer provides reasonable accommodation, such as purchasing
a telephone headset for a person with a hearing impairment.

The following list will familiarize you with typical obligations
employers must generally follow during the hiring process:

1. Employers cannot ask disability-related questions (such as "Do you
   presently have a disability?" or "Do you have any impairments which
   prevent you from performing the job you've applied for?") in interviews.

2. Employers cannot inquire about the kind of accommodation a person
   needs in order to perform the job properly if hired.

3. A medical exam can be requested only after hiring provided it is an
   essential condition for employment for all entering employees in that
   position.

4. All contracts with employment agencies, unions, and insurance plans
   cannot be discriminatory.

5. Employers cannot deny employment opportunities to an applicant or
   employee because of the need to make reasonable accommodation
   for a disability.

6. Employers must avoid employment tests or selection criteria that
   have a disparate impact on individuals with disabilities unless the test
   or criteria are shown to be job-related and supported by business
   necessity.

7. Employers may deny jobs to handicapped workers if they can demonstrate the position poses a danger to the individual's health and welfare or that the hiring would significantly interfere with productivity
   or create dangers to others.

The main object of the ADA is to protect any person with a
physical or mental impairment that substantially limits one or more
life activities. This covers a broad range of disabilities, including

deafness, AIDS, cancer, and learning disabilities. It does not include compulsive gambling or pregnancy. (Note: State law may be more inclusive as to what constitutes a covered disability, so speak to a lawyer for more details if applicable.)

In addition to job applications and screening procedures, every aspect of the employment relationship is protected, from employee compensation, terms, and privileges to job classifications, fringe benefits, promotions, training opportunities, and discharge.

Although ADA does not require an employer to give preferential consideration to persons with disabilities, such persons cannot be excluded for consideration for a raise, promotion, or on-the-job opportunity because of an inability to perform a marginal function. The law also states that persons associated with those who have a disability, such as an individual who does volunteer work with AIDS patients, cannot be discriminated against because of that relationship or association.

> **TIP:** The law does not cover workers who cannot work because of a total disability; the law only protects workers with disabilities who are capable of *continuing* working if the employer provides reasonable accommodation. On-the-job accommodations that must be provided to handicapped employees include:

- Restructuring or modifying work schedules
- Offering part-time work
- Permitting the employee to work at home
- Reassigning an individual to a vacant position
- Providing readers or interpreters for blind or deaf persons
- Acquiring or altering equipment or devices
- Making existing facilities readily accessible to the disabled
- Adjusting marginal job requirements
- Allowing flexibility in arrival and departure times for people who require special vehicles for transportation or who are confined to wheelchairs

> **COUNSEL COMMENTS:** Employers are required to make such accommodations only if the disability is known, if the accommoda-

tion requested is reasonable, and if the employee is truly partially disabled. An employer is relieved of responsibility to accommodate a disabled employee when to do so would impose an undue hardship. Factors considered in determining whether undue hardship exists include the nature and the costs of the accommodation to the employer, the overall financial resources of the employer (i.e., number of employees, overall size of the business, etc.), and other related factors. Courts will look at the type of the operation, overall size, budget, profitability of the employer, and the financial impact of the suggested accommodation in determining whether undue hardship exists. The facts concerning what constitutes undue hardship vary from case to case; however, if the employer can afford to accommodate, it must generally do so.

FINAL TIPS

As a result of the ADA and various state laws, employers now have enhanced obligations to current employees who develop disabilities while working. Wrongful discharge of such persons could result in severe penalties, particularly for workers who contract the AIDS virus, develop alcohol problems affecting their attendance or performance, or even become obese. (Note: Although the ADA defines drug addiction as a disability, which means that you cannot be refused a job or be fired because of past drug addictions, there is no protection for current drug users. You can be legally terminated for using drugs on the job or working in an impaired state because of current drug use.)

While employers are generally permitted to terminate workers who become completely disabled, every opportunity must be extended to give handicapped workers the opportunity to work at less demanding jobs or offer other accommodations. Employers must also provide you with existing short- or long-term disability benefits and other existing medical coverage (as well as an enhanced severance package if you can negotiate it) before you leave. Thus, always try to obtain the best post-termination benefits if you are fired and possess a disability. Contact a lawyer immediately to discuss your rights and options.

RACIAL DISCRIMINATION

Title VII of the Civil Rights Act and various other federal and state laws prohibit intentional discrimination based on ancestry or ethnicity. Some employers practice blatant forms of minority discrimination by paying lower salaries and other compensation to blacks and Hispanics. Others engage in quota systems by denying promotions and jobs to individuals on the basis of race or color. Federal laws prohibit employers of 15 or more employees from discriminating on the basis of race or color. Virtually all states have even stronger antidiscrimination laws directed to fighting job-related race and minority discrimination. In some states, companies with fewer than eight employees can be found guilty of discrimination.

Both federal and state laws generally forbid private employers, labor unions, and state and local government agencies from:

- Denying an applicant a job on the basis of race or color
- Denying promotions, transfers, or assignments on the basis of race or color
- Penalizing workers with reduced privileges, reduced employment opportunities, and reduced compensation on the basis of race or color
- Firing a worker on the basis of race or color

Typically, the EEOC or related state agency will investigate charges of race discrimination or race-related retaliation. The EEOC has broad power to secure information and company records via subpoena, field investigations, audits, and interviewing witnesses, both employees and outsiders. Statistical data may be presented to demonstrate a pattern or practice of discriminatory conduct. As in other forms of discrimination, the contents of an individual's personnel file and the files of others in similar situations are often examined. Data on workplace composition may reveal a pattern or practice of exclusion or channeling. Regional or national data may shed light on whether a decision locally made was, in fact, racially discriminatory.

In cases where circumstantial evidence is presented to prove race discrimination, the burden is on the plaintiff to raise an inference of discrimination. This is often done through the use of statistics and payroll records.

COMMON AREAS OF EXPLOITATION

Although it is legal for employers to pose questions at the hiring interview that test your motivation, maturity, willingness to accept instruction, interest in the job, and ability to communicate, inquiries made to further discriminatory practices are illegal. Common areas of exploitation encompass questions pertaining to color, national origin, citizenship, language, and relatives. For example, it is illegal to ask the following questions under federal Equal Employment Opportunity Commission guidelines and state regulations:

Color:	What is your skin color?
National Origin:	What is your ancestry? What is your mother's native language? What is your spouse's nationality? What is your maiden name?
Citizenship:	Of what country are you a citizen? Are your parents or spouse naturalized or native-born citizens? When did they acquire citizenship? Are you a native-born citizen?
Language:	What is your native tongue? How did you acquire the ability to read, write, and speak a foreign language?
Relatives:	Names, addresses, ages and other pertinent information concerning your spouse, children, or relatives not employed by the company. What type of work does your mother or father do?

TIP: You have the right to refuse to answer any of the above questions at the hiring interview. If you choose not to answer them, you can politely inform the interviewer that you believe the questions are illegal and refuse to answer them on that basis. If you are then denied the job, you may have a strong case for damages after speaking with a representative from the EEOC, the Human Rights Commission, or a knowledgeable lawyer provided you can prove the denial stemmed from a refusal to answer such questions.

Another common area of race discrimination occurs when companies deliberately impose higher hiring standards than necessary, which tends to exclude minorities. All employment criterion requirements must be directly related to the job; minorities cannot be excluded unnecessarily.

> **TIP:** Proving you were individually excluded from a job based on
> your race or color may be difficult. It is often helpful to obtain sta-
> tistical data to show that the employer's practices are illegal. For
> example, if 10 positions for an engineering job were filled and none
> of the jobs was offered to a minority (or a woman), that may be
> sufficient to infer that the company violated the law. You would
> need assistance from a competent lawyer or discrimination specialist
> to prove this because the rules necessary to prove statistical dispari-
> ties are complex.

You may have an easier time of demonstrating race discrimination when you are directly treated unfairly on the job. For example, if you are repeatedly harassed and called names on the job, or are treated differently from nonminorities (e.g., you are absent several days from work and are suspended or placed on formal probation, while white workers with the same or a greater number of absences are only given an informal warning), it is best to gather this factual information for discussion with an executive or officer in your company's personnel department. In light of the Supreme Court decision *Wards Cove v. Antonio*, you may have an easier time proving race discrimination on an individual basis as opposed to relying on statistical disparities. This is because in certain cases employers now only have to offer a business justification for actions that are shown by statistics to have an unfair impact on minorities. The burden then shifts to the complainant to demonstrate that the alleged business justification is not legitimate.

AFFIRMATIVE ACTION PLANS

The Supreme Court recently cast doubt on the constitutionality of Federal affirmative action programs that award benefits on the basis of race. The Court ruled that any such programs will be subject to the most searching judicial inquiry and will survive only if they are narrowly tailored to accomplish a compelling governmental interest.

This ruling is a clear defeat for employers who take positive steps to recruit individuals on the basis of personal characteristics and classifications, including race, sex, religion, and veteran status, when the number of such individuals within the company is far below the number of such individuals within the community where the company is located. It is also a setback for employers who seek to ensure that such individuals, when employed, have an equal opportunity for benefits and promotions within the company.

The effect of the Supreme Court decision has been immediate. For example, the Office of Federal Contract Compliance Programs (OFCCP), charged with overseeing and administering the largest affirmative action program in the U.S., (more than 90,000 organizations have contracts with the federal government valued at $50,000 or more), recently announced that the requirement for "goals and timetables" in mandatory affirmative action plans for federal government contractors is not to be construed as a quota system to be achieved through race-based or gender-based preferences. The OFCCP is trying to clarify that its affirmative action program is different from preferences or set-asides and does not amount to reverse discrimination.

Employers are now eliminating any race or gender-based preferences in their hiring policies; if a formal plan has already been established, companies are considering eliminating any reference to formal goals and/or timetables (such as not requiring that any specific position be filled by a person of a particular race, gender or ethnicity) and not establishing a minimum number of minority employees which must be employed by a certain date.

For companies acting as government contractors, all that is now required is that an employer is responsive to the needs of underrepresented groups and makes informal good faith efforts to hire those best suited for the job. This is not even necessary for other private employers since there is no affirmative duty for companies hiring minority employees to institute affirmative action policies.

Most companies with formal EEO policies contained in company handbooks and manuals are now modifying or deleting the language which guarantees the institution of any formal plan.

COUNSEL COMMENTS: It is unclear just what kind of affirmative action programs are still permissible since all plans are now under a cloud of uncertainty. Those favoring affirmative action argue that the Supreme Court decision did not kill affirmative action, particularly in cases where no women or minority workers are included in a company's workforce. Even if this is not true, your company still cannot take illegal action towards minorities. But any employment program with numbers, goals or timetables that can even remotely lead to quota-preferences is now probably illegal. Speak to an employment lawyer to determine your rights and options where applicable.

RELIGIOUS DISCRIMINATION

The Civil Rights Act of 1964 prohibits religious discrimination and requires employers to reasonably accommodate the religious practices of employees and prospective employees. Various state laws also prohibit discrimination because of a person's observance of the Sabbath or holy day. In many states employers may not require attendance at work on such a day except in emergencies or in situations in which the employee's presence is indispensable. Absences for these observances must be made up at some mutually agreeable time or can be charged against accumulated leave time.

A United States Supreme Court decision illustrates just how costly a lack of knowledge in this area can be for an employer. A terminated worker sued after she was fired for refusing to work overtime on Saturdays due to her religious beliefs. In this particular case, an auto manufacturer hired the woman to work on an assembly line. The job did not initially conflict with her religious beliefs (which required that she not work from sunset Friday to sunset Saturday) because the assembly line operated only from Monday through Friday. However, when the company began requiring mandatory overtime on Saturdays, the worker refused on religious grounds, and she was fired after missing a series of Saturday work shifts.

The woman brought suit in federal court, alleging the company violated Title VII of the Civil Rights Act, which makes it unlawful to fire or discriminate against an employee on the basis of "race, color, religion, sex or national origin," and that a 1972 amendment to the law requires employers to prove they are unable to accommodate an employee's religious practice without "undue hardship."

The primary issue before the trial court was whether the company had made a bona fide attempt to meet the needs of the employee. The court ruled that the woman's absence did not injure the company and that her request was not unreasonable. She was awarded $73,911 in back pay and benefits, despite the employer's argument that the proper running of the business would be affected by high absenteeism rates on Saturday, complaints from co-workers that she not receive special privileges (i.e., it was unfair to require them to work on Saturday while allowing the woman to take time off), and waiting lists of more senior employees requesting transfers to departments with no Saturday work.

The Supreme Court let the lower ruling stand, commenting that the company could have acted on the employee's request without undue hardship through the use of people employed specifically for absentee relief.

The following summarizes what companies are obligated to do to avoid lawsuits:

1. Employers have an obligation to make reasonable accommodations to the religious needs of employees.
2. Employers must give time off for the Sabbath or holy days except in an emergency.
3. If employees don't come to work, employers may give them leave without pay, may require equivalent time to be made up, or may allow the employee to charge the time against any other leave with pay, except sick pay.

Employers may not be required to give time off to employees who work in key health and safety occupations or to those whose presence is critical to the company on any given day. Employers are not required to take steps inconsistent with a valid seniority system to accommodate an employee's religious practices. They are not required to incur overtime costs to replace an employee who will not work on Saturday. Employers have no responsibility to appease fellow employees who complain they are suffering undue hardship when a co-worker is allowed not to work on a Saturday or Sabbath due to a religious belief while they are required to do so. Finally, employers are generally not required to choose the option the employee prefers, as long as the accommodation offered is reasonable. However, penalizing an employee for refusing to work on Christmas or Good Friday most likely constitutes religious discrimination, depending on the facts.

> **COUNSEL COMMENTS:** The definition of a "religious belief" is quite liberal under the law. If your belief is demonstrably sincere, the belief can be considered religious even though not an essential tenet of the religion of which you are a member. The applicant's or employee's knowledge that a position would involve a conflict does not relieve the employer of its duty to reasonably accommodate absent undue hardship.

In most cases, the court weighs the facts to determine whether the employer offered a reasonable accommodation or that undue hardship existed; the plaintiff will attempt to show that the hardship was not severe or that the accommodation offered was not reasonable. What constitutes undue hardship varies on a case-by-case basis. Generally, undue hardship results when more than a de minimis cost (i.e., overtime premium pay or a collective bargaining agreement is breached) is imposed on the employer.

> **TIP:** The "undue hardship" defense is an exception that companies try to assert to successfully circumvent current law in this area. When you request time off for religious practices, document the date and nature of the request and the reasons given by the employer (or the alternatives considered by the company) in meeting or denying that request. If your request is denied, insist on an explanation. Speak to counsel to fully explore your options, such a filing a charge of religious discrimination with the EEOC or a state agency, or suing the employer in either state or federal court, where applicable. You have certain rights if you are a true religious observer whose beliefs conflict with your work schedule.

RETALIATION DISCRIMINATION

Employees who legitimately assert discrimination rights by filing charges in federal or state court, with the EEOC, or through state agencies, or who complain to the employer before taking action, are protected from adverse retaliation by an employer. If you reasonably believe that a Title VII violation was committed, an employer cannot take any action adverse to such rights, such as failing to promote, discharging, or unduly criticizing you as a direct result of that action.

Acts taken by an employer as a direct result of your filing charges or threatening to go to the EEOC or bringing a lawsuit are viewed by the courts as retaliatory. Many employers who are accused of discrimination have valid defenses and can overcome such charges. However, they foolishly take steps deemed to be in retaliation against an individual's freedom to pursue such claims and eventually suffer damages resulting from the retaliatory actions, not the alleged discrimination!

The following list identifies common areas where retaliation occurs:

- Transfer or reassignment that is undesired (even with no loss in pay or benefits)
- A transfer out of the country
- Threats, when repeatedly made and when disruptive to your job performance
- Harassment on the job
- Giving unfavorable references to a prospective employer, or otherwise interfering with your efforts to obtain a new job
- Attempting to persuade a current employer to discharge a former employee
- Firing you or forcing retirement by eliminating the position and offering only lesser alternative positions
- Denying or suspending severance payments
- Retroactively downgrading your performance appraisals and placing derogatory memos in your personnel file
- Refusing to promote or reassign you or adding preconditions for a requested reassignment
- Transferring you to a job with poorer working conditions
- Increasing your workload without good reason
- Adversely changing the company's vacation or benefits policy
- Delaying the distribution of tax and social security forms
- Interfering with an employment contract

TIP: Never falsely accuse an employer of a wrongful act in the attempt to obtain leverage, because you may not be legally protected if you then suffer harmful retaliation. However, you are protected against retaliation in a variety of nondiscriminatory areas such as

Robin has been sexually harassed on the job. Before being harassed she was given a poor work evaluation and told she was being placed on probation. Although she disagreed with the company's position, she is trying her best to demonstrate satisfactory work to remove herself from probation status.

Robin is concerned that if she complains to management about the sexual harassment she will be fired. She consults an employment lawyer. Robin learns that by sending a letter to her company documenting and complaining about the illegal incidents, she may be *protecting* her job because if she is then accused of poor work performance and fired, she can assert that the employer's adverse action was in retaliation of her filing a valid discrimination charge (and not for prior performance ratings).

complaining about overtime policies, safety (OSHA) violations, and filing a workers' compensation claim. Speak to a lawyer for advice and guidance if you believe you were treated unfairly as a result of complaining about an employer's illegal acts.

STRATEGIES TO ENFORCE YOUR RIGHTS

Recognizing discrimination is only part of the battle; proper steps must also be taken to enforce your rights. As previously mentioned, the law entitles victims of discrimination to recover a variety of damages. This may include reinstatement or job hiring; receiving wage adjustments, back pay, and double back pay; receiving promotions and future pay; recovering legal fees, filing costs and fees paid for expert witnesses; receiving punitive damages and compensatory damages up to $300,000 depending on the size of the employer, and other damages depending on the facts of your case. Even if you work in a right-to-work state and can be fired easily, it is illegal to be fired because you belong to a protected class, such as being a woman, over 40, a minority, handicapped, or a religious believer.

In seeking to enforce your rights, you will not be alone. More than 100,000 formal complaints are filed each year with the EEOC and approximately 10,000 private discrimination lawsuits are tried in court annually. This does not include the many hundreds of thousands of complaints brought to state and local agencies and other institutions.

To start the ball rolling, it is necessary to file a formal charge. No one can stop you from filing a complaint; the law forbids employers from threatening reprisals or retaliation (such as loss of a promotion) when action is taken. The following facts must be included in the complaint:

1. Your name

2. The names, business addresses, and business telephone numbers of all persons who committed and/or participated in the discriminatory act(s)

3. Specific events, dates, and facts to support why the act(s) were discriminatory (e.g., statistics, whether other employees or individuals were discriminated against, and if so, the person(s) victimized, and by whom)

The complaint must be signed and sworn to by the complainant. However, it is not necessary for the complaint to be lengthy or elaborate. The main purpose is to allege sufficient facts to trigger an investigation. That is the advantage of filing charges with an appropriate agency; charges of discrimination are initiated and investigated at no cost to you. An investigator from the EEOC or state agency prepares and types the complaint. If your claim seems plausible, the EEOC or other agency will develop the claim on your behalf. A copy of the complaint, together with a request for a written response, is then sent to the employer. The employer must respond to the charges within several weeks. This is done either by a general denial of the claim or by the filing of specific facts and reasons to support the employer's position.

The following text illustrates the brevity of a valid complaint:

"*I am a female. On (date) I was notified by my supervisor (name) at (name of employer) that I was fired. I asked (name) to tell me why I was fired; he said it was because I called in sick six times in the past year. I know of several male employees who called in sick more than six times and who were not fired.*

Based on these facts I believe I have been discriminated against on the basis of my sex."

After charges and countercharges have been examined by an investigator, the employer and the complainant eventually may be invited to attend a no-fault conference if the investigator believes the complainant's charges possibly have merit. Cases that are deemed to be too far-fetched or insufficient on their face are dismissed before the no-fault conference. If you receive a notice from the EEOC that your case has been dismissed (sometimes referred to as lacking probable cause), it must advise you of your rights. The letter will state that if you wish to proceed with your case, you must file a formal lawsuit in federal court within 90 days or forfeit your claim. This is called a "right-to-sue" letter.

The purpose of a no-fault conference is to discuss your case. At that time the investigator may make arrangements to visit the employer's premises, examine documents and other pertinent records, and interview key employees and witnesses. Because an employer may have an incentive to dispose of the matter early on to save excessive legal fees, lost manpower time, and potential damages, approximately 40% of all complaints are disposed at the settlement conference.

> **TIP:**   Although it is not necessary to retain a lawyer to represent you at or before the no-fault conference, the chances of settling your case are much higher with a lawyer present. An employer will bring its counsel, and you may be intimidated. Additionally, an experienced lawyer can evaluate your claim and advise how much it is realistically worth. Since many EEOC claims take years to eventually be heard, a lawyer will advise you whether a settlement offer is valid and should be accepted, particularly after considering the lengthy delays that are frequently involved.

The conference is conducted by an investigator. Pressure may be placed on the employer to offer a monetary settlement or some other form of restitution (such as a promotion) to avoid the large legal expenses that would be incurred in the course of an ongoing investigation and eventual hearing. Also, some employers may be fearful that the investigator will examine its business records, including employment applications, inter-office memos, and pay records if a settlement is not reached.

If your case cannot be settled at the conference, many options are available, including:

■ Hiring a lawyer privately and suing the employer in a civil lawsuit, typically in federal court

■ Representing yourself *pro se* (without a lawyer) and suing the employer in federal or state court

■ Having the agency act on your behalf to protect your rights and proceeding to a fact-finding hearing and determination

■ Having the EEOC or Department of Justice commence a lawsuit for you and/or others similarly situated in a class action lawsuit

■ Hiring a lawyer and commencing a private lawsuit in state court and, if applicable, alleging other causes of action as well as violations of discrimination laws

The advantage of suing an employer privately is that you may receive a quicker settlement. The EEOC and other agencies have many thousands of claims to process and follow; your case could take years before it is acted upon. Even if you receive a favorable decision (referred to as a finding of "probable cause"), the employer can appeal the agency's decision, adding years to the delay before an administrative trial is commenced. A lawyer working for you may be able to move the matter along more quickly. However, private lawsuits can be very expensive. That is why it is best to initially contact the nearest district office of the EEOC or state agency and speak with an intake person or investigator, or contact a lawyer and discuss your options before taking action.

> **TIP:** State and local laws are often more favorable than federal law in terms of the standards of proof required, the amount of damages awarded, and other factors. It may be advantageous to file charges with these agencies instead, so do not automatically assume your case must be filed with the EEOC. Talk to an employment lawyer to discuss your options and maximize a claim.

When you retain a lawyer, he or she may first contact the employer by letter. The letter may specify the potential charges and invite the employer to discuss settlement before the matter proceeds to the next step. Cases are often settled this way before a formal discrimination charge is filed. The letter on the following page illustrates the kind of letter that a lawyer may send on your behalf.

Author's Note: The tone, language, and substance of an initial demand letter will vary depending on your lawyer's style, preference, and the facts. The purpose is to get the company's attention

Sample Letter Sent by a Lawyer on Behalf of a Terminated Client

Law Offices of Sack & Sack
135 East 57th Street, 12th Floor
New York, N.Y. 10022
Telephone (212) 702-9000
Facsimile (212) 702-9702

Date

Name of Company Officer
Employer's Name
Address

Re: Termination of (name of client "Wilma Jones")

Dear Name:

This office has been retained by Wilma Jones concerning her dismissal from employment with your company. On (specify date), Ms. Jones was summarily discharged without cause by (name of supervisor), an officer with your company. Ms. Jones, who is 61 years of age, was dismissed from employment after twelve years of exemplary service in the highly competitive and sophisticated field of publishing. She was replaced by an inexperienced, unqualified younger man (specify name).

No articulable reason was provided to Ms. Jones at the time of her discharge other than the company was downsizing. (Name of supervisor) told my client she was to be terminated and Ms. Jones was only given one hour to clean out her desk and vacate the premises. Upon further inquiry Ms. Jones learned that your company has not engaged in a downsizing as stated.

My client demonstrated a wide array of valuable skills in her work. She was never criticized or warned that her job was in jeopardy. The man who replaced her is much younger (under 40), is not technically skilled in her field, and is inexperienced. Ms. Jones always received favorable performance evaluations during her tenure.

The manner of my client's discharge was both humiliating and distressful. Ms. Jones is confused, deeply pained, and upset at what prompted her dismissal without explanation or notice. Your offer to pay only four weeks' severance is inadequate in light of my client's long-term contributions and achievements. Furthermore, I have been advised that other male executives with similar long-term service have received substantially greater severance packages.

My client's replacement by a much younger, less competent male causes me to conclude that your company terminated Ms. Jones primarily because of her age and sex. Under this state's laws and federal laws, the circumstances surrounding her discharge and replacement reflect a strong indication of sex and age discrimination. As such, I have advised my client she is entitled to be compensated for the arbitrary manner in which she was treated.

As a result of the termination, Ms. Jones also suffered the loss of her medical, dental and profit-sharing benefits she was receiving while employed and which she relied on for her future welfare. At her age it is doubtful she will obtain gainful employment soon and she was counting on working several more years before her retirement. The discharge is even more damaging in view of the fact that Ms. Jones is a widow with little means of support.

Finally, the manner in which she was terminated caused her additional harm and distress in that she was not notified of her continuation of medical benefits under federal COBRA law.

In light of the foregoing, I request that either you or your representative contact this office immediately in the attempt to resolve these and other issues in an amicable fashion to avoid expensive and protracted litigation.

Hopefully this can be avoided and I thank you for your immediate attention and cooperation in this matter.

Very truly yours,

Steve Mitchell Sack

Send Via Messenger

so that the lawyer will receive a favorable response. Hopefully, a dialogue and appropriate settlement will ensue prior to the institution of further legal proceedings.

Additional information and strategies on how to properly hire and work effectively with a lawyer are discussed in Chapter Ten.

FINAL TIP

No matter what course of action is considered, do not delay unnecessarily. In many situations, you must file a formal complaint within 300 days of the time the alleged act(s) occurred to avoid the expiration of the statute of limitations. Some complainants take their time and unfortunately discover their cases are dismissed because they waited too long to file.

WHAT TO DO
IF YOU ARE FIRED

Hundreds of thousands of workers are fired unfairly or illegally each year. Millions of dollars are forfeited by women who fail to assert themselves or recognize what they are legally entitled to. Many state and federal laws protect workers in this area. This chapter will help you detect if you have been fired illegally or unfairly and what to do about it. You will learn how to negotiate extra benefits regardless of your position, industry, or salary level, plus other strategies to maximize your post-termination claims.

In the past, employees had few options when they received a "pink slip" because a legal principle called the employment-at-will doctrine was generally applied throughout the United States. Under this rule of law, employers were free to hire workers at will and fire them at any time with or without cause or notice. However, in the past thirty years, courts and legislatures began handing down rulings and enacting legislation to safeguard the rights of workers. Commentators suggest this occurred primarily to offset the harsh treatment of the employment-at-will doctrine. Now, many forms of dismissals may be illegal, even if you were hired at will without a written contract.

Although the law varies from state to state, and each case warrants attention based on its particular facts, the categories to be discussed may be useful in recovering greater benefits or damages when you are fired. These categories often serve as exceptions to the traditional employment-at-will rule in certain circumstances.

When a discharged employee consults an employment lawyer, the following areas should be carefully analyzed to determine if they apply in the state where you live and/or work.

FIRED TO DENY ACCRUED BENEFITS

The law obligates employers to deal in good faith with longtime employees. If you are fired just before you are supposed to receive anticipated benefits such as an earned bonus, vested stock option rights, accrued pension, profit sharing, or commissions due, consult a lawyer immediately. However, if an employer fires you for a lawful reason, that is, for cause, the fact you are about to become eligible for a substantial benefit may not make the firing illegal.

> **COUNSEL COMMENTS:** The duty of employers to act in good faith and deal fairly applies generally to cases where an employee has been working for the company for many years or where an employee is fired just before she is supposed to receive anticipated financial benefits. For example, in one case, a salesperson with 40 years of service claimed he was fired so his company could avoid paying commission otherwise due on a $5 million sale. The court agreed even though he had been hired at will. He was awarded commissions for the sale, notwithstanding the firing.
>
> Another employee was fired after working 14 years without a written contract or job security. The court ruled that the main reason for the sudden discharge was to deprive her of the vesting of valuable pension benefits commencing several months into her fifteenth year of service.

> **TIP:** If you are fired at the end of the year and are denied a year-end bonus or other benefits about to vest in the following year, consult a lawyer immediately to enforce your rights. Pension or stock option benefits about to vest within six months to a year of a firing often can be obtained via negotiations. For a bonus, a stronger claim can be made if you are fired within three months of the expected payment date. Sometimes a company will agree to keep you on unpaid leave status during the appropriate period as a way of qualifying. Speak to your lawyer about this negotiating strategy for more details if applicable.

If you cannot get your job back using a violation of good faith and fair dealing argument, you or a lawyer may be able to negotiate for you to obtain benefits you were expecting and would have received but for the firing. You should also consider asserting a claim for benefits based on ERISA rights (discussed below).

FIRED DUE TO A LEGITIMATE ILLNESS OR ABSENCE

You cannot be fired if you were injured on the job and file a workers' compensation claim, or are absent for a medical reason relating to pregnancy or for taking maternity leave of less than 12 weeks in any given one-year period (in violation of the federal FMLA if you work for an employer with more than 50 full-time employees). However, an employer may have the right to fire a worker who is excessively absent due to illness. In that case a viable option might be for you to file for and collect benefits under the company's short- or long-term disability plan.

FIRED FOR VOTING OR SERVING ON JURY DUTY

Many federal and state statutes restrict an employer's freedom to discharge employees. For example, the Consumer Credit Protection Act forbids employers from firing workers whose earnings have been subjected to a wage garnishment arising from a single debt. The Employee Retirement Income Security Act (ERISA) prohibits the discharge of any employee who is prevented thereby from attaining immediate vested pension rights or who was exercising rights under ERISA and was fired as a result. The Jury System Improvements Act forbids employers from firing employees who are empaneled to serve on federal grand juries or petit juries. A number of states have enacted similar laws. Additionally, the Federal Railroad Safety Act prohibits companies from firing workers who file complaints or testify about railroad accidents and the Federal Employer's Liability Act makes it a crime to fire an employee who furnishes facts regarding a railroad accident.

FIRED FOR WHISTLE-BLOWING

Various state Whistle-blower's Protection Acts protect workers who reveal abuses of authority. These statutes penalize employers who retaliate against workers who report suspected health, safety, or financial violations and provide specific remedies, including reinstatement with back pay, restoration of seniority and lost fringe benefits, litigation costs, attorney fees, and fines. To find out if your state has such a law, speak to a knowledgeable labor lawyer, legal referral service, or the Civil Liberties Union in your area. People who work for federal agencies are also protected from reprisals from whistle-blowing.

> **TIP:** The law is often complicated in this area. For example, some
> state statutes would not protect you if you correctly reported that a
> vice-president was embezzling funds. They only protect employees
> from reporting safety violations that affect the community-at-large
> and the president could legally fire you for asserting such a charge,
> even if it was true! Thus, always research applicable state law or
> speak to a knowledgeable lawyer to understand your rights before
> reporting alleged violations.

FIRED FOR ATTEMPTING TO UNIONIZE, COMPLAINING ABOUT HEALTH OR SAFETY VIOLATIONS, OR FOR LEGAL OFF-PREMISES CONDUCT

The National Labor Relations Act prohibits the firing of any employee because of her involvement in union activity, because of filing charges, or because of testifying pursuant to the act. Contact the closest regional office of the National Labor Relations Board if you believe you were fired for any of these reasons.

If you were fired for banding together to protest wages, hours, or working conditions, contact your nearest OSHA office for assistance. Federal OSHA law prohibits employers from firing you in retaliation for asserting safety and related violations.

FIRED FOR MILITARY DUTY

Several federal laws, including the Veterans' Re-employment Rights Act and the Military Selective Service Act, protect the rights of veterans and military personnel. These laws provide that employees who are in military service be regarded as being on an unpaid leave of absence from their civilian employment. For example, if you are on extended reserve duty (up to four years) or called up for short-term emergency duty merely to serve in a motor pool across town, you must be offered a job with the same pay, rank, and seniority upon your return. An employer is prohibited from forcing an employee to use vacation time for military training. Employers are obligated to assist employees who return from military service and cannot deny promotions, seniority, or other benefits because of military obligations. Thus if an employee was promoted or promised a raise right before a call-up, she must receive a job in line with the promised promotion and raise upon return, together with reinstatement of all benefits and those benefits (e.g., additional pay) that would have been earned if she had continued to work.

> **TIP:** Companies that receive job applications from military personnel and reservists relating to work after termination of active duty status and don't hire them must fully document the reasons for denial. Any employer not following these rules is subject to investigation and action by the local U.S. Attorney's office or a private lawsuit filed by the claimant in the federal district court sitting in any county where the employer maintains a place of business. Charges can also be brought under the Veterans' Benefits Improvement and Health Care Authorization Act. These laws prohibit discrimination in all aspects of employment, including hiring, promotion, and discharge on the basis of military membership.

FIRED IN A MANNER INCONSISTENT WITH COMPANY HANDBOOKS, MANUALS, AND DISCIPLINARY RULES

Some employers have written progressive disciplinary programs for employees that are supposed to be followed before a firing. Failure to follow these rules, such as the right to be given a formal warning or be placed on 90 days' probation before a firing, may give rise to a lawsuit based on violation of an implied contract in some states.

> **TIP:** To successfully assert this claim, it is essential to have previously received a copy of the company's manual and read it carefully. If you can prove that promises are clearly contained in a manual, and you relied on them to your detriment, you may be able to assert a valid lawsuit under the laws of some states. Remember, if a company fails to act in accord with published work rules or handbooks, it may be construed as violating an important contract obligation in some states.

Types of promises to look for (which may give you additional rights during and after a firing) include:

- Allowing you to appeal or mediate the decision through an internal nonbinding grievance procedure
- Requiring the employer to give reasonable notice before any firing
- Stating you can be fired for cause only after internal steps toward rehabilitation have been taken and have failed
- Guaranteeing the right to be presented with specific, factual reasons for the discharge before the firing can be effective

FIRED AS A RESULT OF DISCRIMINATION

It is illegal to be fired because you are over 40, belong to a protected minority, are female, handicapped, or due to a religious observance, primarily because of such personal characteristics. Also, if you are fired for an infraction (such as reporting to work late) but other male workers with worse attendance records are only given a warning, you may allege discrimination based on preferential treatment.

FIRED BECAUSE YOU ASSERT A SEXUAL HARASSMENT CLAIM OR CHARGE OF RETALIATION AFTER FILING A DISCRIMINATION COMPLAINT

Federal law prohibits employers from retaliation after an employee complains about sexual harassment, files formal charges with the EEOC or a state agency, or commences a lawsuit in court. Consult Chapter Six for more information about this subject.

FIRED AS PART OF A LARGE LAYOFF

If you are part of a massive layoff and not given at least 60 days' notice or 60 days' severance pay, this is a violation under the federal Worker Adjustment and Retraining Notification Act (WARN). This law prohibits employers from ordering a plant closing or massive layoffs until 60 days after the employer has given written notice of this to affected employees or their representatives, the state dislocated worker unit, and the chief elected official of the unit of local government where the closing or layoff is to occur. If you are fired suddenly and are part of a massive layoff, consult a lawyer immediately to discuss your rights and options under WARN.

> **COUNSEL COMMENTS:** This claim does not only apply to union employees working at plants. It can be asserted when a private employer (such as IBM or AT&T) lays off hundreds of executives at one time or when a company discharges large numbers of secretaries or dismantles an accounting, business, or financial department due to a re-organization.

FIRED INCONSISTENT WITH A VERBAL PROMISE

In some states it is illegal to be fired or treated differently when you receive a verbal promise of job security or other rights which the company fails to fulfill. When promises of job security are offered at the hiring interview, they may be enforceable provided they can be proved. This is another exception to the employment-at-will doctrine. For example, if a company president tells you at the hiring interview, "Don't worry, Jean, we never fire anyone around here except for a good reason," a legitimate case might be made to fight the firing provided you could prove that the words were spoken and that it was reasonable to rely on them (i.e., that they were spoken seriously and not in jest).

This occurred in a case decided in Alaska. At the hiring, an employer stated that an applicant could have the job until reaching retirement age so long as she performed her duties properly. When the employee was suddenly fired, she argued that her job performance was excellent and that she had relied on the promise of job security in deciding to accept the job. She won the case after proving the words were spoken. Several witnesses had overheard the promises at the job interview and testified to this fact at the trial.

In another case, a New Jersey employee complained that, relying on an employer's oral promise that he could be fired only for cause, he turned down a position offered by a competitor. Several months later he was summarily fired. The court, noting that promises were made inducing him to remain in the company's employ, ruled that the employer had made specific factual representations that transformed the employment-at-will relationship into employment with termination for cause only. After finding that the employee's decision not to accept the competitor's offer was significant, binding the employer, the court ruled in the employee's favor.

> **COUNSEL COMMENTS:**   Not all oral promises are enforceable against a company, particularly when an employee is promised "a job for life." Promises of lifetime employment are rarely upheld due to a legal principle referred to as the statute of frauds. Under this law (recognized in many states) all contracts with a job term exceeding one year must be in writing to be enforceable. As a result, courts are generally reluctant to view oral contracts as creating permanent or lifetime employment. Often, depending on the facts, such contracts are viewed as being terminable at will by either party.

> **TIP:**   Some states have laws that limit the duration of an employment contract to a specified maximum number of years (e.g., seven). Thus, where applicable, if you anticipate obtaining and enforcing a lengthy agreement, consult a lawyer and have a formal, comprehensive, unambiguous document prepared and signed by all significant parties (such as the president) to reduce problems.

FIRED IN BREACH OF CONTRACT RIGHTS

If you are fired in a manner inconsistent with or different from rights in a written contract or collective bargaining agreement (if you belong to a union), you may be entitled to damages. If a contract exists, examine it upon termination. The failure to give timely notice as required by a contract, or failure to follow the requirements set forth in a contract, may expose a company to a breach of contract claim. In some instances, it can even cause the agreement to be extended for an additional period.

> **TIP:**   All the preceding topics describe areas to help in detecting if you have been fired illegally. Armed with this knowledge, you can be in a better position of recognizing when you are being treated unfairly and knowing when to speak to a competent employment lawyer. Since the above topics are merely a summary of key areas the law protects, seek advice from a professional to explore all your rights and options whenever you have been fired from an important job.

Judith is a fashion designer who works for a small company. Several years ago, desiring job security, she negotiated and received a one year written contract before beginning work. The benefit of having a one-year agreement was that Judith could not be fired prior to the expiration of the one-year term unless she was fired for cause (which Judith knew was hard to prove.)

Judith's contract stated that if timely notice of termination was not sent by either party at least 60 days prior to the expiration of the original one-year term, the contract would be automatically renewed, under the same terms and conditions, for another year. Her company apparently forgot about the contract's existence and notified her two weeks prior to the expiration date that the agreement would not be renewed.

Judith immediately advised the company of the existence of the written agreement. She consulted and hired a lawyer to protect her rights. The lawyer told Judith that the company breached the agreement but if Judith found another job during the next year, her damages would be reduced by the amount of compensation she received from the new job plus any unemployment benefits she obtained.

Judith felt confident she would find another job quickly. Thus, rather than sue, she authorized her lawyer to accept a settlement immediately equal to four months of her salary to resolve the matter. The experience taught her that a few favorable words on a piece of paper can mean thousands of dollars in additional benefits when an employer fails to act according to the terms of a contract.

STEPS TO TAKE WHEN YOU ARE FIRED

Most employers fire people without warning. The fact you are terminated suddenly does not mean you should accept fewer benefits than you are entitled to. The following strategies can help increase severance benefits and/or damages in the event of a firing. Often, you do not need an employment lawyer to actually negotiate additional benefits on your behalf. You can do this yourself, and the following information will tell you how.

1. *Stall for time.* Do not panic or scream at your boss when informed of the bad news. Stay calm. Request extra time to think things over. This may allow you to learn important facts and negotiate a better settlement. If possible, always avoid accepting the company's first offer.

2. *Review your employment contract or letter of agreement.* If you signed a written contract, reread it. Review what it says about termination, because if the company fails to act according to the contract, your rights may be violated.

3. *Discover why you are were fired.* This can help in the event you decide to sue your former employer. For example, once you receive a reason for the firing, the employer may be precluded from offering additional reasons at a trial, arbitration, or unemployment compensation hearing. Some states have service letter statutes requiring companies to specify in writing the reasons for an employee's termination. If the employer refuses to tell you why you were fired, or tells prospective employers other reasons later, you may have grounds for a lawsuit under the laws of these states.

   TIP: Send a letter similar to the one on page 212 if you work in a service-letter-statute state. If the company fails to respond to your request, you may be entitled to damages after sending such a letter.

4. *Learn who made the decision to fire you.* You may discover you were fired for petty reasons (such as jealousy) and can be reinstated. Or perhaps the punishment for a long-term worker "did not fit the crime" since other male workers were not similarly treated. Often, however, short of commencing a lawsuit, there may be little you can do other than negotiate a better severance package.

5. *Ask to see your personnel file.* Some states permit terminated workers to review and copy the contents of their personnel files. Sometimes these files do not support firing decisions because they contain favorable recommendations and comments. If you can be fired only for cause and the company gives you specific reasons why you were fired, your file may demonstrate that such reasons are factually incorrect and/or legally insufficient. If this occurs, you may have a strong case against the former employer for breach of contract. If you have received excellent performance reviews and appraisals and the file indicates you received merit salary increases, you can use this information to contest the firing, negotiate more severance, obtain a favor-

able letter of recommendation, or better prepare you for future interviews with prospective employers.

6. *Reconstruct promises.* If promises regarding job security were previously given, recall the time, place, and whether these statements were made in the presence of witnesses. Some courts are ruling that oral promises from high-ranking officers (such as the president) concerning job security are binding.

7. *Request an additional negotiating session to discuss your severance package.* Generally there is no legal obligation for an employer to pay severance unless:

   ■ You have a written contract stating that severance will be paid

   ■ Oral promises are given regarding severance pay

   ■ There is a documented policy of paying severance in a company handbook or manual

   ■ The employer voluntarily offers to pay severance

   ■ Other employees in similar positions have received severance pay in the past

Although lower-level employees sometimes have difficulty arranging a negotiating session, most managers, employees in supervisory positions, executives, and officers generally are granted another interview.

TIP: Do not automatically acquiesce to a denial of benefits if you are fired and not offered severance, whatever your particular situation. Most salaried employees working for mid-to-large-size companies are now receiving severance when they are fired due to a layoff or business reorganization (but not for cause); others are negotiating and receiving greater severance than the company's first offer. Statistics from the author's own law practice after 18 years support this. The vast majority (more than 75%) of all clients who retain the author to negotiate firings obtain more severance and other benefits than the amount first offered directly to them by the ex-employer.

8. *Negotiate the package.* At the meeting it is often best to avoid threatening litigation. At first, appeal to corporate decency and fair play instead. For example, it is better to say "As you know I recently became a widow and have to pay for two children in college right now; your offer of four weeks' severance is inadequate since it is unlikely I can find a comparable job in the next four weeks" rather than say "If you don't pay more money, I will sue."

**Sample Letter
Demanding True Reason for Discharge**

Your Name
Address
Date

Name of Officer of Employer
Title
Name of Employer
Address

Re: My termination

Dear (Name of Officer),

On (date) I was fired suddenly by your company without notice, warning, or cause. All that I was told by (name of person) was that my services were no longer required and that my termination was effective immediately.

To date, I have not received any explanation documenting the reason(s) for my discharge. In accordance with the laws of this state I hereby demand such information in writing immediately.

Thank you for your prompt attention and cooperation in this matter.

Very truly yours,

(your name)

(Send certified mail, return receipt requested.)

(Author's note: Many states have no laws requiring an employer to furnish a true reason for the discharge upon demand. Thus, use this letter only where state law permits.)

TIP: Generally ask for an amount of severance pay equal to one month for each year on the job. Although the employer may initially balk at this request, especially if you have worked many years (e.g., more than 15), it will give you adequate room to bargain. Discuss an additional bonus, pension and profit sharing benefits, medical coverage, and other benefits paid by the company for an extended period of time. Discuss a favorable letter of reference, entitlement to unemployment insurance benefits, and how the company will announce the separation (called your "cover story"). The comprehensive checklist of negotiating strategies included later in this chapter will provide numerous details and points to ask for.

9. *Confirm all agreements in writing to document the final deal.* Insist on receiving more money and other benefits before signing any release or waiver of a discrimination claim. Exit agreements, releases, and covenants not to sue can deprive you of valuable rights. Never sign one without the advice of a lawyer. The sample release beginning on page 262 is included for your review.

   If the company fails to summarize your severance package in writing, it is a good idea to send a letter similar to the one beginning on page 214 which accurately reflects the final arrangement. Such a letter can eliminate confusion, particularly when the terms of the settlement are extensive.

10. *Apply for unemployment benefits.* Unemployment benefits are available under state law. However, you may be denied benefits if you voluntarily left your job without a good reason, were fired for misconduct, or refused a valid job offer. You can request a hearing if you feel benefits were unfairly denied. Speak to a lawyer or a representative from your local Department of Labor if:

   ■ you are fired but the employer requests your resignation (Note: by resigning you may be unknowingly forfeiting unemployment benefits.);

   ■ your benefits are contested by the employer; or

   ■ you require representation at an unemployment hearing.

   Information on how to maximize an unemployment compensation claim is discussed in the next chapter.

11. *Do not be intimidated or forced into early retirement.* Recognize that you may have rights, particularly if your early retirement causes you to lose large, expected financial benefits. Federal and state age discrimination laws protect older workers from early retirement pressure.

Sample Letter Documenting Severance Arrangement

> Your name
> Address
> Date

Name of Corporate Officer
Title
Name of Employer
Address

Re: Our Severance Agreement

Dear (Name of Corporate Officer):

This will confirm our discussion and agreement regarding my termination:

1. I will be kept on the payroll through (specify date) and will receive (specify) weeks' vacation pay, which shall be included with my last check on that date.

2. (Name of Company) shall pay me a bonus of (specify) within (specify) days from the date of this letter.

3. (Name of Company) will purchase both my nonvested and vested company stock, totaling (specify) shares at a price of (specify $) per share, or at the market rate if it is higher at the time of repurchase, on or before (specify date).

4. (Name of Company) will continue to maintain in effect all profit-sharing and retirement plans, medical, dental, hospitalization, disability and life insurance policies presently in effect through (specify date). After that date, I have been advised that I may convert said policies at my sole cost and expense and that coverage for these policies will not lapse. I will receive information concerning the conversion of my retirement plan savings within the next few weeks.

5. I will be permitted to use the company's premises at (specify location) from the hours of 9:00 A.M. until 5:00 P.M. This shall include the use of a secretary, telephone, stationery, and other amenities at the company's sole cost and expense to assist me in obtaining another position.

6. I will be permitted to continue using the automobile previously supplied to me through (specify date) under the same terms and con-

ditions presently in effect. On that date, I will return all sets of keys in my possession together with all other papers and documents belonging to the company.

7. (Name of Company) will reimburse me for all reasonable and necessary expenses related to the completion of company business after I submit appropriate vouchers and records within (specify) days of presentment.

8. (Name of Company) agrees to provide me with a favorable letter of recommendation and reference(s) and will announce to the trade that I am resigning for "personal reasons." I am enclosing a letter for that purpose which will be reviewed and signed by (specify person) and returned to me immediately.

9. Although unanticipated, (name of Company) will not contest my filing for unemployment insurance benefits after (specify date), and will assist me in promptly executing all documents necessary for that purpose.

10. If a position is procured by me prior to (specify date), a lump sum payment for my remaining severance will be paid within (specify) days after my notification of same. Additionally, the stock referred to in Paragraph 3 will be purchased as of the date of my employment with another company if prior to (specify date) and will be paid to me within (specify) days of my notification.

If any of the terms of this letter are ambiguous or incorrect, please advise me immediately in writing specifying the item(s) that are incorrect. Otherwise, this letter shall set forth our entire understanding in this matter, which cannot be changed orally.

(Name of Corporate Officer), I want to personally thank you for your assistance and cooperation in this matter and wish you all the best in the future.

Very truly yours,

(your name)

(Send certified mail, return receipt requested.)

12. *Enforce your ERISA rights.* The Employee Retirement Income Security Act of 1974 (ERISA) prohibits the discharge of any employee who is prevented from attaining immediate vested pension benefits, or who was exercising rights under ERISA and was fired as a result. ERISA also entitles employees to certain rights as participants in an employer's pension and/or profit-sharing plans. Plan participants are entitled to examine without charge all plan documents, including insurance contracts, annual reports, plan descriptions, and copies of documents filed by the plan with the U.S. Department of Labor. If you have not received a proper accounting or payment of your retirement benefits, send a letter to the employer certified mail, return receipt requested, requesting summaries of each plan's annual financial report. The letter on page 219 illustrates this. If you do not receive the information within 30 days, you can file a lawsuit in federal court.

    In such a case, the court may require the plan administrator to provide the materials and pay you up to $100 a day until you receive them (unless the materials were not sent for reasons beyond the administrator's control). Thus, find out the name and address of the administrator of any of your retirement plans. If the company is stonewalling by not returning your calls, providing information, or paying your retirement benefits, consult a lawyer for advice.

13. *Enforce your COBRA rights.* The federal Consolidated Omnibus Budget Reconciliation Act of 1985 (COBRA) requires private employers who employ more than 20 workers on a typical business day to continue to make group health insurance available to workers who are discharged from employment. All employees who are discharged as a result of voluntary or involuntary termination (with the exception of those who are fired for gross misconduct) may elect to continue plan benefits currently in effect at their own cost provided the employee (or beneficiary) makes an initial payment within 30 days of notification and is not covered under Medicare or any other group plan. The law also applies to qualified beneficiaries who were covered by the employer's group health plan the day before the discharge. For example, if you choose not to continue such coverage, your spouse or dependent children may elect to continue coverage at their own expense. The extended coverage period is 18 months after termination of the covered employee; upon the death, divorce, or separation of the covered employee, the benefit coverage period is 36 months for spouses and dependents.

    TIP: Be sure you know your rights under COBRA in the event you are fired. If an employer refuses to negotiate continued health benefits as a part of a severance package, fails to explain your rights and options, or fails to notify you of the existence of such benefits within 30 days of the discharge, contact the personnel office immediately. Follow up the telephone call with a letter sent certified mail, return receipt requested. The sample demand letter on page 220 illustrates this. If the employer refuses to offer continued COBRA benefits after a discharge for any reason, consult an experienced employment lawyer immediately.

14. *Take action if the employer is providing negative references to prospective employers.* This includes sending letters by certified mail, return receipt requested, to protect your rights. The letter can document what you have learned and put the employer on notice of your desire to take prompt legal action if the problem persists. Many states have enacted antiblacklisting statutes that punish employers for maliciously or willfully attempting to prevent former employees from finding work. In some states, untruthful job references are treated as crimes. You can also assert a lawsuit based on defamation and emotional distress if you discover that private employment data and confidential personnel records (such as medical information) were leaked to outsiders without your consent. More information on this subject is discussed in the next chapter.

15. *Resign from a job properly.* It is best to request and sign a written contract with your new employer before resigning. This protects you if the new employer changes its mind and decides not to hire you, or tries to fire you after a short period of time. If you signed a prior contract, learn what it says regarding termination and comply with those terms. For example, if the contract states you can resign provided written notice is sent certified mail 60 days prior to the effective termination date, you must send timely notice. Failure to do so could result in the employer suing you for breach of contract.

16. *Return company property.* Items such as automobile keys and samples must be returned to avoid claims of misappropriation, fraud, and breach of contract. When returning items by mail, get a receipt to prove delivery. If the company owes you money, you may consider holding the company's property to force a settlement. However, speak to a lawyer before taking such action since some states permit employees to retain company property as a lien but others don't.

TIP: In most states, an employer cannot withhold earned salary or accrued vacation benefits for any reason. Thus, assert your rights and demand your money where applicable.

17. *Speak to a lawyer to enforce your rights* especially if you are owed wages, accrued overtime pay, vacation pay, an earned bonus, commissions, stock options, or other compensation, or believe the employer violated the law.

> **TIP:** The lawyer may first advise you to send letters of protest on your own in the attempt to obtain an amicable settlement. The sample letters beginning on page 219 illustrate the kind of letters to send (always by certified mail, return receipt requested). If the employer fails to respond, or you are unsuccessful in resolving a dispute informally, it may be necessary to hire a lawyer. Information on how to hire a lawyer properly and work effectively with one is presented in Chapter Ten.

NEGOTIATING STRATEGIES TO MAXIMIZE POST-TERMINATION SEVERANCE

There is no law requiring employers to pay severance unless they have done so in the past, if promises were made in a company handbook or manual, or if your contract has a clause requiring the company to pay a specified amount of severance. Stay calm when the boss calls you in and informs you of the termination. *It is best to say as little as possible initially.* Write down everything the company offers you. After receiving an initial offer, tell the employer you need time to think it over. Ask for the employer to confirm the proposed terms in writing. Avoid accepting the company's first offer if you can help it. Try to stay on the payroll while negotiations ensue. Stalling for time can help you learn important facts, including what other similarly situated terminated employees received in severance. Most importantly, your goal is to continue receiving regular wages as long as possible while negotiations are proceeding (before the severance package "kicks in"). If you are a salaried employee who works on a full-time basis, you have everything to win if you negotiate forcefully but quietly; thus, request another negotiating session to obtain more benefits.

> **TIP:** Employers sometimes violate discrimination laws by paying different severance packages to terminated workers. When they fail to act consistently, they commit illegal acts. For example, say you are fired suddenly due to a business reorganization and had worked at the company for four years. You are initially offered eight weeks'

Sample Demand Letter for ERISA Retirement Benefits

Your Name
Address
Telephone Number
Date

Name of Officer or Employer
Title
Name of Employer
Address

Re: My ERISA Retirement Benefits

Dear (Name of Officer):

As you know, I was terminated (or resigned) on (specify date). However, I have not received a written description of all my retirement benefits under federal ERISA law. (Or, if applicable, state: I have not received the correct computation of all benefits due me. Or, I believe I was fired shortly [i.e., two months] before the vesting of a pension, in violation of my ERISA rights.)

Your company has a legal obligation to provide me with accurate information concerning all applicable profit-sharing, pension, employee welfare, benefit, and other plans. Therefore I would like you to send me (specify what you want, such as to receive a copy of the employer's formal pension and/or profit-sharing plans, recompute your benefits, or offer you a pension, if applicable).

It is imperative that I receive a response to my request immediately in writing to avoid having me take prompt legal action to enforce my rights.

Hopefully, this will not be necessary and I thank you for your prompt attention in this matter.

Very truly yours,

(your name)

(Send certified mail, return receipt requested.)

Author's Note: Under federal ERISA law, if you request materials from a plan and do not receive them within 30 days, you may file suit in federal or state court. Contact the plan administrator for the company immediately in writing if your claim is denied or if you do not receive an adequate response shortly after a firing. If no adequate response is received, seek assistance from the U.S. Department of Labor or a competent employment lawyer to protect your rights.

Sample Demand Letter for COBRA Medical Benefits Coverage

Your Name
Address
Telephone Number
Date

Name of Officer or Employer
Title
Name of Employer
Address

Re: My COBRA Medical Benefits

Dear (Name of Officer):

As you know, I was terminated on (specify date) due to a job elimination (or specify, such as business reorganization). However, more than 30 days has elapsed from the date of my discharge and I have not yet received official notification from either your company or your medical carrier that my medical benefits have been maintained and/or extended under federal COBRA law.

It is imperative that I receive such notification immediately in writing, specifying my cost at the group rate for such coverage.

I trust that such information will be forthcoming immediately so that I am not required to take prompt legal action to enforce my rights.

Hopefully, such additional legal action will not be necessary and I thank you for your prompt attention to this apparent oversight.

If you wish to discuss this matter with me, feel free to contact me immediately.

Very truly yours,

(your name)

<u>(Send certified mail, return receipt requested.)</u>

Author's Note: Federal COBRA law requires that most employers offer continuation of coverage for an additional 18 months to former employees who were discharged as a result of a voluntary or involuntary termination (with the exception of gross misconduct); all terminated employees have the option to continue medical plan benefits at their cost. You must be notified within 60 days of your right to continue such coverage. Send a similar letter whenever you do not receive such a notification shortly after a firing. A well-drafted letter can spur the company into action and protect your rights.

Sample Demand Letter for Earned Commission

Your Name
Address
Telephone Number
Date

Name of Officer or Employer
Title
Name of Employer
Address

Re: My Commissions

Dear (Name of Officer):

It has been (specify) days from the effective termination date of our agreement. Despite our discussions and your earlier promises that all commissions presently owed would be paid immediately, I still have not received my money.

Please be advised that under this state's law, unless I am provided a final, accurate accounting, together with copies of all invoices reflecting shipment of my orders (or state if you require anything else) and payment of commissions totaling (specify $X if you know), within (specify, such as five days) from your receipt of this letter, your company will be liable for additional damages, attorney fees and costs upon my institution of a lawsuit to collect same.

Hopefully this will not be necessary and I thank you for your prompt attention to this apparent oversight.

If you wish to discuss this matter with me, feel free to contact me immediately.

Very truly yours,

(your name)

<u>(Send certified mail, return receipt requested.)</u>

Author's Note: Most states require that salespeople receive earned commissions immediately after a firing. Many of these laws provide independent reps up to three times additional damages in excess of the commission owed, plus reasonable attorney fees and costs, when monies are not promptly paid. Thus always send a detailed written demand for unpaid commissions. This should always be done by certified mail, return receipt requested, to document your claim and prove delivery. Such a demand will "start the clock" for the purpose of determining the number of days that commissions remain unpaid and put the employer on notice that additional damages and penalties may be owed if money is not received immediately. A written demand is essential in enforcing your rights and typically will get the employer to contact you and resolve the matter amicably.

Sample Demand Letter for Earned Bonus

Your Name
Address
Telephone Number
Date

Name of Officer or Employer
Title
Name of Employer
Address

Re: My Bonus

Dear (Name of Officer):

Please be advised that I am currently owed a bonus of (specify $X if you know). I was fired on (specify date, such as January 15) suddenly for no valid reason and not as a result of any negative or detrimental conduct on my part. Prior to my termination, I complied with all company directives and was expecting to receive a bonus for the work I rendered in the preceding year.

This expectation was in accordance with our previous understandings and practices since I have regularly received bonuses for the past (specify) years ranging from (specify dollar amounts).

Therefore, to avoid further legal action, I request prompt payment of my earned bonus. Hopefully, additional legal action will not be necessary and I thank you for your prompt attention to this apparent oversight.

Feel free to contact me immediately.

Very truly yours,

(your name)

<u>(Send certified mail, return receipt requested.)</u>

Author's Note: Some employers fire workers right before they are scheduled to receive a bonus by requiring workers to be employed on the day bonus checks are issued as a condition of payment. If this happens to you, or you are denied a bonus for any reason, send a letter similar to the one above to protect your rights. Argue that you would have received the bonus but for the firing. Demand that you are entitled to receive a pro rata share of the bonus if you are fired close to but before the end of the year. For example, if you are fired on December 1, negotiate to receive eleven-twelfths of the bonus you were expecting, if you cannot receive the full bonus.

Sample Demand Letter for Accrued Vacation Pay

Your Name
Address
Telephone Number
Date

Name of Officer or Employer
Title
Name of Employer
Address

Re: My Earned Vacation Pay

Dear (Name of Officer):

Please be advised that I am currently owed vacation pay totaling (specify number of days or weeks due or $X if you know). As you know, I resigned (or was fired) on (specify date). According to your company's policy specified in (state, such as a handbook or manual), I am entitled to (specify) weeks per year.

To avoid having me take legal action, including my contacting this state's Department of Labor and requesting a formal investigation, I expect to receive my earned, accrued vacation pay immediately.

Hopefully, additional legal action will not be necessary and I thank you for your prompt attention to this apparent oversight.

Very truly yours,

(your name)

<u>(Send certified mail, return receipt requested.)</u>

Author's Note: Most states require employers to pay accrued vacation pay in all circumstances, even after resignations by employees or terminations for cause. Although each company is free to implement its own rules governing vacation pay, employers must apply such policies consistently to avoid charges of discrimination and breach of contract. To avoid problems, be sure you understand how long you must first work to qualify, whether vacation days must be taken in a given year, can they be carried over to the next year, or can you be paid in cash for unused, earned vacation days? Also, how much notice is required before being allowed to take vacation time?

If the ex-employer fails to respond to your initial letter and even a second, final request, contact the Department of Labor or a competent employment lawyer for assistance.

Sample Demand Letter for Accrued Overtime Pay

Your Name
Address
Telephone Number
Date

Name of Officer or Employer
Title
Name of Employer
Address

Re: My Earned Overtime Pay

Dear (Name of Officer):

Please be advised that I am currently owed (specify hours) of overtime pay totaling (specify $X). As you know, I resigned (or was fired) on (specify date). Under federal law, since I was an hourly worker for your company, overtime at one and one half times my regular pay rate must be paid for hours worked in excess of 40 hours per work week.

I am enclosing copies of time sheets for overtime work approved by my supervisor from (specify date) to (specify date). To avoid having me take prompt legal action, including my contacting this state's Department of Labor and requesting a formal investigation into your company's violation of the Fair Labor Standards Act, I expect to receive my earned overtime pay immediately.

Hopefully, additional legal action will not be necessary and I thank you for your prompt attention to this matter.

Very truly yours,

(your name)

(Send certified mail, return receipt requested.)

Author's Note: Overtime is not generally available for salaried workers who work in executive, administrative, or professional jobs (called "exempt employees"). But if you are a salaried worker, your company is not generally allowed to deduct a few hours off your weekly paycheck for time off for any reason, including personal time. If they do, you may be determined to be an hourly worker, capable of receiving overtime for up to three years.

If you have kept proper records and took authorized overtime, contact a representative at your state's Department of Labor or the Wage and Hour Division of the U.S. Department of Labor for help if the ex-employer fails to respond to your initial letter or a second final written request.

severance pay but learn that a male employee in your department who was fired last year after working one year was given one month's severance. This could constitute sex discrimination if you are not paid four months' severance pay (the same pro rata rate) unless the company's policy is to pay terminated employees a minimum of four weeks' severance no matter how long they worked for the company. Remember this and act accordingly.

The golden rule is to never quit. Refuse an employer's offer to resign whenever possible. This is because if you resign you may be waiving a claim to unemployment and other severance benefits, including earned commissions. This is a trap many employees fall into.

Sandra is called into her boss's office and told that she is being summarily discharged. However, the company states she can resign by signing a letter of resignation, which it has prepared and presents to her.

Sandra thinks it is better to resign than be fired so she signs the letter of resignation and leaves the premises. When she files for unemployment benefits, she learns she is not entitled to benefits unless she can prove that she was forced to resign. The company introduces the letter of resignation as evidence that no pressure or undue influence was forced on Sandra and it was her voluntary decision; she is denied unemployment insurance benefits.

Sandra consults an employment lawyer. She learns had she not resigned she would have received severance. She also learns that she could have made a deal with her employer (and confirmed it in writing) that although the company would agree to inform prospective employers she resigned for personal reasons ("her cover story"), it would not contest her unemployment benefits or deny paying her other benefits she would have received had she allowed the company to fire her. The lawyer also explained that if she was close to earning a vesting pension, profit-sharing benefits, or year-end bonus, her resignation would seriously undermine a claim for those expected benefits.

IMPORTANT NEGOTIATING POINTS

The following strategies can help you obtain a better severance package, whatever your situation, often without a lawyer's assistance.

1. *Wages* (also referred to as salary continuation)

   a. Try to stay on the payroll as long as possible.

   b. Negotiate for the employer to continue to provide medical, dental, and hospitalization coverage (paid for by the employer) while you are receiving severance wages.

   c. Avoid arrangements where you are offered severance for a specified period of time (e.g., six months) which automatically ceases when you obtain a new job. Rather, make the offer noncontingent on new employment. If that is not possible, arrange that differential severance will be paid in a lump sum if you obtain a new job prior to the expiration of the severance period. (For example, request that three months' worth of severance will be paid in a lump sum if a new job is obtained any time before the six months' of salary continuation expires.)

   d. If severance pay is to be paid in a lump sum, consider asking for it immediately, not in installments over time.

   e. Consider the tax ramifications of postponing a lump sum payout until the following year, when your tax base will be lower if you do not find employment quickly.

   f. Recognize that if you receive salary continuation rather than a lump sum payment you may be ineligible for unemployment benefits until the salary continuation payments cease in some states; thus, always contact your local Department of Labor for guidance and consider the benefits of a lump sum payment rather than extended salary continuation (unless you are not adversely affected under your state's unemployment compensation policies).

   g. Avoid accepting the employer's first offer; always *negotiate, negotiate, negotiate.*

   h. Attempt to receive at least four weeks' severance for every year of employment.

2. *Other Compensation*

   a. If you have relocated recently at the request of the employer, try to obtain additional relocation allowances.

   b. Discuss accrued vacation pay, overtime, and unused sick pay. Be sure you are paid for these items.

    c. If you were fired without notice, ask for two additional weeks of salary in lieu of the employer's lack of notice.

    d. If commissions are due or about to become due, insist that you be paid immediately; do not waive these expected benefits.

3. *Bonus*

    a. Understand how your bonus is computed.

    b. If you were entitled to receive a bonus at the end of the year, ask for it now.

    c. If the employer refuses to pay, argue that the firing deprived you of the right to receive the bonus; or

    d. Insist that your bonus be prorated according to the amount of time you worked during the year if the above arrangement is rejected. For example, if you are fired on November 30, ask to receive 11/12 of your expected bonus. Do not accept the employer's argument that you must be on the payroll the day the bonus is paid in order to receive it; some employers fire workers to deprive them of these expected benefits.

4. *Pension and Profit-Sharing Benefits*

    a. Ask for details regarding the nature of your benefits. You are entitled to an accurate, written description of all benefits under federal law.

    b. Be aware of all plans, funds, and programs that may have been established on your behalf.

    c. If you are fired just before the vesting of a pension or stock options (e.g., two months before the vesting date), argue that the timing is suspect and that public policy and fairness requires the employer to grant your pension or stock options. If the employer refuses, consult an experienced labor lawyer immediately.

5. *Other Benefits*

    a. Request continued use of an office, secretary, telephone, or mail facilities to assist you in your job search if appropriate.

    b. Consider requesting a loan to tide you over while looking for a new job.

    c. Consider requesting continued use of your company car or ask to buy the car or take over the lease at a reduced rate, if appropriate.

    d. Request that the employer pay for outplacement guidance, career counseling and resume preparation services, including typing and incidental expenses. Some employees negotiate to receive a smaller cash settlement in lieu of the cost of outplacement services where applicable.

6. *Medical, Dental, and Hospitalization Coverage*

   a. Does coverage stop the day you are fired or is there a grace period? Ask for a copy of the applicable policy.

   b. Can you extend coverage beyond the grace period?

   c. Be sure your benefits are explained to you if you do not understand them.

   d. Can you assume the policy at a reduced personal cost? This is sometimes referred to as a conversion policy.

   e. If you are married and your spouse is working, you may be covered under your spouse's policy. If so, do you want to continue paying for your own policy?

   f. Be sure the employer has notified you regarding your rights under COBRA. If you receive no notification within 30 days of your discharge, contact the employer immediately.

7. *Life Insurance*

   a. Can you convert the policy to your benefit at your own cost? Don't forget to inquire about this.

   b. Is there any equity in the employer's life insurance plan that accrues to you on termination? Inquire about this and ask for a copy of all policies presently in effect.

8. *Your Cover Story*

   a. Clarify how the news of your departure will be announced. Discuss and agree with management the story to be told to outsiders.

   b. Consider whether you want it to be known that you resigned for personal reasons or that you were terminated due to a "business reorganization." These are neutral explanations that are preferable to firings for misconduct or poor performance.

   c. Request that a copy of a favorable letter of recommendation be given to you before you leave the company if possible.

   d. Request that key members of the company be notified of your departure in writing. If possible, approve the contents of such a memo before distribution. The news of a firing spreads rapidly and written memos can dispel false rumors about your termination.

9. *Golden Parachutes*

   a. Determine if you are entitled to receive additional benefits under a severance contract or golden parachute. Generally, golden parachutes are arrangements between an executive and a corporation that are contingent on a change in control of the corporation.

b. Speak to an experienced employment lawyer immediately to protect your rights if the employer refuses to provide all the benefits specified in your contract or there is a merger and a successor company advises it will not honor prior commitments of severance and other expected benefits.

FINAL POINTS

After you have negotiated the severance package and are satisfied that you have adequately covered all your options and benefits, you must decide whether to accept the company's final offer or retain a lawyer in the attempt to obtain additional compensation.

Before retaining a lawyer, be sure you feel comfortable with him or her and that the lawyer will render competent services on your behalf. This can be accomplished by following many of the strategies contained in Chapter Ten. A qualified lawyer can coach you, advise what payouts are standard in your industry, and help draft your severance agreement. If you receive a comprehensive document like the one beginning on page 230, consider retaining a lawyer to review the document for errors or inconsistencies. If you do not receive a written offer after terms are discussed, it is advisable to send a letter to the employer to confirm the deal. The letter on page 214 illustrates this.

> **TIP:** Whomever you retain, it is important that the lawyer commence work on your matter immediately. Time is crucial in all termination cases; action must be taken quickly to demonstrate the seriousness of your resolve. The longer the lawyer waits before contacting the employer, the weaker the case often becomes and the chances of receiving more compensation and benefits in negotiations may diminish. In fact, the author prefers to contact the employer no more than several weeks after a female client has been fired. Sometimes, the author will not represent a client in a termination settlement when she has been fired many months before. (Note: If negotiating a severance package is not the issue, such as seeking to collect commissions or breach of contract damages that may be owed, the time frame to contact an employer or principal on behalf of client is not as important.)

Sample Letter Confirming Severance Benefits

Date

Name of Employee
Address

Dear (Name of Employee):

This will confirm our agreement regarding your employment status with (Name of Employer).

We agreed as follows:

1. Your services as Vice President of (specify division) will terminate by mutual agreement effective (date).

2. Although your services as Vice President will not be required beyond (specify date), you agree to be available to (Name of Employer) through (specify termination date) to render advice, answer any questions, and provide information regarding company business.

3. Through (specify termination date) except as provided in Paragraph 4 below, you will continue to receive your regular bi-weekly salary of (specify) and you may continue to participate in those company benefit plans in which you are currently enrolled. In addition to your final paycheck, you will receive from the company on or about (specify termination date) or given as provided for in Paragraph 4 hereunder, the sum of (specify) less applicable deductions for local, state, and federal taxes, as a bonus for the present year.

4. If you obtain other regular, full-time employment prior to (specify termination date), then, upon commencement of such employment (date of new employment), your regular bi-weekly salary payments and your participation in company benefit plans, as described in Paragraph 3 above, shall cease; however, medical and dental coverage previously provided you shall be continued for an additional period of three months at a cost to be borne by (Name of Employer). In such event, you will receive in a lump sum (less applicable deductions for taxes) the remaining amount you would have received on a bi-weekly basis from the date of new employment through (specify termination date) plus the (specify sum) bonus (less taxes) payment referred to in Paragraph 3 within two weeks of your date of new employment. You agree to notify the company immediately of the date on which such regular full-time employment will commence.

5. You acknowledge that the sums referred to in Paragraphs 3 and 4 above include any and all monies due you from the company, contractual or otherwise, to which you may be entitled, except for any vested benefit you may have in the (Name of Employer) Savings and Investment Plan and the Pension Plan.

6. (Name of Employer) will provide you with available office space, telephone service, and clerical help on an as-needed basis at (address) until you obtain other regular full time employment or (date), whichever occurs first.

7. You agree to cooperate fully with (Name of Employer) in their defense of or other participation in any administrative, judicial, or collective bargaining proceeding arising from any charge, complaint, grievance, or action which has been or may be filed.

8. You, on behalf of yourself and your heirs, representatives, and assigns, hereby release (Name of Employer), its parents, their subsidiaries and divisions, and all of their respective current and former directors, officers, shareholders, successors, agents, representatives, and employees, from any and all claims you ever had, now have, or may in the future assert regarding any matter that predates this agreement, including, without limitation, all claims regarding your employment at or termination of employment from (Name of Employer), any contract, express or implied, any tort, or any breach of a fair employment practice law, including Title VII, the Age Discrimination in Employment Act, and any other local, state, or federal equal opportunity law.

9. You acknowledge that you have had the opportunity to review this agreement with counsel of your own choosing, that you are fully aware of the agreement's contents and of its legal effects, and that you are voluntarily entering into this agreement.

10. You agree that any confidential information you acquired while an employee of the company shall not be disclosed to any other person or used in a manner detrimental to the company's interests.

11. Neither you nor anyone acting on your behalf shall publicize, disseminate, or otherwise make known the terms of this agreement to any other person, except to those rendering financial or legal advice, or unless required to do so by court order or other compulsory process of law.

12. The provisions of this agreement are severable and if any provision is held to be invalid or unenforceable it shall not affect the validity or enforceability of any other provision.

13. This agreement sets forth the entire agreement between you and the company and supersedes any and all prior oral or written agreements or understandings between you and the company concerning this subject matter. This agreement may not be altered, amended, or modified except by a further writing signed by you and (Name of Employer).

14. In the event (Name of Employer) becomes insolvent, bankrupt, is sold, or is unable in any way to pay the amounts due you under the terms of this agreement, then such obligations shall be undertaken and assumed by (specify Parent Company) and all such sums shall be guaranteed by (Name of Parent Company).

15. In the event that any monies due under this agreement are not paid for any reason, then the release referred to in Paragraph 8 shall be null and void and of no effect.

If the foregoing correctly and fully recites the substance of our agreement, please so signify by signing in the space below.

Dated:
Very truly yours,

Name of Employer   Accepted and agreed:
By: _____   Name of Employee
Name of Officer, Title
                                                                   _____

Summary of Things to Know If Your Job Is in Jeopardy

1. It may be illegal for a company to fire you to deprive you of large commissions, vested pension rights, a year-end bonus, or other expected financial benefits.

2. It may be illegal for a company to fire you after returning from an illness, pregnancy, or jury duty.

3. It may be illegal to fire you after you have complained about a safety violation or other wrongdoing.

4. It may be illegal to fire you in a manner inconsistent with company handbooks, manuals, written contracts, and disciplinary rules.

5. It may be illegal to fire you if you are over 40, belong to a protected minority, or are a female, primarily because of such personal characteristics.

6. It may be illegal to fire a large number of workers and/or close a plant without giving *at least* 60 days notice or 60 days severance pay.

7. It may be illegal to fire you if you received a verbal promise of job security or other rights which the company failed to fulfill.

8. It may be illegal to fire a long-term worker when the "punishment does not fit the crime" and other workers were not similarly treated, particularly if you are over 40, belong to a protected minority, or are a female.

9. If you signed a written contract, reread it. Review what it says about termination, because if the company fails to act according to the contract, your rights may be violated.

10. Try to make copies of all pertinent documents in your personnel file while working. If you have received excellent performance reviews and appraisals and the file indicates you received merit salary increases, you may be able to use this information to successfully negotiate more severance than the company is offering.

11. *Refuse* the company's offer to resign whenever possible. This is because if you resign you may be waiving your claim to unemployment and other severance benefits.

12. *Avoid* accepting the company's first offer of severance. Stall for time and follow the negotiating strategies given in this chapter. By doing so, you can increase the chances of obtaining more severance pay and other post-termination financial benefits than the company initially offered.

Finally, since the above 12 strategies are merely suggestions and are not intended to be legal advice per se, always seek competent legal advice where warranted.

Summary of Negotiating Strategies to Maximize Severance Pay and Retirement Benefits

1. Generally, there is no *legal* obligation for a company to pay severance unless you have a written contract stating that severance will be paid, oral promises are given regarding severance pay, there is a documented policy of paying severance in a company manual or handbook, the employer voluntarily offers to pay severance, or other employees in similar positions have received severance pay in the past.

2. If you are fired, request an additional negotiating session to discuss your severance package.

3. Stall for time and try not accept the company's first offer.

4. Appeal to corporate decency and fair play; avoid threatening litigation at the initial meeting. For example, it is better to say "I am 58 years old and have to pay for two children in college right now, and your offer of just 4 weeks' severance will probably put me on the road to financial ruin, since it is unlikely that I can find another comparable job in 4 weeks" rather than "if you don't pay me more money, I will sue."

5. Follow the negotiating strategies contained in this chapter to maximize your chances of obtaining additional financial and other post-termination benefits. Recognize that by asking for many (e.g., 15) items, you may be able to get the company to settle for some (e.g., 5).

6. Confirm all arrangements in writing to document the final deal of severance and post-termination benefits; do not accept the company's promise that "Everything will work out."

7. Insist on receiving more money and other benefits before signing any release or waiver of age or sex discrimination claims.

8. Do not rely on promises from the company that you will receive a favorable job reference. Rather, draft your own favorable letter of reference and get an officer or your supervisor to sign the letter of reference before you depart.

9. Do not be intimidated or forced into early retirement. Recognize that you may have rights, particularly if your early retirement causes you to lose large, expected financial benefits.

10. Be cautious when the employer asks you to sign a release because you may be waiving valuable rights and benefits in the process.

    Finally, since the above 10 strategies are merely suggestions and are not intended to be legal advice per se, always seek competent legal advice where warranted.

CHAPTER EIGHT

POST-EMPLOYMENT MATTERS

Workers experience numerous post-employment problems. Many people do not know how to file for unemployment benefits or resign from a job properly. Sometimes they are victims of defamatory job references or are forced to honor onerous restrictive covenants and suffer resulting damages. This chapter will discuss a variety of concerns that often impact female employees after the job has ended.

UNEMPLOYMENT BENEFITS

Each state imposes different eligibility requirements for collecting unemployment benefits (e.g., the maximum amount of money that may be collected weekly, the normal waiting period required before payments begin, the length of such benefits, and the maximum period you can wait before filing and collecting). States also differ on standards of proof required to receive such benefits. You must know such essential details before filing. Do this by contacting your nearest unemployment office for pertinent information.

The following are some of the questions to ask:

- How quickly can I file?
- When will I begin receiving payments?
- How long will the payments last?

- What must I do (i.e., must I actively look for employment?) in order to qualify and continue receiving benefits?
- How long did I have to work for my former employer in order to qualify?
- What must I prove to collect if my ex-employer contests my claim?
- When and where will the hearing be held?
- Will I have the opportunity to review the employer's charges and documentation opposing my claim (often contained in the official file) before the hearing?
- How can I learn whether witnesses will appear on the company's behalf to testify against me?
- How can I obtain competent legal counsel to represent me?
- How much will this cost?
- Will a record be made of the hearing? If so, in what form?
- Can the hearing examiner's decision be appealed?
- Can I recover benefits if I was forced to resign?
- Is the burden on the employer to demonstrate I was fired for a good reason (e.g., misconduct) or is the burden of proof on me to demonstrate I did not act improperly?
- Can I subpoena witnesses if they refuse to appear voluntarily on my behalf? Will the hearing examiner assist me in this regard?
- Are formal rules of evidence followed at the hearing?

TIP: Collecting unemployment benefits is not always a simple matter, especially if your claim is contested by an ex-employer. In most states, you can collect benefits if you were fired due to a business reorganization, massive layoff, job elimination, or other reasons that were not your fault. In many situations you can even collect if you were fired for being unsuited, unskilled, or for overall poor work performance. However, you generally cannot collect if you voluntarily resigned from a job (unless you were forced to resign for a good reason) or were fired for misconduct.

The following are common examples of acts that justify the denial of unemployment benefits based on misconduct:

- Insubordination or fighting on the job
- Habitual lateness or excessive absence
- Drug abuse on the job

- Disobedience of company work rules or policies
- Gross negligence or neglect of duty
- Dishonesty

COUNSEL COMMENTS: Although these examples appear to be relatively straightforward, employers often have difficulty proving that such acts reached the level of misconduct. This is because hearing examiners typically seek to determine whether a legitimate company rule was violated and whether or not that rule was justified.

PREPARING FOR THE HEARING

Once you file for unemployment insurance benefits and learn the employer is contesting your claim, it is your responsibility to follow the progress of the case carefully.

TIP: Consider whether you require representation by experienced counsel at the hearing (especially if you are considering suing the employer in court over other issues and do not wish to lose the first battle). If you are anticipating receiving the maximum benefits allowed (which in some states can exceed $325 per week) and expect to be unable to find gainful employment for a long period of time (e.g., six months), it may be advantageous to hire a lawyer when the amount of money being contested is significant.

Many people do not know how to act at unemployment hearings. Claimants are often told by unemployment personnel that a lawyer or other representative is not required and that prehearing preparation is unnecessary. They then attend the hearing and are surprised to learn that the employer is represented by counsel who has brought witnesses to testify against their version of the facts. Some are unprepared for the grueling, possibly humiliating cross-examination lasting several hours that they are subjected to. Other claimants lose at the hearing because they don't understand the purpose of their testimony or what they must prove to receive benefits.

Plan on being able to attend the hearing on the date in question. If you cannot be present, speak to a representative responsible for scheduling, explain your reasons, and ask for another convenient date. This should preferably be done in person. Include future dates when you know you can appear. Call that individual the day before the old hearing date to confirm that your request has been granted.

An unemployment hearing is often no different from a trial. Witnesses must testify under oath. Documents, including personnel information, warnings, and performance appraisals, are submitted as exhibits. The atmosphere is rarely friendly. Thus, you must prepare in advance what you will say, how you will handle tough questions from the employer, and what you will try to prove to win the case.

When preparing for the hearing, be certain that all your friendly witnesses (if any) will attend and testify on your behalf. If necessary, ask a representative from the unemployment office to issue a subpoena compelling the attendance of key disinterested witnesses (e.g., co-workers) who refuse to testify and voluntarily attend. If the unemployment representative has no power to do this, wait until the first day of the hearing. Explain to the judge or hearing examiner the necessity of compelling the appearance and testimony of key witnesses. The judge may grant your request depending on its relevance and reasonableness.

Organize the case the day before the hearing to maximize your chances of success. If you have a lawyer, meet with him or her to learn the correct way to testify and what you must prove to win benefits. Collect all evidence so it can be produced easily at the hearing. Practice what you will say. Prepare an outline of key points to be discussed and questions to ask each witness and employee of the ex-employer.

THE HEARING

Arrive early on the hearing date and advise a scheduling clerk of your appearance. Bring your evidence and come properly attired (preferably in business clothes). In some states you can review the entire contents of your file before the hearing; don't forget to ask for this if appropriate. When your case is called, all witnesses will be sworn in. Show the judge your evidence and never argue with the hearing examiner. Listen to the judge's or your lawyer's questions before answering. Avoid being emotional and arguing with your opponent at the hearing.

After the employer finishes testifying, you will have the opportunity to cross-examine the witnesses and refute what was said. If the employer is represented by an attorney and you feel intimidated because you are not represented by counsel, tell the judge you are not familiar with unemployment hearing procedures. Ask the judge to intercede on your behalf if you feel your opponent's attorney is treating you unfairly.

OBTAINING A DECISION

Decisions are not usually obtained immediately after the hearing. You will probably be notified by mail (sometimes two to four weeks later). Be sure to continue filing for benefits while waiting for the decision. Many people forget to do this and lose valuable benefits.

SHOULD YOU APPEAL?

If you are notified that you have lost the decision, read the notice carefully. Most judges and hearing examiners give specific, lengthy reasons for their rulings. If you feel the ruling was incorrect or disagree with the judge's opinion, you may want to file an appeal and have the case reconsidered. However, it is best to speak with an experienced employment lawyer to get an opinion before doing so. You may discover that your chances of success with an appeal are not as good as you think. Appeals are not granted automatically as a matter of right in many states. If the judges on the Appeals Board believe that the hearing judge's decision was correct factually or as a matter of law, the decision will go undisturbed.

> **TIP:** The odds of winning an appeal are not in your favor if you lose at the initial hearing. The amount of time needed to review the transcript or tape of the proceedings, prepare an appeal brief, and reargue the case often makes it expensive and time-consuming. Depending on the particular facts of your case, appealing the hearing may not be worth it. However, if new material facts come to light, if relevant witnesses are willing to come forward and testify at an appeal hearing, or if the success of another case (such as a discrimination lawsuit that was previously filed) depends on a successful outcome of the unemployment matter, this could make a difference.
>
> Typically, you have only a specified period of time (say 30 days) to file the appeal, so do this timely to avoid having the appeal dismissed due to a technical error.

TIP: Speak to an employment lawyer if you have already received benefits and now are being asked to return the money because you lost the hearing. In some states, the failure to return benefits is a crime and you can be prosecuted. The author has structured settlements for many clients with a small payout over time (and often no interest charges imposed) to diminish the burden of having to pay all the money back immediately. Women out of work with insufficient funds can do this with a lawyer's assistance, so inquire about this where appropriate.

HOW TO RESIGN FROM A JOB PROPERLY

Many women do not know how to resign properly. The slightest mistake can expose you to a lawsuit or cause the forfeiture of valuable benefits. Some people resign without receiving a firm job offer from a new employer. Later, after learning the new job did not materialize, they are unable to be rehired by their former employers and spend months out of work unnecessarily without collecting unemployment benefits. To avoid this and similar problems, review and implement the following strategies where possible.

SIGN A WRITTEN CONTRACT WITH A NEW EMPLOYER BEFORE RESIGNING

A written contract with a definite term of employment (for example, six months or one year) can protect you from situations where the new employer changes its mind and decides not to hire you, or fires you after a short period of time. This often happens with devastating consequences but can be avoided by insisting on a valid agreement with job security before starting work. If the new employer does not agree to this, think twice before jumping ship.

REVIEW YOUR CURRENT CONTRACT OR LETTER OF AGREEMENT

If notice is required to be given, do this so you will not violate the contract's obligations.

GIVE NOTICE ONLY WHERE NECESSARY

In many jobs, giving notice is not required or necessary (contrary to the public's misconception) especially if you are hired at will. However, the employer will usually benefit when you offer notice because it may then have time to seek and train a replacement. It may also give you the opportunity to bargain for additional severance benefits before walking out the door.

> **TIP:** Two weeks' notice is probably more than adequate; avoid giving more notice than necessary. Do not offer notice if you must start a new job immediately and believe this will jeopardize your new position. However, if you are entitled to a large bonus or commission in the near future, postpone resigning until you have received such a benefit.

Many employers often summarily reject an employee's notice and ask you to leave the minute they are notified of your intentions. The reason is that some employers believe you will copy pertinent documents or cause trouble. Don't be surprised if this occurs. Anticipate this may occur and plan ahead.

SHOULD YOU RESIGN BY LETTER?

Only when it is used to clarify resignation benefits, request prompt payment of monies previously due, or put you on record that the resignation will not be effective until some later date. If this is important, *always* resign by letter. When you do, keep the letter brief and avoid giving specified reasons for the resignation without having a lawyer review the letter first. The reason is that the letter may be used as evidence at a later trial or proceeding and can preclude you from offering other reasons for the resignation or tipping your hand in the event of a lawsuit.

The example on page 242 is the kind of resignation letter you may wish to draft. Notice that it is hand-delivered or sent by certified mail, return receipt requested. This is done to prove delivery.

Sample Letter of Resignation

Date

Name of Officer
Title
Name of Employer
Address

Re: My Resignation

Dear (Name of Officer):

Please be advised that I am resigning from my job as (title) effective (date).

As of this date, I believe that (describe what salary, commissions, other benefits) are due and I look forward to discussing my termination benefits with you.

I shall be returning all property belonging to the company (specify) by (date) and will be available to assist you in a smooth transition if requested.

Thank you for your attention to these matters.

Very truly yours,

Your Name

HAND DELIVERED or SENT CERTIFIED MAIL
RETURN RECEIPT REQUESTED

NEVER RESIGN IF GIVEN THE CHOICE

Many employers have written policies that state that no severance or other post-termination benefits will be paid to workers who resign. Additionally, you are not entitled to unemployment insurance benefits after voluntarily resigning from a job for a good reason (e.g., because the employer wants you to work the midnight shift or drastically cuts your pay) in many states. If you are a commission salesperson, it is often more difficult to argue that you are entitled to commissions due on orders shipped after a resignation (as opposed to after a firing).

> **TIP:** Think twice if the employer gives you the option of resigning or discharge. Talk to a lawyer for advice where applicable. The author generally prefers that his clients be fired rather than resign whenever possible, since potential damage claims and severance benefits may remain intact. You can always negotiate that the employer will tell outsiders you "resigned for personal reasons" (even if you were fired) if you are worried what outsiders may think.

KEEP QUIET

Tell friends and business associates of your decision to resign after telling your current employer, not before.

AVOID BADMOUTHING

It is not a good idea to tell others about the circumstances surrounding a resignation, particularly if you are leaving on less than pleasant terms. Many employers have sued former employees for defamation, product disparagement, and unfair competition on discovering that harmful oral or written comments were made. Additionally, when the statement disparages the quality of a company's product and at the same time implies that an officer or principal of the employer is dishonest, fraudulent, or incompetent (thus affecting the individual's personal reputation), a private lawsuit for personal defamation may be brought. Some companies withhold severance pay and other voluntary benefits as a way of getting even. Thus, avoid discussing your employer in a negative way with anyone.

RETURN COMPANY PROPERTY

Disputes sometimes occur when property belonging to the employer is not returned. You generally must return such property (automobile keys, confidential customer lists, samples, etc.) immediately on resignation to avoid claims of conversion, fraud, and breach of contract.

> **TIP:** If returning items by mail, get a receipt to prove delivery. Recognize that a few states permit you to retain company property as a lien in the event you are owed money which the employer refuses to pay. However, since many states do not recognize this, speak to an employment lawyer before taking such action.

JOB REFERENCES AND DEFAMATION CLAIMS

Employers are not legally obligated to furnish prospective employers with positive or negative job references. After a firing, management may apologetically advise at the termination interview "not to worry, you'll be given a positive reference." Weeks later, however, the person making the promise may refuse to take or answer calls from prospective employers or merely confirm your dates of employment and title.

> **TIP:** To avoid similar problems, request that a copy of a favorable letter of recommendation be given to you before you leave. The letter should state the dates of your employment, the positions held, and that you performed all your job duties in a diligent and satisfactory fashion. If possible, the letter should be signed by a qualified officer or supervisor who worked with you and knows you well. Do not rely on promises that the employer will furnish prospective employers with a favorable recommendation, since many do not once you are out the door. Always attempt to have such a letter in hand before you leave (see the letter on page 245 as an example).

To ensure receiving a favorable reference, knowledgeable employees type the letter themselves on company letterhead after being fired but before leaving the premises. With a signed, favorable letter of reference in hand, you can reduce the chances of receiving a poor reference.

**Sample Letter
of Recommendation**

Date

To whom it may concern:

I am pleased to submit this letter of recommendation on behalf of (Name of Employee).

(Name of Employee) worked for the company from (date) through (date). During this period, (Name of Employee) was promoted from (specify title) to (specify title).

During the past (specify) years, I have had the opportunity to work closely with (Name of Employee). At all times I found her to be diligent and dependable and (Name of Employee) rendered competent and satisfactory services on the company's behalf.

I heartily recommend (Name of Employee) as a candidate for employment of her choosing.

Very truly yours,

Name of Officer

Title

If you cannot obtain a written letter of reference, try to choose the person who will field inquiries from prospective employers. Rehearse what will be said about you. Give only that person's name and telephone number to reduce the chance that harmful or damaging information will be discussed about you by other people at the company. Request that person to only handle inquiries on your behalf.

COUNSEL COMMENTS: Employers are supposed to avoid discussing the decision to terminate or criticize you in front of nonessential third parties. The reason is that fired employees are increasingly suing former employers for defamation. For example, the Minnesota Supreme Court awarded four employees $570,000 because they had to reveal in job applications that their former employer had fired them. The plaintiffs had been fired for alleged gross insubordination for failing to comply with their manager's request to falsify certain expenditure reports. Following termination, the employees sought other positions of employment. In response to inquiries about their previous positions, the four employees stated that they had been fired for gross insubordination.

The Minnesota court ruled that a defamation had occurred because the terminated employees, when asked, would truthfully reply they were fired for insubordination. Any explanations the plaintiffs tried to provide prospective employers could not compensate for the highly negative impression caused by the words "gross insubordination." To make matters worse, the company's policy of withholding information after a job referral request only added to the innuendos.

TIP: This case is significant because it indicates that, in some states, employees fired on false charges of bad conduct can sue their former employers for defamation, even if it is the workers themselves who reveal the charges. Thus, it is important to understand what defamation is; if you are forced to repeat a defamatory job reference, speak to a lawyer immediately.

DEFAMATION

Defamation occurs when a communication (either oral or written) is made about a person that tends to so harm that person's reputation as to lower her in the estimation of the community or to deter others from associating or dealing with her. Defamatory statements in written form constitute libel; defamatory statements in oral form constitute slander and the penalties are similar for each. Defamatory acts are quite common, such as when a newspaper reporter misstates a private person's comments during an interview, when a former employer maliciously provides an improper job reference, and when false gossip is repeated.

For defamation to occur there must be:

- A false statement made about someone;
- to a third party;
- which injures the person's reputation; and
- no absolute or qualified privilege exists as a legal bar to the lawsuit.

No defamation exists when a poor opinion about someone is given. To be actionable, the comment offered must be a statement of fact and not an opinion. If the statement is true, this is a valid defense. If the person alleging defamation is not mentioned by name, a valid case will exist if it is clear that she was the one being talked about and the statement was made to a third party.

Damages do not have to be proved in all instances. The law treats certain statements as defamatory per se, which means that the person or business does not have to prove actual damages to win a verdict; money can be recovered simply because the statement is untrue.

Examples of per se statements are:

- Accusing a person of serious misconduct in her business, trade, or profession (e.g., that a doctor or group medical practice she is affiliated with has trouble paying its bills, is discontinuing its operations and filing for bankruptcy, is financially unstable, incompetent, of poor moral character, unreliable or dishonest.)
- Imputing to a person the commission of a criminal offense.
- Charging a person with dishonesty (e.g., "She is a crook and steals money from the company").
- Accusing a person of serious sexual misconduct (e.g., "She is a whore").
- Stating that a person has a loathsome or deadly disease (such as AIDS).

In certain situations, such as in court proceedings and the employment context, people have an absolute or qualified privilege to make defamatory statements without legal consequences. For example, statements made about people by judges, witnesses and lawyers during trials are absolutely privileged. Employers have a qualified privilege to talk about former employees when giving job references. However, this doesn't mean an employer can talk maliciously about a former employee and tell untruths in an attempt to embarrass and scuttle future job opportunities.

To avoid problems, think first before disclosing private information concerning others. For employers, potentially damaging information in performance reviews and comments to prospective employers should be reviewed by a supervisor. Avoid having damaging memos about a person read by nonessential third parties. In many states, such as Connecticut, any dissemination of private employment data to prospective employers other than the dates of employment, position held and latest salary figures is illegal. Many states prohibit the dissemination of confidential private medical information as well.

> **TIP:** Avoid disseminating any information about someone that can remotely be considered private. Do not repeat unconfirmed gossip or trade gossip, especially about the financial condition of a competitor, business or product. If you might be a victim of defamation, speak to a lawyer immediately to protect your rights.

To reduce the risk of defamation claims by ex-employees, employers are being advised by management attorneys to:

1. Never stand in the way of a terminated employee's future employment.
2. Maintain tight control over personnel files and avoid distributing personal information without an employee's consent.
3. Avoid giving negative references to prospective employers.
4. Avoid criticizing an individual in front of others at the exit or firing interview.

> **COUNSEL COMMENTS:** Some states treat untruthful job references as crimes. Also, as the Minnesota case demonstrates, if your ex-company refrains from releasing information, it may still be vulnerable in a suit in some states if you are forced to tell a prospec-

tive employer the reason why you were let go and the reason later proves to be false.

Protection for defamation may extend also to physical acts. For example, if you are suspected of theft and forcibly searched and interrogated when leaving the premises after a firing, the rough treatment observed by others may defame your reputation by holding you up to ridicule and scorn.

Recognize, however, that in any defamation lawsuit, truth is an absolute defense. This means that if a harmful but true statement is disseminated about you, you will probably not prevail. And, in most states, if the statement later proves to be untrue but was not spoken with an intentional attempt to harm you (i.e., proving malice) an employer's qualified privilege may exculpate it from liability.

> **TIP:** If you suspect your efforts to obtain new employment are being sabotaged by an ex-employer, there are several steps to take. Have a friend contact the ex-employer and pretend that he or she is interested in hiring you. In many states, such telephone conversations can be legally taped without the permission of the other party. In fact, there are companies that specialize in acquiring information for terminated employees. Consult your yellow pages for pertinent firms.

Once you determine what is being said, write a letter similar to the one on page 250 to protest unfavorable job references and preserve your rights. If you do not receive a satisfactory response to your letter, if your letter is ignored, or if you suspect damaging information continues to be disseminated, contact a lawyer immediately for advice on how to protect your rights. The lawyer may recommend that he or she send a cease and desist letter to the company demanding that any alleged misconduct stop immediately to avoid expensive and protracted legal proceedings. Such a letter may do the trick.

RESTRICTIVE COVENANTS AND RELATED PROBLEMS

As discussed in Chapter Three, restrictive covenants are clauses in agreements that prohibit you from directly competing with or working for a competitor of your employer. They also are drafted to pro-

Sample Letter Protesting Unfavorable Job Reference

Your Name
Address
Telephone Number
Date

Name of Employer
Address

Dear (Name),

   On (specify date), I applied for a job with (name of potential employer). At the interview, I was told that your firm had submitted an inaccurate, unfavorable reference about me.

   (Specify name) supposedly said the reason I was fired was that I was an uncooperative and complaining worker (or specify facts).

   This is untrue. In fact, my personnel file, which I copied, contains not one derogatory comment about me.

   You are hereby requested to cease making inaccurate statements about my job performance to anyone. If you do not comply, I will contact my lawyer and take appropriate legal action. Hopefully this will be avoided and I thank you for your cooperation in this matter.

Very truly yours,

(Your name)

cc: potential employer

(Send certified mail, return receipt requested.)

tect employers against the dissemination of confidential trade secrets and other information.

Each state has its own rules for deciding whether to enforce a restrictive convenant. Obviously, where possible, avoid signing any such clause in an employment agreement before you begin working. The reason is that even if the company cannot validly restrain you from using confidential information (such as a customer list) or prohibit you from earning a living in the future, the threat of a lawsuit or the filing of a lawsuit will cost you time, money, aggravation, and expensive legal fees.

> **TIP:** Avoid signing any document with significant restrictions. Always consult a lawyer before deciding to execute such a document. (Note: Signing a document prohibiting you from revealing trade secrets or confidential information is often not as serious as one prohibiting you from calling on customers you previously serviced or working for a competitor. Trade secret covenants are often difficult to enforce. Thus, weigh the relative risks and benefits before signing.)

Additionally, consult an experienced lawyer immediately when an ex-employer threatens to sue you to enforce a restrictive convenant. You may be surprised to learn that the employer will be unsuccessful in a lawsuit. However, the lawyer may suggest a settlement (such as reducing the time of the covenant from six months to two months or agreeing to refrain from competing provided you are paid your regular salary during this period) with the employer to spare you the additional expense.

> **COUNSEL COMMENTS:** When companies are in breach of important contract terms, the law sometimes presumes they have unclean hands; often in such situations, restrictive covenants will not be applied against you.

For example, the author once defended several sales employees who had gone into business in competition with an ex-employer. Previously, they contacted me to review an employment agreement they had signed with the ex-employer. The agreement contained a restrictive covenant. During the consultation I learned that the employer had reduced their salary contrary to the agreement. My clients had protested this unfair, unilateral action, both orally and in writing.

The employees were sued after commencing business operations. At the trial, the judge heard testimony regarding this unauthorized unilateral cut of pay. The judge ruled that the employer was obligated to pay a specified, predetermined salary per the contract. Since the employer had unfairly reduced their compensation, the restrictive covenant was not enforceable.

The issue of whether a restrictive covenant cannot be applied against you depends on the unique circumstances and facts of your particular case. Often the issues are not clear-cut and the results cannot be predicted easily. For example, a New York Supreme Court justice recently upheld a six-month anticompetition clause in an employment agreement. New York courts have traditionally been reluctant to enforce noncompete clauses that prevent someone from earning a living unless the former employee is "unique" or could use the employer's trade secrets. However, the covenant was enforced against four terminated foreign exchange brokers because the employer agreed to pay the employees their full salary during the six months that the covenant was in effect.

> **TIP:** The case might have been decided differently if the covenant was longer than six months. However, the case illustrates the importance of always consulting with an experienced employment lawyer for advice where applicable.

CHAPTER NINE

EMPLOYMENT LITIGATION AND ALTERNATIVES

Tens of thousands of employment-related lawsuits are filed in state and federal courts annually. Common lawsuits are for discrimination complaints and breach of contract actions to collect wages, commissions, and benefits. Lawsuits are brought in either a state or a federal court, depending on the facts. This chapter will provide you with an explanation of the various legal forums you may be exposed to when asserting your rights. Strategies will be provided to help win a case in court, after an appeal, through arbitration, and through small-claims court, and how to settle a matter out of court through mediation.

LITIGATION PROCEDURES AND THE COURTS

The party commencing a lawsuit (called the plaintiff) must have proper subject matter and personal jurisdiction to avoid having the case initially dismissed. Having subject matter jurisdiction means filing the action in an appropriate court. For example, an ERISA benefits claim must be filed in a federal district court; a case involving significant wages cannot be filed in small-claims court. Speak to a lawyer to be sure you are filing your case in the proper court before starting a lawsuit.

It is also necessary to demonstrate personal (*in personam*) jurisdiction. Typically, if the person or business being sued (called the defendant) lives or works in the state where the action is filed, or has close ties with that state (e.g., ships goods into or travels to that state to conduct business), then personal jurisdiction may be determined to exist by a judge. It will also be necessary to select the correct venue (the proper county) where the lawsuit should be filed. For example, in a wrongful discharge lawsuit, the proper venue is the county where the plaintiff or defendant resides. Since venue laws vary from state to state, ask your lawyer where the suit should be brought to avoid having the case dismissed.

COUNSEL COMMENTS: Where applicable, ask your lawyer about the advantages and disadvantages of commencing the lawsuit in either state or federal court. Some experts believe that federal court judges are generally more highly regarded for their legal skills than state judges and that litigants are often able to obtain a trial quicker in federal court. However, if a dispute is with an employer located within your state, you may not be able to file a lawsuit in federal court unless you are asserting a discrimination charge or other matter dealing with federal laws (such as a wage and hour or overtime violation). Conversely, if you are being sued, it may be advantageous to keep the case in a state court to "slow down" its progress.

Before starting any action, it is important to thoroughly analyze whether your case has merit. For example, does the defendant have a strong defense? Will you be able to prove your case? Will the defendant be interested in settling the matter before protracted and expensive litigation occurs? Carefully examine the strengths and weaknesses of any case before starting. Analyze whether the defendant has sufficient assets (such as money in the bank and property). After going through lengthy litigation and expense if the matter is not settled out of court, you don't want to win the case but be unable to collect the award.

TIP: There are investigative companies who, for a fee, can advise you about the defendant's asset picture. Your lawyer can tell you where such companies are located. You may also find them listed in the telephone yellow pages. Always discuss these concerns with your lawyer before the decision to litigate is made.

COURTS

A court is a place where trials are held and/or the law is applied. Depending upon one's choice and other factors, a trial may be conducted and decided by a judge only, or a judge and jury. In some appellate courts and the United States Supreme Court, only judges are present to hear arguments and make decisions.

A court can only preside over matters to which it has jurisdiction. Courts of original jurisdiction are the first courts to preside over a matter. A court of appellate jurisdiction is a higher court that reviews cases removed by appeal from a lower court.

Each state has its own court system, which operates separately from the federal court system. There are basically two levels of state courts: trial courts and appellate courts. General trial courts are typically divided into two separate, distinct courts, one to hear criminal matters and one to adjudicate civil matters. Civil trial courts may be further divided depending upon the amount of money or the subject matter at issue. In New York, for example, original jurisdiction small claims courts adjudicate civil matters up to $3,000; the Civil Court adjudicates matters up to $25,000, and the Supreme Court presides over civil matters involving more than $25,000 or other issues. The Family Court hears issues pertaining to support, domestic violence, and problems affecting juveniles, while the Surrogate's Court is involved in matters affecting probate, estates, and wills.

The federal court system is divided into 12 districts or circuits and has jurisdiction over the following:

- When a federal law is at issue such as bankruptcy, copyright and patents, maritime, and postal matters
- When one state is suing another state
- When a person or entity (i.e., a corporation) is suing a person or entity residing in another state and the amount in controversy exceeds $50,000

Within the federal system are separate limited jurisdiction courts that hear matters exclusively pertaining to bankruptcy (U.S. Bankruptcy Court), tax issues (U.S. Tax Court), suits against the federal government (U.S. Court of Claims), and disputes concerning tariffs and customs (U.S. Court of International Trade).

The United States Supreme Court is the country's highest court. It considers cases from the highest courts of each state, decisions of the U.S. Court of Appeals (the highest federal appeals court) and cases where the constitutionality of federal laws comes into play.

The vast majority of lawsuits, including unemployment and worker compensation hearings, originate in state courts. If you are thinking of filing a lawsuit, speak to an employment lawyer or visit the clerk of any local court to determine where the correct place is to start. Each state has its own unique filing, procedural, and jurisdictional requirements, which must be correctly followed so the case will not be dismissed. It is essential to get proper advice from a lawyer before starting any legal process.

STARTING AN ACTION

A civil lawsuit must be commenced (i.e., filed) within a certain period of time after the dispute arose to avoid dismissal on the basis of being untimely (called the statute of limitations). Each state and federal court has its own rules concerning the maximum amount of time you can wait before a lawsuit must be filed; it is crucial to know how much time you have before contemplating litigation, If you wish to join others in one suit (called a class action), it is necessary to contact the law firm representing the class within the required period of time to be able to join and be included in the lawsuit.

A lawsuit is started by preparing and filing a summons and complaint with the court. A summons is a single piece of paper typically accompanied by the complaint that, when served on the defendant (e.g., an employer), notifies the defendant of a lawsuit. A complaint is a legal document that starts the lawsuit. It alleges pertinent facts and legal causes of action that the plaintiff will rely on in her attempt to collect damages. For a lawsuit to proceed, it is necessary that the summons and complaint be served on the defendant either in person (typically with the help of a process server or sheriff) or by certified mail, return receipt requested, in states that permit mail service. If the defendant is not notified of the existence of the lawsuit or if the complaint is not drafted accurately and fails to state a legally recognized cause of action, the case may be dismissed. If a lawsuit is dismissed without prejudice it may be started over; lawsuits dismissed with prejudice may never be brought again.

Once the summons and complaint is served on the defendant, it must be filed with the proper court together with the payment of the initial filing fee (which can be as much as $250 in some states). Filing these documents is rather easy. At the courthouse, a clerk accepts the fee and documents, stamps the papers to indicate the date and time received, and issues a receipt. The documents then become part of a file, which is stored at the court. The file is given to the presiding judge of the case when appropriate (such as during oral arguments before trial and at the trial). A judge is randomly assigned to preside over every filed case. The judge will rule on various pretrial motions, move the case along to the trial, conduct the trial, and render a judgment based on the evidence when a jury is not involved.

After the complaint is served, the defendant has a period of time (usually no more than 30 days) to submit an answer. An answer is the defendant's reply to the plaintiff's charges in a civil lawsuit. Properly drafted answers typically deny most of the plaintiff's charges, list a number of legal reasons (called affirmative defenses) why the case should not proceed, and may or may not contain counterclaims. A counterclaim is a claim asserted by the defendant in a lawsuit. Sometimes the plaintiff loses her case and the defendant wins the case through its counterclaim.

Each case is decided by its unique facts. The fact that you are the plaintiff means only that you filed the lawsuit first; it does not guarantee success of the matter in any way. However, if the defendant fails to respond to the lawsuit by filing an answer, it may lose the case by default. (Note: If you are sued, *always* consult an attorney after receiving a complaint to ensure that a timely answer will be filed.)

KINDS OF DAMAGES

Damages are compensation or relief awarded to the prevailing party in a lawsuit. Damages can be in the form of money or a directive by the court for the losing party to perform or refrain from performing a certain action. The following briefly describes various forms of damages.

Compensatory damages. This is a sum of money awarded to a party that represents the actual harm suffered or loss incurred. To collect compensatory damages, one must prove what the actual out-of-pocket losses are since damages cannot be presumed. For example, projections of future lost profits will not be awarded unless they are definite and certain.

Incidental damages. Incidental damages are traditionally direct out-of-pocket expenses for filing a lawsuit and related court costs (such as process server fees). These direct costs of litigation are sometimes awarded to the prevailing party in a litigation as part of the party's loss.

Liquidated damages. This is an amount of money agreed on in advance by parties to a written contract to be paid in the event of a breach or dispute. If it is not possible to compute the amount of the loss, a judge may uphold the amount specified. However, in many circumstances, when the amount specified has no actual basis in fact, a judge may disregard it, viewing the amount merely as a penalty.

Nominal damages. This is a small amount of money (e.g., $1.00) awarded by the court. Sometimes, a party may win the lawsuit but not have proved suffering or any actual damages.

Punitive damages. Also called exemplary damages, punitive damages represent money awarded as punishment for a party's wrongful acts beyond any actual losses. When punitive damages are awarded, a judge is often sending a signal to the community that similar outrageous, malicious, or oppressive conduct will not be tolerated. Under the laws of many states, punitive damages can be awarded only in certain types of lawsuits, such as personal injury and product liability actions, and not lawsuits to enforce employment contracts or business agreements.

Specific performance. This is a directive by the court for the party being sued (i.e., the defendant) to perform a certain action such as sell a business or not work for a competitor pursuant to a clause in an employment contract. Specific performance is typically not awarded if monetary damages can make the party seeking the relief whole.

Injunction. This is a court order restraining one party from performing or refusing to perform an action or contract.

Mitigation of damages. This is a legal principle that requires a party seeking damages to make reasonable efforts to reduce damages as much as possible; for example, to secure comparable employment or file for unemployment benefits if a job cannot be obtained in the short term.

Sometimes an employer is interested not only in obtaining damages, but in seeking to stop you from establishing a competing business or working for a competitor. An action can be commenced called a preliminary injunction. The employer (as the moving party) will request a hearing immediately after the lawsuit is filed. A request for an immediate hearing is called an *order to show cause*. If a judge rules in favor of the motion, the injunction will be granted. If a judge decides in favor of the defendant, the injunction will be denied but, depending on the circumstances, the case may be allowed to proceed like any other lawsuit to ascertain damages.

After the answer is received from the defendant, the discovery phase of the case begins. Several pretrial devices, including interrogatories, depositions, and motions, are used by lawyers to elicit information from the opposing side, gather evidence, and prepare for the trial. The discovery phase can last several years in a complicated case and can be very expensive in terms of attorney fees and the costs of taking depositions, procuring documents, and paying for postage and related expenses.

Interrogatories are written questions sent to an opponent to be answered under oath. One problem with interrogatories is that the opposing party's attorney may draft the responses to prevent, insofar as possible, damaging statements from being conveyed.

Depositions often lasting several days are taken by both sides in complicated labor cases. A deposition is a pretrial proceeding in which one party is questioned under oath by the opposing party's lawyer. A stenographer is present to record all statements and preserve the testimony. Depositions are used to collect information and facts about the case, narrow the issues to be proven at trial, and discredit (impeach) the testimony of the witness.

It is essential that your lawyer properly prepare and advise you before your deposition is taken. Many cases have been lost due to unprepared responses elicited from a witness at a deposition. If your testimony is materially different (inconsistent) at the trial from statements you gave at the deposition, your credibility may be seriously undermined; giving a totally different statement about something at the trial could dramatically reduce the chances of success. Also, incorrect answers at the deposition might give the opposing attorney grounds to file a motion to dismiss the case in its entirety or throw out various causes of action. A motion to dismiss requests that even if the plaintiff's allegations are true and there is no genuine issue as to important facts, no legal basis exists for finding the defendant liable.

Sometimes attorneys file motions to get a ruling on admissibility of evidence or ask the court to assist in obtaining documents and records that have not been turned over by the other side (although promised).

Once the discovery phase of the case is completed, a judge will order a pretrial conference. Both attorneys are asked to appear to discuss the case and the possibility of settlement. Some judges make active attempts to settle cases at these conferences. If the conference is successful and the case is settled, the parties will prepare a written stipulation that describes the terms of the settlement. Typically the judge will review and approve all settlements before they are implemented.

> **TIP:** Think carefully before accepting any settlement. Most civil actions take up to five years to be tried. By accepting a fair settlement early on, you have use of the money, which can be invested to earn more money. You may eliminate large legal fees, court costs, and the possibility of eventually losing the case after a trial. However, if you have a good case, it may pay to wait before discussing and accepting a settlement. Most trial attorneys believe that large settlements are obtained for their clients by waiting until the case reaches the courthouse steps.

The decision on whether to accept a settlement should always be made jointly with your attorney, who knows the merits, pitfalls, and true value of the case better than you. However, do not allow a lawyer to pressure you into accepting a smaller settlement than you deserve. Some attorneys seek smaller immediate settlements out of laziness because the settlement represents money in the bank to them.

Instruct your attorney to provide you with a detailed explanation of the pros and cons of settling your case. Inform her that you prefer to control your affairs, including the decision of settling a claim. Do not let your attorney push you around. Your attorney cannot settle the case without your approval. If she does, she can be sued for malpractice. If you are not satisfied with your lawyer's advice or conduct, consult another attorney for a second opinion before settling the matter. Do this before taking action, because once you sign the settlement papers you probably cannot change your mind and continue with the case, since release language contained in such documents generally prohibits you from doing so.

On page 262 is an example of a general release in an employment discrimination case.

If a matter cannot be settled, the judge will discuss with both attorneys how the case will proceed. The identity and order of witnesses and exhibits to be submitted at the trial will be agreed to before the trial begins. In many types of labor cases, either party can request that a jury decide the case rather than a judge. A jury trial usually involves 12 people, although some states allow as few as 6. Some states permit a civil jury's decision to be less than unanimous.

The first step of the trial begins with jury selection if a jury has been requested by either side. Prospective jurors are questioned (referred to as the voir dire) to see if they are qualified to sit on the panel. Lawyers seek answers to certain questions in the attempt to learn if a person has an open mind and is not biased. After attorneys for both sides dismiss certain people and retain others, the jury is picked and the trial begins. The plaintiff's lawyer will begin the trial with an opening statement. This is a speech designed to tell the judge or jury about the nature of the case, what the plaintiff intends to prove from the facts, and what kind of damages are sought.

After the defendant's attorney gives his opening statement, the trial begins. Witnesses are called by the plaintiff, and witnesses give their direct testimony under oath. The opposing attorney has the right to question (cross-examine) each witness in turn. All other evidence such as documents and exhibits, is submitted and other witnesses are questioned.

EVIDENCE

Evidence is information in the form of oral testimony, exhibits, physical items, or affidavits used to prove a party's claim. Evidence can be presented in many forms. For example, exhibits are tangible evidence presented in a court proceeding for the purpose of supporting factual allegations or arguments. Testimony from expert witnesses may be introduced as evidence. In certain kinds of criminal cases, physical evidence such as fingerprints or hair samples can be

General Release

FOR GOOD AND VALUABLE CONSIDERATION, the adequacy of which is hereby acknowledged, in the form of payment to Employee of a severance benefit in the amount of ($XX) salary less withholding for federal and state taxes, FICA, and any other amounts required to be withheld, Employee agrees that he/she, or any person acting by, through, or under Employee, RELEASES AND FOREVER DISCHARGES (Name of Employer), and its parent company and subsidiaries, affiliates, successors, and assigns, as well as the officers, employees, representatives, agents and fiduciaries, *de facto* or *de jure* (hereinafter collectively referred to as "Released Parties"), and covenants and agrees not to institute any action or actions, causes or causes of action (in law unknown) in state or federal court, based upon or arising by reason of any damage, loss, or in any way related to Employee's employment with any of the Released Parties or the termination of said employment. The foregoing includes, but not by way of limitation, all claims which could have been raised under common law, including retaliatory discharge and breach of contract, or statute, including, without limitation, the Age Discrimination in Employment Act of 1967, 42 U.S.C. Sections 621-634, as amended by the Older Workers Benefit Protection Act of 1990, Title VII of the Civil Rights Act of 1964, 42 U.S.C. Sections 2000e *et seq.* and the Employee Retirement Income Security Act of 1974, 29 U.S.C. Sections 1001 *et seq.* or any other Federal or State Law; except that this General Release is not intended to cover any claim arising from computational or clerical errors in the calculation of the severance benefit provided to Employee, or retirement benefit to which Employee may be entitled from any plan or other benefits to which Employee may be entitled under any plan maintained by any of the Released Parties.

Employee covenants and agrees to forever refrain from instituting, pursuing, or in any way whatsoever aiding any claim, demand, action, or cause of action or other matter released and discharged herein by Employee arising out of or in any way related to Employee's employment with any of the Released Parties and the rights to recovery for any damages or compensation awarded as a result of a lawsuit brought by any third party or governmental agency on Employee's behalf.

Employee further agrees to indemnify all Released Parties from any and all loss, liability, damages, claims, suits, judgments, attorneys' fees and other costs and expenses of whatsoever kind or individually Employee may sustain or incur as a result of or in connection with matters hereinabove released and discharged by Employee. Employee warrants that he/she has not filed any lawsuits, charges, complaints, petitions, or accusatory pleadings against any of the Released Parties with any governmental agency or in any court, based upon, arising out of, or related in any way to any event or events occurring prior to the signing of this General Release, including, without limitation, his/her employment with any of the Released Parties or the termination thereof.

Employee acknowledges, understands and affirms that: (a) This General Release is a binding legal document; (b) (i) Released Parties advised him/her to consult with an attorney before signing this General Release, (ii) he/she had the right to consult with an attorney about and before signing this General Release, (iii) he/she was given a period of at least 21 calendar days in which to consider this General Release prior to signing, and (iv) he/she voluntarily signs and enters into this General Release without reservation after having given the matter full and careful consideration; and (c) (i) Employee has a period of seven days after signing this General Release in which he/she may revoke this General Release, (ii) this General Release does not become effective or enforceable and no payment shall be made hereunder until this seven-day-revocation period has elapsed, and (iii) any revocation must be in writing by Employee and delivered to (specify), Human Resources, within the seven-day-revocation period.

IN WITNESS WHEREOF, the Employee signs this General Release this day of _____.

Employee's Name (please print)

WITNESS:

Signature:_____Date: _____

helpful in proving who harmed a victim if no witnesses were present.

In a civil case, the plaintiff has the burden of proving its case by a legal standard called preponderance of the evidence ("more likely than not") through witnesses, charts, documents, photographs and other forms of physical evidence. In a criminal case, the prosecution must prove a person's guilt beyond a reasonable doubt. This is a more difficult standard to achieve.

During the trial one side will try to get evidence admitted into the court record for consideration by a judge or jury when deciding the case. The other party, through his or her lawyer, will seek to exclude such evidence through objections; for example, by stating that the evidence is irrelevant or inadmissible. A judge will either deny the objection and allow the evidence to be admitted or sustain the objection and exclude the evidence. The introduction of evidence in any case depends upon an attorney's arguments and the judge's interpretation of that state or federal court's rules. Certain types of evidence, such as hearsay evidence (a witness's testimony about what someone else said outside of the courtroom), must be excluded (and may be excluded in advance of a trial).

Each party has the opportunity to discover what evidence the other intends to introduce at the trial to prove its version of the facts. This is done through depositions where a witness's testimony is taken under oath and during discovery procedures whereby records and other physical information is turned over to the other side for evaluation. In most states it is against the law to destroy evidence.

> **TIP:** Because the success or failure of a case often depends on the type of evidence introduced and admitted (or excluded) from the record at a trial, it is important to hire an employment lawyer who is very knowledgeable about the rules of evidence. For maximum success, always hire an employment lawyer who possesses competent trial skills.

After the plaintiff's case is completed, the defendant presents its side of the case. When both sides are finished, each attorney gives a summation. This is a review of the facts, testimony, and other evidence. If no jury is involved, the judge will render a decision. Typically, both parties have to wait a period of time (up to 30 days) before receiving the judge's written decision.

If a jury is involved, a judge will instruct its members as to what *law* is applicable to the facts and statements they have heard. The jury will then leave the courtroom and return with its determination. In rare cases, a judge may disregard the jury's findings and grant a motion for judgment notwithstanding the verdict (called a JNOV) when she believes there was insufficient evidence to support a jury's conclusion.

After the judgment is made, either party can appeal the decision by filing a written document called a brief. Information about appeals is discussed in the next section. It is also important to take proper steps to collect the judgment if the losing party doesn't pay. This may involve placing a lien on real estate property owned by the losing party or attaching such property to prevent the transfer, assignment, or sale without your consent. Speak to your attorney for more information about how this can be accomplished.

> **TIP:** Litigation is complicated, time-consuming, and subject to many hazards. Unless absolutely necessary, or involving a small amount of money that can be handled by yourself in small-claims court, do not attempt to file papers and represent yourself (pro se) in a lawsuit without an attorney.

The following is a summary of key strategies to follow in any lawsuit, whether you are the plaintiff or the defendant:

1. Hire a lawyer skilled in conducting trials. Many attorneys do not litigate cases, which is a specialty.

2. Play an active role in all phases of the case. Request that your attorney routinely send you copies of all incoming and outgoing correspondence on a regular basis. This will help you monitor and question the progress of your case.

3. Never ignore a summons and complaint if you are served. Ignoring a summons and complaint can result in the imposition of a default judgment with huge damages, penalties, and interest assessed against you without your filing a defense. Speak to a lawyer immediately to protect your rights.

4. Never ignore a subpoena if you are summoned to court to appear as a witness. A subpoena is an order requiring your presence to testify. If for some reason you cannot be present on the date specified, speak to the clerk of the court for advice and guidance. Ignoring a subpoena can result in a fine, imprisonment, or both.

5. Be prepared at all times. Competent attorneys work with their clients in anticipation of the upcoming deposition and trial. There should be no surprises in what you will testify to and what the opposing lawyer will ask you. Your lawyer should advise you how to react if you do not understand a question or do not wish to answer.

6. Consider alternative methods to settle your dispute. This includes arbitration and mediation (which are discussed in other sections of this chapter). Ask your lawyer to actively seek and encourage a settlement where warranted.

7. Determine if the opposing party has sufficient assets to pay a successful verdict before starting an action.

8. Assess the chances of winning or losing and how much a lawsuit will cost to commence or defend before getting in too deep.

APPEALS

The vast majority of employment-related lawsuits never go to trial; they are either discontinued or settled. However, every case that is tried has a loser, and the losing party must decide whether or not to appeal the unfavorable decision.

An appeal is a request that a higher court review the decision of a lower court. In those states that have an intermediate appellate court, the losing party challenging a trial court decision first brings the appeal to the intermediate court. In the federal court system, the losing party brings the appeal to the court of appeals in the appropriate circuit. For serious criminal cases (i.e., felonies), the right to an appeal is mandatory. In civil cases, an appeals court may have the discretion not to consider the appeal in certain circumstances. After the appeal is decided by an intermediate appellate court, the case can be further reviewed by the highest state appeals court (although some state cases are reviewed by the U.S. Supreme Court). In the federal system, after the appeal is decided by the U.S. Court of Appeals, the Supreme Court of the United States has the power and discretion to review and rule on the history of the case and the most recent appeal.

Appeals judges read the transcript of the trial together with legal documents called briefs to determine if the trial judge or jury erred in their decision. Typically, the intermediate appellate court will concern itself with issues of law as opposed to facts. It is rare that the appellate court will overturn a jury's factual decision. Rather, a verdict can be reversed if the wrong law was applied, incorrect jury instructions were given by the judge, or significant legal mistakes occurred, such as important evidence being mistakenly excluded by a judge from the trial.

Less than 20 percent of all criminal cases and 30 percent of all civil cases are reversed on appeal. Most decisions do not get reversed but if a person or business has spent several years and thousands of dollars pursuing or defending a valid claim, the additional money spent on an appeal can be worth it, particularly if the delay caused by the appeals process works to an appellant's advantage.

Speak to a lawyer immediately if you receive an unfavorable trial verdict. There is a limited period of time (i.e., often 30 days) in which to file a notice that you intend to appeal. This must be done without delay to preserve your rights. To evaluate the chances of a successful appeal, it is necessary to carefully reconstruct (in an objective fashion) the reason the case was lost. Consider whether to hire a specialist in appeals matters. Although your current attorney is familiar with the case, there are distinct advantages to hiring an attorney who makes a living writing briefs and arguing oral appeals (it is an art). Be certain you know how much the appeal will cost. Always sign a retainer agreement similar to the example on page 269 that clearly spells out attorney fees, costs, and disbursements.

Remember that no matter which lawyer handles the appeal, it is generally costly, time-consuming, and frequently does not produce anticipated results. However, if you win a big case and the employer appeals, there is little you may be able to do but contest the appeal.

MEDIATION PROCEDURES

Mediation is an alternative to resolving employment disputes via formal litigation or arbitration. A neutral intermediary (the mediator) defines the conflicting interests of the parties, explains the legal implications, and attempts to help the parties reach and prepare a fair settlement. When settlements are achieved, they are typically reached more quickly and cheaply because opposing parties have not hired opposing counsel to fight it out in court. More and more employment-related cases are now being resolved this way. For example:

- When an employer alleges it was justified in firing an executive for cause prior to the expiration of the stated term in an employment agreement

- When an employer is confronted with a breach of contract or wrongful discharge case
- When a worker threatens to file a lawsuit alleging sex harassment
- When there is a significant dispute over the terms of an important clause in an employment contract

the parties may prefer to work out their problems in the privacy of a business suite instead of a crowded public courtroom and negotiate the terms of a settlement based on their best mutual interests. If a mediator (usually a trained lawyer, businessperson, or retired judge) is hired to assist in the process, he or she will not make decisions for the parties but will help them reach an agreement within the realistic limits of their budget.

Resolving a dispute by mediation requires that both parties agree to mediate the dispute. It also requires a good faith effort by the parties to resolve the dispute, not to determine who is right and who is wrong. Nonbinding mediation may not work when one party strongly believes he or she is entitled to punitive or extra damages that can be awarded only by a judge via litigation.

How it works. Various community associations, private enterprises, and the American Arbitration Association (AAA) offer mediation services. The AAA is often selected to assist parties in the mediation process. It is a public-service, nonprofit organization that offers dispute-settlement services to business executives, employers, trade associations, unions, and all levels of government. Services are available through AAA's national office in New York City and through 25 regional offices in major cities throughout the United States.

A list of various mediation and dispute-resolution organizations is included at the end of this chapter.

Once both parties agree to try to solve their differences through mediation, a joint request for mediation is sometimes made through an AAA regional office. The request identifies the parties involved in the dispute, gives their current addresses and phone numbers, and briefly describes the controversy and the issues involved. The employee and the company should include whatever information is helpful to appoint a mediator.

The AAA assigns a mediator from its master list. The parties are then given information about the mediator. Typically, the mediator has no past or present relationship with the parties. A mediator is free to refuse the appointment or resign at any time. Likewise, the

Sample Retainer Agreement with Attorney for Appeal

Date

Name of Client
Address

Dear (Name of Client):

This letter confirms that you have retained me as your attorney to represent you in the defense of an appeal of a judgment granted in your favor by Justice (specify name) on (specify date) in the (specify trial court) and entered on (specify date) in the office of the Clerk. The appeal will be defended in (specify court).

You have agreed to pay to me promptly a retainer of (specify $) as a down payment for legal services to be rendered in this matter. This fee shall be applied against my standard hourly rate of (specify amount). If additional retainers are required, you agree to promptly pay same after receiving and reviewing accurate time sheets sent to you on a monthly basis. However, we have agreed that your final legal bill for all of my services will not exceed (specify $).

In addition to my fee, you also agree to pay for all incidental costs and disbursements incurred in connection with your appeal. Disbursements include, but are not limited to (specify), such as the cost of the trial transcript estimated by the court reporter to be (specify) and the printing of our briefs on appeal. All of these costs and disbursements are estimated to be (specify $) but the actual disbursements may vary from this estimate.

I promise to keep you informed of all developments as they occur and to send you copies of all incoming and outgoing correspondence immediately after it is generated/received. Additionally, I will supply you with drafts of the brief for your comments and approval before it is submitted.

I will personally handle the drafting of your brief and the arguing of any motions or the appeal in court if necessary.

I look forward to working with you on this matter. Kindly indicate your understanding and acceptance of the above terms by signing this letter below where indicated.

Very truly yours,

Name of Attorney

I, (Name of Client), have read and understand the above letter, have received a copy, and accept all of its terms:

_____

Name of Client

parties are free to stop the mediation or ask for the services of a different mediator. If a mediator is unwilling or unable to serve, or if one of the parties requests that the mediator resign from the case, the parties may ask the AAA to recommend another mediator. The mediator is compensated on either an hourly or daily basis. Both parties are informed of potential mediator fees and are sometimes requested to sign a document evidencing approval of the compensation arrangement and an agreement to share fees.

Before choosing a mediator, inquire if the mediator's approach is suited to your needs. Ask the following questions at the initial interview:

- How does the mediator operate?
- How much experience and training does the mediator have?
- What is the mediator's background?
- How many sessions are required?
- How much will mediation cost?

After the initial interview takes place and the mediator is found to be acceptable, he or she will arrange the time and place for each conference with the parties. At the first conference, the parties will be asked to produce information required for the mediator to understand the issues. The mediator may require either party to supplement such information. The mediator will explain what the parties should expect. Good mediators explain that the process is entirely voluntary, that they are not judges and have no power to dictate solutions, and that the parties are free to terminate the mediation process at any time.

A mediator does not have authority to impose a settlement but will attempt to help the parties reach a satisfactory resolution of their dispute. Although usually trained in law, the mediator is not supposed to give legal advice. While parties do not have to be represented by counsel at the mediation sessions, most claimants and employers retain attorneys in employment and business disputes.

Conferences are private. The mediator will meet with both parties, and then sometimes with each privately. Other persons including witnesses, may attend only with the permission of the parties and at the invitation of the mediator.

COUNSEL COMMENTS: The mediator is hired as a consultant, jointly retained, to help the parties work their way through their problems to resolution. At some point the mediator may make a recommendation or proposal. Both parties can agree or disagree or come to a compromise of their own. The mediator will draft a report confirming the agreement. The report is then submitted to the parties for submission to their attorneys for incorporation into a formal document, such as a settlement agreement.

If the parties fail to agree, or do not agree with the mediator's recommendation, they can break off the mediation, consult another mediator, give up, settle their dispute without a mediator, or go to court. The following is a typical mediation scenario from start to finish:

1. The mediator and parties meet at the initial conference. The mediator's role is explained and the responsibilities and rights of the parties are set forth.
2. The mediator designs a schedule for the sessions.
3. The parties sign a formal retainer agreement with the mediator.
4. A method is adopted for obtaining whatever information is required to understand the parties' problems.
5. The mediator identifies the various areas of agreement, defines the issues to be resolved, and assists the parties in their negotiations.
6. A final settlement may be proposed.
7. The mediator arranges for the terms of the settlement to be transmitted to the attorneys of the parties for filing in court, if necessary.

COUNSEL COMMENTS: Some mediators do not possess sufficient skills or training to be effective. Others have been criticized for not ending the process when the interests of each party are not receiving balanced treatment. If the mediator is a lawyer, he or she often has to make an adjustment in attitude. Unlike the lawyer, who tells the client what to do, a mediator must allow the parties enough freedom to structure their own unique solutions to problems. Mediation by attorneys has raised the concern of whether one lawyer can adequately advise two parties with opposing interests and whether a mediator can invoke the attorney-client privilege in any future litigation. For example, if lawyers are present with the parties at mediation sessions and incriminating or damaging statements are made by a client, a lawyer may seek to prevent a judge or jury from hearing such statements in court when the mediation fails. A judge may not allow such oral testimony to be admitted in court depending on a number of facts, such as whether the parties formally agreed beforehand that such statements were confidential and could not be introduced in subsequent court hearings.

TIP: To avoid problems, interview the mediator carefully; be sure to hire the mediator only on the basis of a written retainer agreement. If you believe the process is not working or do not feel comfortable with the person hired, terminate the relationship immediately and discuss further options with your attorney or other professional advisor. Understand that mediation will not work unless both parties are willing to cooperate and recognize the savings and other benefits to be achieved versus litigation, such as:

- eliminating the anxiety of preparing a case before going to court
- avoiding potential poor publicity
- maintaining privacy
- obtaining a quicker result
- eliminating uncertainty as to outcome when the case is tried in court
- maintaining a desire to maintain good business relationships

If either party has a great need to even the score, mediation will probably fail. Speak to your professional advisor to determine if mediation is a proper means of resolving any employment dispute before resorting to litigation or arbitration. Once involved in mediation with a company representative, inquire if that person has sufficient authority to resolve and settle the matter on the company's behalf once a resolution is imminent. Finally, since your lawyer may be able to meet and question important witnesses, the benefits of learning more about your adversary's case may make the exercise worthwhile even if a settlement is not forthcoming. (Note: In some employment lawsuits, nonbinding court-ordered mediation is required before a trial begins. Speak to your lawyer for more details if applicable.)

ARBITRATION PROCEDURES

Arbitration is a formal mechanism for resolving disputes that differs from litigation. Hearings are conducted by arbitrators rather than by judges and are not limited by strict rules of evidence. They can consider all relevant testimony when making an award, including some forms of evidence (e.g., hearsay, questionable copies of documents, etc.,) that would be excluded in a regular court, Arbitrators have the authority to hear witnesses out of order. Their decision is usually final and unappealable. (Note: Limited circumstances for appeals are mentioned later in this section.)

To obtain an arbitration the law requires both parties to agree to the arbitration process beforehand in writing to prevent claims of unfairness by the losing side. Typically in an employment contract, lease, loan agreement, or other document, the relevant clause may state some version of the following:

> *"Any controversy or claim arising out of or relating to this agreement or the breach thereof, shall be settled by arbitration in accordance with the rules of the American Arbitration Association and judgment upon the award rendered by the arbitrator(s) may be entered in any court having jurisdiction thereof."*

ADVANTAGES OF ARBITRATION

Expense. Substantial savings can be achieved through arbitration. Attorney fees are reduced because the average hearing is shorter than the average trial (typically less than a day versus several days). Time consuming and expensive pre-trial procedures, including depositions, interrogatories, and motions, are usually eliminated. Out-of-pocket expenses are reduced because stenographic fees, transcripts, and other items are not required.

Time. Arbitration hearings and final awards are obtained quickly; cases are usually decided in a matter of months, compared to several years in formal litigation.

Privacy. The arbitration hearing is held in a private conference room, rather than a courtroom. Unlike a trial, the hearing cannot be attended by the general public.

Expertise of arbitrators. Arbitrators usually have special training in the area of the case. In a breach of an entertainment contract dispute, for example, arbitrators serving on the panel are typically respected lawyers or other professionals with significant experience in the entertainment industry. Their knowledge of trade customs helps them identify and understand a problem more quickly than a judge or jury.

Increased odds of obtaining an award. Some lawyers believe that arbitrators are more likely than judges to split close cases down the middle. The theory is that arbitrators bend over backwards to satisfy both parties to some degree since their rulings are final and binding. This tendency to compromise, if true, benefits claimants with weaker cases.

DISADVANTAGES OF ARBITRATION

Finality. Arbitrators, unlike judges, need not give formal reasons for their decisions. They are not required to maintain a formal record of the proceedings. The arbitrator's decision is binding. This means that an appeal cannot be taken if you lose the case or disagree with the size of the award except in a few extraordinary circumstances where arbitrator misconduct, dishonesty, or bias can be proved.

Arbitrator selection. The parties sometimes agree that each will select its own arbitrator. In such cases it may be assumed that the chosen arbitrators are more sympathetic to one side than the other. However, arbitrators are usually selected from a list of neutral names supplied by the AAA. This method generally eliminates bias.

Loss of sympathetic juries. Some knowledgeable lawyers believe that juries tend to empathize more with certain kinds of people such as fired employees, destitute wives, and older individuals. Arbitrators are usually successful lawyers and business people whose philosophical orientation may lean more toward companies rather than individuals.

Loss of discovery devices. Some claimants must rely upon an adversary's documents and records to prove their case. For example, sales agents, authors, patent holders, and others often depend upon their company's (or licensee's) sales figures and accurate record keeping to determine how much commission and royalties they are owed. The same is true for minority shareholders who seek a proper assessment of a company's profit picture.

These people may find a disadvantage in the arbitration process. Trial lawyers have ample opportunity to view the private books and records of an adversary long before the day of the trial. This is accomplished by pre-trial discovery devices, which include interrogatories, depositions, and notices to produce documents for inspection and copying. However, these devices are not readily available to litigants in arbitration. In many instances, records are not available for inspection until the day of the arbitration hearing, This makes it difficult to detect whether they are accurate and complete. And, it is often up the arbitrator's discretion whether to grant an adjournment for the purposes of reviewing such records. Such requests may be refused.

Sexual harassment and sex discrimination issues are currently being resolved in arbitration as well as by litigation. Often an employee prefers that her matter *not* be resolved through arbitration because punitive and other special damages are not granted in an arbitrator's award in many states. However, if you signed an employment agreement containing an arbitration clause, you may be forced to arbitrate your case (including claims made by a fired employee for age discrimination under the Age Discrimination in Employment Act).

TIP: Courts favor resolving cases through arbitration when agreed beforehand by the parties. Thus, it is essential to understand the ramifications of signing any employment agreement or contract containing an arbitration clause.

Angela is a salesperson working for an investment banking firm. She complains that her superiors created a hostile atmosphere designed to discriminate against female employees at the firm where she works. She hires a lawyer and files a sex discrimination lawsuit in federal court.

The employer seeks to stay the litigation and compel binding arbitration. It argues that she signed a Form U-4, common to people working in the securities industry. The Form U-4 contains an arbitration clause which states that the parties agree to settle all disputes via arbitration.

Angela's lawyer argues she was never told that the Form U-4 precluded her from commencing an action for sex discrimination. However, the court rules against Angela and states that her matter must be resolved through arbitration. Angela is very disappointed because she cannot obtain a jury trial, reimbursement for her lawyer and expert witness fees, or punitive and large compensatory damage awards via arbitration.

SUMMARY OF STEPS LEADING TO THE HEARING

Commencing the hearing is a relatively simple matter once arbitration has been selected as the method of resolving a dispute. A party or her lawyer sends a notice called a Demand for Arbitration to the adversary. See page 278 for an example of this notice. Copies of the demand are sent to the American Arbitration Association, along with the appropriate administrative fee. The AAA is most often selected to arbitrate disputes. It is a public service nonprofit organization which offers dispute settlement services through the national office in New York City and dozens of regional offices in major cities throughout the United States.

The notice briefly describes the controversy. It specifies the kind of relief sought, including the amount of monetary damages requested. A response to the charges is then sent by the opposing party, usually within seven days. This may also assert a counterclaim for damages. Either party can add or change claims in writing until the arbitrator is appointed. Once this occurs, changes and additional claims can only be made with the arbitrator's consent.

After the AAA receives the Demand for Arbitration and reply, an AAA administrator usually supplies the parties with a list of potential arbitrators. The list contains the arbitrator's name, current occupation, place of employment and appropriate background information. The parties mutually agree to nominees from this list. Potential arbitrators are obligated to notify the AAA immediately of any facts likely to affect their impartiality (e.g., prior dealings with one of the litigants), and disqualify themselves where appropriate. (Note: If the parties do not agree beforehand to the number of arbitrators, the dispute is decided by one arbitrator, unless the AAA determines that three arbitrators is appropriate.)

Once the arbitrator is selected, the AAA administrator schedules a convenient hearing date and location. There is no direct communication between the parties and the arbitrator until the hearing date; all requests and inquiries are received by the administrator and relayed to the arbitrator. This avoids the appearance of impropriety. The parties are free to request a pre-hearing conference to exchange documents and resolve certain issues. Typically, however, the parties, administrators, lawyers, and arbitrator meet face-to-face for the first time at the actual hearing.

THE ARBITRATION HEARING

Most hearings are conducted in a conference room at an AAA regional office. A stenographer is present, if requested. (Note: The requesting party generally bears the cost.) The arbitrator introduces the parties and typically asks each side to briefly summarize its version of the dispute and what each intends to prove at the hearing.

The complainant's case is presented first. Witnesses are called to give testimony (usually under oath). After witnesses finish speaking, they are usually cross-examined by the opposing party's lawyer. They may also be questioned by the arbitrator. The complainant introduces all its witnesses, documents, and affidavits until it has finished presenting its side of the case.

The opposing party then introduces its witnesses and documents to defend its case and/or prove damages. After the opposition has concluded its case, both sides are usually requested to make a brief summary of the facts (i.e., what they felt was proved at the hearing). Sometimes the arbitrator may request that legal briefs be submitted that summarize the respective position of the parties before rendering a final decision.

Arbitrators are generally required to render written decisions within 30 days unless the parties agree to some other time period. The arbitrator can make any award that is equitable. She can order the losing party to pay additional costs, including AAA filing fees and arbitrator fees. Legal fees may be awarded if the arbitration clause so provides. See page 279 for an example Award of Arbitrator.

Arbitrators volunteer their time for hearings lasting under two full days; they are paid a reasonable per diem rate (up to $750) for additional hearings. If the parties settle their dispute prior to a decision, they may request that the terms of the settlement be embodied in the consent award.

Arbitrators have no contact with the parties after the hearing is concluded. The parties are notified in writing by the AAA administrator and are sent a copy of the award. The decision in a typical employment case is brief — usually no formal reasons are given to explain why a particular award was rendered or the basis on which damages were calculated.

It is practically impossible to appeal a losing case. The arbitrator has no power once the case is decided. The matter can be

American Arbitration Association

Commercial Arbitration Rules
Demand for Arbitration

Date:

TO: Name of Employer
(Name of party upon whom the Demand is made)
(Address)
(City and State) (Zip Code)
(Telephone)

Named claimant, a party to an arbitration agreement contained in a written contract, dated _____ providing for arbitration, hereby demands arbitration thereunder.

(attach arbitration clause or quote hereunder, such as)

"Any controversy or claim arising out of or relating to this contract, or any breach thereof, shall be settled in accordance with the Rules of the American Arbitration Association, and judgment upon the award may be entered in any court having jurisdiction thereof."

NATURE OF DISPUTE: Breach of contract action

CLAIM OR RELIEF SOUGHT: (amount, if any) $50,000 plus attorney fees as payment of salary through the termination date of employment agreement

TYPE OF BUSINESS:

Claimant/<u>Executive</u> Respondent/<u>Financial</u>

HEARING LOCALE REQUESTED: <u>New York City - NY</u> (City and State)

You are hereby notified that copies of our arbitration agreement and of this demand are being filed with the American Arbitration Association at its <u>New York</u> Regional Office, with the request that it commence the administration of the arbitration. Under Section 7 of the Commercial Arbitration Rules, you may file an answering statement within seven days after notice from the Administrator.

Signed
(May Be Signed by Attorney)

Name of Claimant _____

Home or Business Address of Claimant _____

City and State _____ Zip Code _____
Telephone _____

Name of Attorney <u>Steven Mitchell Sack, Esq.</u>
Attorney's Address <u>135 East 57th Street, 12th floor</u>
City and State <u>New York, NY.</u> Zip Code <u>10022</u>
Telephone <u>212-702-9000</u>   FAX <u>212-702-9702</u>

To institute proceedings, please send three copies of this Demand with the administrative fee, as provided in Section 48 of the Rules, to the AAA. Send original Demand to Respondent.

Award of Arbitrator

In the Matter of Arbitration between

_____

Sally Smith
And
Doe Corporation Inc.   Case No.

_____

I, the undersigned Arbitrator, having been designated in accordance with the Arbitration Agreement entered into by the above named Parties, and dated (specify), and having been duly sworn and having heard the proofs and allegations of the Parties, AWARD as follows:

    1. Within ten (10) days from the date of this AWARD, Doe Corporation Inc. ("Doe") shall pay to Sally Smith ("Smith"), the sum of Twenty Five Thousand Eighteen Dollars ($25,018.00), plus interest in the amount of Two Thousand Two Hundred Dollars ($2,200.00).

    2. The counterclaim of Doe against Smith is hereby denied in its entirety.

    3. The administrative fees of the American Arbitration Association totaling Eleven Hundred Dollars ($1,100.00) shall be borne equally by the Parties. Therefore, Doe shall pay Smith the sum of Five Hundred Fifty Dollars ($550.00) representing one half (50%) of the filing fees previously advanced by Smith to the AAA.

    4. Each Party shall pay one half (50%) of the Arbitrator's fee in this arbitration.

    5. This AWARD is in full settlement of all claims and counterclaims submitted in this arbitration.

_____
Signature of Arbitrator

Dated: _____

reviewed only by a judge, and judges cannot overturn the award on the grounds of insufficient evidence. The only ways a case can be overturned on review generally are:

- For arbitrator dishonesty, partiality, or bias
- When no valid agreement was entered into that authorized the arbitration process
- When an issue that the arbitrator was not authorized to decide was ruled upon

Awards are modifiable only if there was a miscalculation of figures, or a mistake in the description of the person, property, or thing referred to in the award.

How To Increase The Chances of Success in Arbitration

Since the arbitrator's award is final and binding, it is essential to prepare and present a case properly the first time around, because you won't get a second chance. The following strategies may help increase the chances of success.

Hire a lawyer. People have the right to appear themselves (pro se), but it's best to have a lawyer represent you at the hearing, particularly if the dispute involves a large amount of money or complicated legal questions. The familiar expression, "He who represents himself has a fool for a client," is certainly applicable in arbitrations. Seek the services of an experienced lawyer who is familiar with the intricacies of the arbitration process. Ask your prospective lawyer how many times she has represented clients in arbitration within the past several years. If the answer is "never" or "only a few times," look elsewhere for representation.

Prepare for the hearing. It is important that both you and your lawyer submit evidence to prove the case, so:

- Organize the facts - Gather and label all documents needed at the hearing so they can be produced in an orderly fashion.
- Prepare a checklist of documents and exhibits so nothing will be forgotten during the presentation.
- Make copies of all documents for the arbitrator and adversary.
- If some of the documents needed are in the possession of the other party, ask they be brought to the hearing or subpoenaed.

- Interview witnesses.

- Be sure that friendly witnesses will attend and testify; if there is a possibility that additional witnesses may have to appear, alert them to be available on call without delay.

- Select witnesses who are believable, who understand the case and the importance of their testimony, and who will not say things at the hearing to surprise you.

- Coordinate the witnesses' testimony so your case will seem consistent and credible.

- Prepare witnesses for the rigors of cross-examination.

- If a translator is required, make arrangements in advance.

- Prepare a written summary of what each witness will hopefully prove and refer to it at the hearing.

- Anticipate what the opponent will say to defeat your claim and be prepared to refute such evidence.

- Practice your story to put you at ease and help organize the facts.

- Prepare a list of questions your lawyer should ask the opponent at the hearing.

- Dress appropriately by wearing conservative business clothes.

- Act professionally and show respect for the arbitrator.

- Listen to the arbitrator's questions and instructions; never argue with the arbitrator.

- If a question is posed while you are speaking, stop talking immediately.

- Answer all questions honestly and directly.

- Avoid arguing with your opponent at the hearing; interrupt his presentation only where absolutely necessary.

Finally, most losing parties voluntarily comply with the terms of an unfavorable award. However, if you win and your opponent decides not to pay, you can enforce the judgment in a regular court. Speak to a lawyer for more details if applicable.

BRINGING SUIT IN SMALL-CLAIMS COURT

Before considering filing a lawsuit in small-claims court, attempt to resolve your dispute in a reasonable fashion. It is often best to write a demand letter to your employer or ex-employer and send it certified mail, return receipt requested. In addition to documenting your claim, the letter will advise the company that the matter must be corrected to your immediate satisfaction or you will take additional action. If there is no response to your letter, send a follow-up letter reporting that your initial letter has not been answered. The letter should also state what your next step will be if this letter is ignored.

If you cannot get satisfaction in an employment, financial, or business dispute by personal negotiations, you might consider suing in small-claims court. Small-claims courts, which help you collect wages, commissions, and money in an inexpensive manner without hiring a lawyer, hear over one million cases a year in the U.S. They can be used in many situations. For example, you may wish to sue for money damages when your employer fails to pay you or someone damages your property and refuses to pay for repairs. Many small-claims courts have night sessions and matters are resolved quickly, sometimes within a month from the time an action is filed. The maximum amount of money you can recover varies from state to state. It is usually up to $3,500.

The following guidelines describe the procedures of a typical small-claims court. However, the rules vary in each city and state. Before you contemplate starting a lawsuit, call the clerk of that court and ask for a written explanation of the specific procedural rules to be followed.

Who can be sued?   Small-claims court can be used to sue any person, business, partnership, corporation, or government body owing you money. If you sue in small-claims court and recover a judgment, you are precluded from suing again to recover any additional money owed to you. Thus, if your claim greatly exceeds the maximum amount of money that might be awarded in small-claims court consider hiring a lawyer and instituting suit in a higher court.

Do you have a valid claim?   In order to be successful, you must have a valid claim. This means that you must:

- identify the person or business that damaged or caused you harm;
- calculate the amount of damages you suffered;
- show that there is some basis in law to have a court award you damages; and
- be sure that you were not the main cause of your own harm, that you haven't waited too long to start the action (statute of limitations), and that you did not sign a written release.

Where to sue. Call your local bar association, city hall, or the county courthouse to discover where the nearest small-claims court is located. (In some states small-claims court is called justice court, district court, municipal court, or justice of the peace court.) In most states, suit must be brought in the county in which the person or business you are suing lives or does business. Confirm this with the small-claims court clerk and ask what days and hours the court is in session. Also find out the maximum amount of money you can sue for, what documents are needed to file a complaint, the filing fee, and whether this can be paid by cash, check, or money order.

What can you sue for? You can sue only to collect money. Thus, before you begin to sue in small-claims court, estimate the amount of money you wish to collect. When calculating the amount of your claim, include all incurred expenses, including gasoline bills, tolls, telephone costs, losses due to time missed from work, sales tax, and interest, if applicable. Save all your receipts for this purpose.

Starting the lawsuit. You begin the lawsuit by paying a small fee (about $5) and either going to the court in person or mailing in a complaint that states the following information:

- your name and address
- the complete name and address of the person, business, or company you are suing (the defendant)
- the amount of money you believe you are owed
- the facts of your case
- the reasons you (the plaintiff) are seeking redress. If you are filing a claim on behalf of an individually owned business, you must list the name of the owner in addition to the name of the business. If you are filing a claim on behalf of a partnership, you must list the name of the partnership as the plaintiff. (Note: some states do not allow a corporation to sue someone in small-claims court.)

Be sure to write the accurate and complete name and address of the defendant on the complaint. Write the corporation's formal name rather than its "doing business as" (d/b/a) name. Thus, if you are suing a corporation, contact the county clerk's office in the county where the corporation does business to obtain its proper name and address. Better still, call the department of corporations in your state to obtain such information.

At this time, you may also be required to prepare another form called a "summons," which notifies your opponent of the lawsuit. Sometimes the clerk will do this. Ask the clerk whether the court will mail the summons by registered or first-class mail, personally serve the defendant on your behalf, or whether you must hire a professional process server. If a professional process server is required, ask what is necessary to prove that service was accomplished. You may have to pay the process server an additional fee (between $20 and $50). However, if you win your case, you can ask the judge to include the process server's fee in the award. When the clerk gives you a hearing date, be sure that it is convenient and you have no other commitments.

The defendant's response.   When the person or company you are suing receives the summons, the defendant or his or her attorney can:

- deny your claim by mailing a response to the court
- deny your claim by personally appearing in court on the day of the hearing
- sue you for money you supposedly owe (this is called a "counter-claim")
- contact you to settle the matter out of court

If an offer of payment is made, ask to be reimbursed for all filing and service costs. Notify the court that you are dismissing the action only after you receive payment. (If you are paid by check, wait until the check clears.) Do not postpone the case. Tell your opponent that unless you are paid before the day of the trial, you are prepared to go to court and either commence with the trial or stipulate the offer of settlement to the judge.

If a written denial is mailed to the court, ask the clerk to read it to you over the phone or go to the court and read it yourself. This is your right and may help you prepare for your opponent's defense. The following is an example of a simple denial in an answer: "I deny each and every allegation in the face of the complaint." Now you must prove your allegations in court to recover your claim.

Your duties as the moving party.   It is up to you to follow the progress of your case. Call the clerk and refer to the docket number to discover whether the defendant received the complaint and whether it was answered. If you discover that the defendant did not receive the complaint by the day of the trial, request that the clerk issue a new complaint to be served by a sheriff or process server. Go to court that day anyway, to be sure that the case is not dismissed because of your failure to appear.

If the complaint is personally served and your employer does not appear at the trial, he will be in default and you may be awarded a judgment automatically. In some states you still have to prove your case in order to be successful. Also, defendants sometimes file motions (legal affidavits) requesting the court to remove the default judgment on the grounds that there was a valid reason for not attending the hearing. If this motion is granted, your trial will be rescheduled.

If you are unable to come to court on the day of the trial, send a certified letter, return receipt requested, to the clerk, asking for a continuance. The letter should specify the reasons you will be unable to appear and include future dates when you will be able to come to court. Send a copy of this letter to your opponent. When you receive a new date, send your opponent a certified letter, return receipt requested, informing the employer of the revised date. Requests for continuances are sometimes not honored. Call the clerk on the day of the original trial date to be sure that your request has been granted. Be prepared to send a friend or relative to court to ask for a continuance on your behalf if a continuance has not been obtained by the day of the trial.

Preparing for trial. You have several weeks to prepare for trial. Use the time wisely. First, be sure that your friendly witnesses, if any, will attend the trial and testify on your behalf. Select witnesses who are believable and who will not say things that will surprise you. In some states, you can present the judge with signed affidavits or statements of witnesses who are unable to appear at the trial. Some states also permit judges to hear testimony via conference telephones.

If necessary, the clerk can issue a subpoena to ensure the attendance of important witnesses who you believe may refuse to attend and testify. A subpoena is a document that orders a person to testify or produce books, papers, and other physical objects on a specified date. If the subpoena is issued and the person refuses to appear, a judge can direct a sheriff to bring the witness into court or even impose a jail sentence for a willful violation of the order.

When you come to court for the trial, check to see if the clerk has received any subpoenaed documents. If such records are crucial to your case and have not been received, you can ask for a continuance. If you have subpoenaed an individual and do not know what he or she looks like, ask the clerk to call out the name to determine if he or she is present so you can proceed with the trial.

To maximize your chances of success, organize your case before the trial. Gather and label all your evidence so that you can produce the documents easily. You may also wish to speak with a lawyer or call a lawyer's referral service for legal advice. Many communities have such advisory organizations, and they are willing to inform you, without charge, about relevant cases and statutes. This may help you know to what damages you are legally entitled. You may cite these laws, if applicable, at the hearing.

The trial. Arrive early, locate the correct courtroom, find the name of your case on the court calendar, and check in with the clerk. You should be properly attired, preferably in business clothes. Come prepared with all relevant documents. Examples are:

- receipts and canceled checks
- correspondence
- contracts
- letters of protest demanding unpaid wages
- unpaid invoices
- contemporaneous memos of promises and statements made to you
- signed affidavits or statements from friends and witnesses unable to appear at the hearing
- an accountant's statement of lost wages
- prior years' tax returns
- diagrams or charts
- copies of applicable statutes, cases, and regulations

When your case is called, you and your opponent will be sworn. The judge or court-appointed arbitrator will conduct the hearing and ask you questions. Be relaxed. Keep your presentation brief and to the point. Tell why you are suing the defendant and what monetary damages you are seeking. Show your evidence. Bring along a short written summary of the case. You can refer to it during the trial, and if the judge does not come to an immediate decision, he or she can use your outline for reference. Talk directly to the judge and respond to his or her questions. Show respect. Always refer to him or her as "Your Honor" or "Judge." Listen to the judge's instructions and never argue. If the judge asks you a question while you are speaking, stop immediately. Then answer the question honestly and to the point. Be diplomatic rather than emotional. Also, avoid arguing with your opponent in court and never interrupt his or her presentation.

After both sides finish speaking, you will have the opportunity to refute what your opponent has told the judge. Do not be intimidated if he or she is accompanied by a lawyer. Simply inform the judge that you are not represented by counsel and are not familiar with small-claims court procedures. Ask the judge to intercede on your behalf if you feel that your opponent's attorney is treating you unfairly. Most judges will be sympathetic, since small-claims courts are specially designed for you to present your case without an attorney.

If you are a defendant. Follow the same procedures as the plaintiff; prepare your testimony, contact your witnesses to be sure that they will appear at the trial and testify on your behalf; collect your exhibits and documents; arrive early on the day of the trial and check in with the clerk. If you have any doubts about your case, try to settle with the plaintiff before the judge hears the case. Request that the case be dismissed if your opponent fails to appear. Your opponent will speak first if he or she appears. Wait until he or she is finished speaking before telling your side of the story. Point out any inconsistencies or flaws in your opponent's story. Conclude your remarks by highlighting the important aspects of the case.

> **TIP:** Some states require that you send a "30-day demand letter" before filing a small-claims action. The letter should briefly describe your money loss and what you want the employer to do to remedy the situation. Add that you are giving the employer 30 days to make a good-faith response; otherwise, you will begin legal action. Send the letter certified mail, return receipt requested, and consider sending copies to your state's attorney general's office and your attorney.

If the letter is answered and the ex-employer refuses to pay, you may learn what position it intends to take at the trial. If your letter is ignored, that is evidence in court.

COUNSEL COMMENTS: In certain states, an employer's willful failure to pay earned vacation money, wages, or other accrued compensation or promised benefits may cause it to be liable for extra statutory damages (such as an additional 25%) plus legal costs and expenses. Check your state's law to ascertain whether this applies in your case.

Obtaining judgment. Some small-claims court judges render oral decisions on the spot. Others issue a decision in writing several days after the hearing. This gives them time to weigh the testimony and exhibits. If your opponent failed to attend the hearing, judges usually render a judgment of default immediately after your presentation.

If you win the case, make sure you know how and when payment will be made. Check to see that all your disbursements, including court costs, filing fees, service of process, and applicable witness fees, are added to the amount of your judgment. Send a copy of the decision by certified mail, return receipt requested, to your opponent, together with a letter requesting payment. Some states require that payment be made to the court; others allow payment to be made directly to you.

Do not hesitate to act if you do not receive the money. First, contact the clerk and file a Petition for Notice to Show Cause. This will be sent to the defendant, ordering the employer to come into court and explain why it has not paid. You should also file an Order of Execution with the sheriff's, constable's, or clerk's office in the county where the defendant is located or owns a business. This will enable you to discover where the defendant has assets. The sheriff or other enforcement agent has the power to go out and collect the judgment either by seizing personal property, freezing the defendant's bank accounts, placing a lien on any real estate, or even garnisheeing an individuals' salary where appropriate. The clerk of your small-claims court should tell you exactly what to do to collect your judgment.

FINAL COUNSEL COMMENTS: By bringing suit in small-claims court, you usually waive your right to a trial by jury. However, the defendant can surprise you. Some states allow defendants to move a small-claims court case to a higher court and/or obtain a trial by jury. If this occurs, you will need a lawyer to represent you, and his or her services could cost as much as your claim in the dispute.

Some states do not allow losing plaintiffs to appeal. Also, an appeals court will overturn the decision of a small-claims court judge only if there is strong proof that the judge was biased or dishonest. This may be difficult to prove.

WORKERS' COMPENSATION

Each state has enacted its own particular laws with respect to workers' compensation benefits, which provide aid for employees who suffer job-related injuries. Compensation may be available for the following kinds of injuries:

- Preexisting conditions that the workplace accelerates or aggravates, such as a bad back, even if pain from the injury is delayed until a later time.

- Injuries caused during breaks, lunch hours, and work-sponsored recreational activities (such as a company-paid New Year's Eve party), and on-the-job injuries caused by company facilities, such as a shower located on premises.

- Diseases such as lung cancer, if contracted by asbestos or other carcinogenic exposure at work as a result of the usual conditions to which the worker was exposed by his/her employment.

- Injuries resulting from mental and physical strain brought on by increased work duties or the stress caused by a requirement that the employee make decisions on other employee dismissals. In some states, this includes employees who develop a disabling mental condition because they cannot keep up with the demands of the job and a supervisor's constant harassment.

In all states, employers with more than several workers are obligated to maintain workers' compensation insurance through a company or be self-insured for the benefit of their employees (not independent contractors). The advantage to employers is that they cannot be sued in court for injuries sustained by workers during the course of employment even if an accident was caused by an employer's fault (negligence). Lawyers representing injured workers typically prefer that their clients not receive workers' compensation benefits because the potential of being awarded money for damages in a personal injury lawsuit is vastly greater.

Not every on-the-job injury is covered under workers' compensation. State courts seem to be divided on whether an injured employee can recover for horseplay. Many states will not award benefits to a person who is injured while intoxicated or who deliberately inflicts injury on herself. Furthermore, an employee who is injured while traveling to or from work is not generally entitled to benefits unless the employer has agreed to provide the worker with the means of transportation, pay the employee's cost of commuting, or if travel is required while performing his/her duties. For example, if the employee regularly dictates office memos into a dictating machine within a vehicle, the car may be deemed part of his/her workplace.

If a worker leaves the employer's premises to do a personal errand, no compensation should be due. However, if an employee is injured while returning from company-sponsored education classes, when an employee goes to the restroom, visits the cafeteria, has a coffee break, or steps out of a nonsmoking office to smoke a cigarette, workers' comp boards and courts typically recognize that employers benefit from these "nonbusiness" employee conveniences and often award compensation.

Always alert your employer immediately if you are injured on the job. Under compensation laws in most states, each employer must promptly provide medical, surgical, optometric, or other treatment for injured employees as well as provide hospital care, crutches, eyeglasses, and other appliances necessary to repair, relieve, or support a part of the body. Your company's medical team may eliminate unnecessary treatment, but an injured employee may select her own physician for authorized treatment, provided that physician is authorized by the state's workers' compensation board.

COUNSEL COMMENTS: Employers may engage the services of a competent physician to review the medical care an injured worker is receiving. Such a person may be able to determine, for example, whether less expensive home care is more appropriate than hospital care. A medical consultant can also evaluate claims from the employee's doctor to see if they are self-serving.

TIP: Do not be afraid of reporting an accident or filing a claim in writing. Most states prohibit companies from firing, demoting, or otherwise punishing an employee for filing or pursuing a valid workers' compensation claim. Do this as quickly as possible so your case is not dismissed as being untimely. While you are receiving medical treatment, save all receipts of drug purchases, trips to the doctor (including tolls and cab fares), and all related purchases. You are generally entitled to full reimbursement for all direct out-of-pocket expenses, including payment for doctors, hospitals, rehabilitation, and related therapy costs. Dependents are entitled to receive death benefits in case of death, and you will be compensated for the loss of a limb or body part (such as an eye) based on a predetermined schedule. You are also entitled to compensation for loss of wages and income. The type of disability you suffered (e.g., temporary, permanent, partial, and/or total disability) will determine the amount of money you receive each week and how long you will receive such benefits. Each state has maximum limits for weekly benefits that typically do not exceed 75% of a worker's regular weekly salary.

Do not hesitate to consult a lawyer specializing in workers' compensation injuries or a personal injury lawyer where applicable, particularly if your employer refuses to provide benefits. A lawyer can protect your rights in many ways. For example, if anyone other than your employer or co-worker was even partly responsible for the accident, you may be free to file your own liability insurance claim against that person or business. If for any reason your accident is not covered by workers' compensation because you are an independent contractor or because the company has no coverage, you may be able to file a lawsuit against your employer in the same fashion that you could sue anyone who causes you personal injury. In such a case, additional damages such as attorney fees, money for mental pain and suffering, loss of companionship to a spouse, and even punitive damages, may be awarded.

Under certain circumstances you may also be able to collect Social Security benefits, retirement benefits or unemployment compensation, and health insurance payments while you are collecting disability benefits. A labor lawyer or one who specializes in workers' compensation law can advise you. A knowledgeable lawyer's services may be required to argue your case at the hearing stage before an administrative law judge, especially when the issues are not clear-cut (such as when and where the accident occurred, to determine initially if workers' compensation is applicable). Lawyers handling workers' compensation matters are generally quite knowledgeable about medical conditions and dealing with doctors. Resolving an issue of whether an accident caused a partial or permanent disability can involve tens of thousands of dollars in future wages.

(Note: Typically workers' compensation lawyers work on a contingency fee basis.) It may also be necessary to retain the services of a lawyer if you want to pursue an unsuccessful verdict at the appeals stage. Thus, consult a specialist for advice and guidance where applicable.

SUMMARY OF STEPS TO MAXIMIZE A DISCRIMINATION CLAIM

1. If you believe you have been victimized by employment discrimination, consider filing a discrimination charge with the EEOC and/or your state agency. In some states, filing a charge with either the EEOC or a state agency will be treated as filing with both. Speak to a labor lawyer for advice because some state statutes provide greater protection and some state agencies have more powers than the EEOC.

2. EEOC offices are listed in the telephone directory under United States Government or you can call 800-669-4000. State agencies can be located by calling your state's department of labor or an EEOC office in your area.

3. Typically you must give your name if you want an investigation to proceed, but you cannot be retaliated against for filing a charge.

4. Although some state agencies permit a longer period (e.g., up to 300 days depending on state law), you must file a charge with the EEOC within 180 days of the date the last incident occurred to be timely.

5. Although you may file a private lawsuit in federal court, once you file a charge with the EEOC you cannot litigate the matter privately until the EEOC dismisses your case (finds "no probable cause") or rules in

your favor. In either situation you then have 90 days to file a private lawsuit to be timely after receiving a final disposition notice (called a "right-to-sue" letter) from the EEOC.

6. Obtaining a favorable decision does not automatically mean that you will receive big bucks. The employer may appeal a state agency or EEOC decision and force you to sue it in federal court.

7. Call the EEOC officer assigned to your case regularly to determine the status of the investigation and action taken in your case. Be assertive and follow the progress of your case. Whenever you receive a request for information, provide this immediately to the investigator.

8. If you are unhappy with the progress of the investigation or how the case is being handled, consult an attorney for guidance and advice. Consider joining a class action lawsuit if one already exists against your employer or ex-employer. By doing so, however, you may have to withdraw from a private action.

9. Be patient. The EEOC often takes years to render its decision and the employer may delay the final outcome years more by refusing to settle and appealing the case further. Some investigators leave the agency while working on your case and a new investigator has to be assigned, causing further delay. Thus, recognize that in most situations, even with a good case, you may not receive justice for many years.

List of Mediation and Dispute Resolution Organizations

American Arbitration Association (AAA)
140 W. 51st Street
New York, NY 10020
212-484-4000

American Bar Association (ABA)
Section of Dispute Resolution
740 15th Street NW
Washington, DC 20009
202-662-1680

National Institute for Dispute Resolution
1901 L Street NW, Suite 600
Washington, DC 20036
202-862-7200

Council of Better Business Bureaus
4200 Wilson Boulevard, Suite 800
Arlington, VA 22203
703-276-0100

Author's Note: The above organizations may be able to provide additional information about specific areas of dispute resolution. Many offer catalogs of publications, as well as brochures of general information.

List of Significant Women's Organizations

Equal Rights Advocates
1663 Mission Street, Suite 550
San Francisco, CA 94103
415-621-0672

Federation of Organizations For Professional Women
2001 S Street NW, Suite 540
Washington, DC 20009
202-328-1415

Formerly Employed Mothers at the Leading Edge (FEMALE)
PO Box 31
Elmhurst, IL 60126
708-941-3553

9 to 5, National Association of Working Women
614 Superior Avenue, NW
Cleveland, OH 44113
216-566-9308 or 800-522-0925

National Women's Law Center
1616 P Street NW, Suite 100
Washington, DC 20036
202-328-5160

U.S. Department of Labor, Women's Bureau
200 Constitution Avenue NW
Washington, DC 20210
800-827-5355

Significant Women's Organizations (continued)

Women's Legal Defense Fund
1875 Connecticut Avenue NW, Suite 710
Washington, DC 20009
202-986-2600

Coalition of Labor Union Women
1126 16th Street NW
Washington, DC 20036
202-296-1200

Author's Note: Many of these organizations give advice and counsel on legal issues impacting women, such as sexual harassment, pregnancy discrimination, and family leave. Excellent referrals and free assistance may be obtained by calling a hotline number.

List of Important Federal and State Agencies to Contact

For Civil Rights Violations

Commission on Civil Rights, Washington, DC

American Civil Liberties Union
132 West 43rd Street
New York, NY 10036
212-944-9800

National Association for the Advancement of Colored People, Washington, DC

National Organization for Women, New York, NY

For Discrimination Complaints

American Civil Liberties Union, New York, NY

Equal Employment Opportunity Commission
1801 L Street NW
Washington, DC 20506
800-669-EEOC; (800-669-4000 for a list of regional offices)
202-663-4264

U.S. Department of Labor
200 Constitution Avenue NW
Washington, DC 20210
202-219-6666

Concerning the Elderly

American Association of Retired Persons, Washington, DC

National Council on the Aging, Washington, DC

Social Security Administration, Washington, DC

Equal Employment Opportunity Commission, Washington, DC

List of Important Federal and State Agencies to Contact (continued)

Concerning the Elderly (continued)

American Association of Retired Persons
601 E Street NW
Washington, DC 20049
800-424-3410

For Discrimination Concerning the Handicapped

Equal Employment Opportunity Commission, Washington, DC

U.S. Department of Transportation, Washington, DC

State Attorney General's office

Pension and Welfare Benefits Administration, Washington, DC

President's Committee on Employment of People With Disabilities
1331 F Street NW
Washington, DC 20004-1107
202-376-6200

Social Security Administration, Washington, DC

For Safety and Health Complaints

U.S. Department of Labor
Occupational Safety and Health Administration (OSHA)
Frances Perkins Building
200 Constitution Avenue NW
Washington, DC 20210
202-219-6091

For Information on Labor Unions

AFL-CIO, Washington, DC

202-637-5000

National Labor Relations Board

1099 Fourteenth Street NW

Washington, DC

202-273-1991

Pension Information

Division of Public Disclosure

U.S. Department of Labor

Room N5507

Washington, DC 20210

202-219-8771

Pension Rights Center

918 16th Street NW, Suite 704

Washington, DC 20006

202-296-3778

Pension Benefit Guaranty Corporation

Case Operations and Compliance

1200 K Street NW

Washington, DC 20005

202-326-4000

Pension and Welfare Benefits Administration

1730 K Street NW, Suite 556

Washington, D.C. 20006

202-254-7013

CHAPTER TEN

HOW TO HIRE
AND WORK EFFECTIVELY
WITH A LAWYER

Labor laws and regulations are unduly complicated and people often need attorneys to guide them properly. The time to determine whether you need an employment lawyer is before legal action is considered. Common situations that might call for legal help include:

- Deciding to resign from a lucrative job
- Considering filing a discrimination case with the EEOC or a state agency, or filing a private lawsuit in federal or state court.
- Before commencing or threatening to file a lawsuit for breach of contract, commissions, wages, bonuses, benefits, or other monies due
- Negotiating severance and other benefits resulting from a firing
- Defending a charge of violating a restrictive covenant
- Reviewing a proposed independent contractor or employment agreement.

The best time to determine whether a lawyer is needed is before legal action is contemplated or necessary, and the best way to decide if a lawyer is needed is to speak to one. Hopefully, you won't be charged for brief information given over the telephone.

HOW TO FIND A LAWYER

Select a lawyer with care. The right choice can mean recovery of thousands of dollars or satisfactory resolution of a conflict or other problem and peace of mind. The wrong choice can cost money and aggravation.

Phone a lawyer you know or who is recommended. Describe your problem and ask whether an interview should be scheduled. Recognize that many attorneys who competently represent clients in one area (e.g., criminal law) are not qualified to represent the same client in an employment matter because most lawyers become familiar with certain types of cases, which they handle promptly, efficiently, and profitably. When lawyers accept matters outside the realm of their daily practice, the chances of making mistakes or not handling matters promptly increases. Ask the attorney what proportion of his working time is spent dealing in the field of law related to your problem. If the lawyer states he does not commonly handle such a matter, ask for the names of other lawyers he is willing to recommend. Clients often receive excellent assistance through attorney referrals.

Ask around for recommendations. If you don't know a lawyer, ask friends or relatives if they can recommend someone.

TIP: Be wary of recommendations from people whose advice may be self-motivated.

Call a local or state bar association. These associations are listed in the phone book, and some maintain lists of lawyers who agree not to charge more than $25 for the first half hour of consultation. If experience is important, tell the person handling the inquiry that you want to contact an experienced practitioner.

Be wary of attorney advertising. Some lawyers have misled the public with their advertising. One common method is to run an advertisement which states that a particular matter costs only $XX. When a potential client meets the attorney, she learns that court costs and filing fees are $XX, but attorney's fees are extra. Also beware of advertisements that proclaim the lawyer is a "specialist." Most state bar associations have not adopted specialist certification programs.

THE INITIAL INTERVIEW

After you find a lawyer who will discuss your case with you, set up an initial interview. This interview will help you obtain a sound evaluation about a legal problem, and helps decide if the attorney you met should be hired. This is also the time to discuss important working details, such as the fee arrangement. Bring all pertinent written information to the initial interview (e.g., copies of contracts, checks, rebuttals to performance reviews, and letters of protest). Tell the lawyer everything related to the matter. Communicate relevant information without inhibition because the discussion is privileged and confidential.

Once the lawyer receives all the pertinent facts, she should be in a position of advising if the matter has any legal validity or consequences depending on state and/or federal law. You should also be advised whether the matter can be resolved through legal assistance. If so, inquire how quickly the lawyer believes the matter can be resolved, what must be done, and how much the lawyer intends to charge for the contemplated services.

If a lawsuit is considered, or if you have been sued and need a lawyer to assist in defense of the case, the attorney will then:

- Decide whether the case has a fair probability of success after considering the law in the state where the suit will be brought
- Give an estimate as to how long the lawsuit will last
- Make a determination of the approximate legal fees and disbursements
- Explain what legal papers will be filed, when, and what their purposes are
- Discuss the defenses an opponent will probably raise, and how to deal with them

If the lawyer sees weaknesses in the case and believes that litigation will be unduly expensive, she may advise to compromise and settle the claim without resorting to litigation. In any event, the chosen course of action should be instituted without delay to be able to receive remuneration as quickly as possible and insure that the requisite time period to start the action (i.e., the statute of limitations) will not have expired.

For all matters, the lawyer should advise what legal work needs to be done, how long it will take, and how much it will cost. Some lawyers neglect to give honest appraisals. Clients are then misled and spend large sums of money on losing causes. Be wary if the lawyer states, "You have nothing to worry about." Prudent attorneys tell clients that "airtight" cases do not exist and that the possibility of unforeseen circumstances and developments is always present.

TIP: If applicable, request an opinion letter, which spells out the pros and cons of a matter and how much money may be spent to accomplish your objectives. Even if you are charged for the time it takes to draft the letter, an opinion letter can minimize future misunderstandings between you and your lawyer and help decide whether or not to proceed with a lawsuit or legal intervention.

It is important to leave the interview feeling the lawyer is open and responsive to your needs, is genuinely interested in helping you, will return your telephone calls promptly, and will prepare and handle your case properly. Although it is difficult to predict how well the attorney will perform, there are certain clues to look for during the interview.

- Does the lawyer present an outward appearance of neatness and good grooming?

- Are you received at the appointed interview hour or kept waiting? Some lawyers believe if a client is kept waiting she will think the lawyer is busy and, therefore, good. Keeping you waiting is merely a sign that the lawyer is not organized or is inconsiderate.

- Does the lawyer leave the room frequently during the interview, or permit telephone calls to intrude? You deserve his complete attention.

- Does he demonstrate boredom or lack of interest by yawning or finger tapping?

- Is she a clock-watcher?

- Does the lawyer try to impress you by narrating other cases he handled? Good lawyers do not have to boast to obtain clients.

- Does he fail to discuss the fee arrangement up front? Some attorneys have a tendency to wait until all work is done before submitting large bills. The failure to discuss fee arrangements at the initial interview may be a sign the lawyer operates this way.

Successful lawyers win cases and make money for their clients. Don't be fooled by appearances. Plush offices, fancy cars, and expensive clothes might be a reason you will pay exorbitant fees for routine legal services. Don't be impressed by the school from which the lawyer graduated. Most law schools do not give their graduates practical training, and many less prestigious "local" law schools provide superior concrete skills, which is what you are paying for.

Be sure the lawyer of your choice will be working on the matter. People often go to prestigious firms expecting their matter to be handled by a partner. They pay large fees and sometimes wind up being represented in court by a junior associate. Be sure the retainer agreement states that the matter will be handled by attorney X (the attorney of your choice).

The major factor in determining whether a particular lawyer should be hired is the amount of experience and expertise he or she has in handling similar legal problems. Use a lawyer who devotes at least 50 percent of her practice to such problems. Avoid inexperienced lawyers if possible. Novices charge less, but often require more time to handle a problem. If you are being charged on an hourly basis, you may pay the same amount of money and not obtain the expertise of a pro.

Hire a lawyer to whom you can relate. Ask the lawyer about his outside activities and professional associations. Inquire if you can speak to any of his previous clients; references will help you learn more about the lawyer. If you do not feel comfortable with the first lawyer you meet, shop around and schedule appointments with others.

CONFIRMING THE ARRANGEMENT

After you decide to retain a lawyer, it is necessary to discuss a variety of points concerning fees to eliminate potential misunderstandings.

Clarify the fee.   Most attorneys generally charge a modest fee for the first visit to the office. Fees should be charged only when actual time is spent working on a matter. Charges are based on the amount of time and work involved, the difficulty of the problem, the dollar amount of the case, the result, the urgency of the problem (for example, an arbitration hearing that the attorney must handle the day after he is contacted will command a higher fee than the same hearing that takes place in a month), and the lawyer's expertise and reputation in handling your type of problem. Operating expenses and office overhead are elements that may also affect the fee arrangement.

Frequently a lawyer cannot state exactly how much will be charged because he is unable to determine the amount of work that is involved. In such a case, ask for an estimate of the minimum and maximum fee you can expect to pay. If it seems high, do not hesitate to question it. If necessary, state that you intend to speak to other lawyers about fees.

The fee arrangement is comprised of several elements, which you must clearly understand. *Costs* are expenses that the attorney incurs while preparing a case or working on a matter (e.g., photocopying, telephone, mailing, fees paid to the court for filing documents). Be certain the fee arrangement specifically mentions in writing which of these costs you must pay.

Attorneys use different forms of fee arrangements. In a *flat-fee arrangement,* the lawyer is paid a specified sum to get the job done. Most lawyers offer a number of services which are performed on a flat fee basis (e.g., review or preparation of an employment contract and other standard services). In a *flat-fee-plus-time arrangement,* a sum for a specified number of hours is charged. Once the lawyer works more hours than are specified, the client is charged on an hourly basis. However, most lawyers use an hourly rate, which can range from $175 to $300 or more. Under this arrangement, you will be charged at a fixed hourly rate for all work done. If you are billed by the hour, ask if phone calls between you and the lawyer are included. If so, ask that you be charged only for calls exceeding a certain amount per month. This can be justified by arguing you should not be charged when the lawyer fails to clarify a point, obtain additional information, or discuss news regarding the progress of the case. (See page 307 for a sample hourly retainer agreement.)

In a *contingency-fee arrangement*, the lawyer receives a specified percentage of any money recovered via a lawsuit or settlement. Contingency-fee arrangements are common in employment-related collection disputes (such as to recover commissions or other monies due). Some clients favor contingency-fee arrangements because they are not required to pay legal fees if their case is unsuccessful. However, some types of contingency fees are not permitted. For example, a lawyer cannot agree to structure the size of his fee based on the type of verdict obtained for a client in a criminal proceeding. Contingency fees are also looked on unfavorably by courts and disciplinary boards in matrimonial actions because they are viewed as encouraging divorces. So, too, are contingency fees in employment suits that exceed maximum allowable percentages (typically 40 percent). (The sample retainer agreement on page 310 illustrates a modified contingency-fee arrangement sometimes used by the author.)

Sample Hourly Retainer Agreement

Date

Name of Client
Address
Re: Retainer Agreement Regarding Doe v. ABC Company

Dear (Name of Client):

This letter confirms that you have retained me as your attorney to (state precise nature of engagement, such as to negotiate a settlement agreement with your ex-employer if that is reasonably possible; or, if not, to represent you in a breach of contract lawsuit). You agree to pay to me promptly an initial retainer of (specify $, such as $2,000). If I devote more than 10 hours to this case based upon accurate time records commencing from the initial conference, which I will prepare and send to you on a monthly basis, you shall pay additional fees counted at the rate of (specify $, such as $200/hour).

If you should decide to discontinue my services in this matter at any time, you shall be liable for my time computed at the rate of $200/hour.

These fees do not include any work in appellate courts, any other actions or proceedings, or out-of-pocket disbursements. Out-of-pocket disbursements include, but are not limited to, costs of filing papers, court fees, process servers, witness fees, court reporters, long-distance telephone calls, travel, parking, and photocopies (billed at 10 cents per copy) normally made by me or requested by you, which disbursements shall be paid for or reimbursed to me upon my request after I furnish you with evidence of same.

I promise to keep you informed of all developments as they occur and to send you copies of all incoming and outgoing correspondence immediately after it is generated/received. I will personally handle all negotiations of your matter, preparing all necessary papers and documents and arguing your case in court if necessary.

I look forward to working with you on this matter. Kindly indicate your understanding and acceptance of the above terms by signing this letter below where indicated.

Very truly yours,

Name of Attorney

I, (name of client), have read and understand the above letter, have received a copy, and accept all of its terms:

Name of Client: _____ Date: _____

Always spell out contingency arrangements in writing to pre-vent problems. The agreement should state who is responsible for costs in the event you are unsuccessful. All provisions should be explained so they are clearly understood; be sure to save a copy for your records.

There are distinct advantages and disadvantages in using different fee arrangements. For example, in a flat-fee arrangement you know how much you will be charged but do not know how much care and attention will be spent on the matter. The hourly rate might be cheaper than a flat fee for routine work, but some dishonest attorneys "pad" timesheets to increase their fees. In addition, although contingency-fee arrangements are beneficial to clients with weak cases, they sometimes encourage attorneys to settle "winner" cases for less money than go to court. This is why, no matter what type of fee is agreed upon, it is essential to hire a lawyer who is honest and has your best interests in mind at all times.

Ask for a receipt if you pay for the initial or retainer in cash. If a retainer is required, inquire whether the retainer is to become part of the entire fee and whether it is refundable. The retainer guarantees the availability of the lawyer to represent you and is an advance paid to demonstrate your desire to resolve a problem via legal recourse. Ask if the retainer and other fees can be paid by credit card. Be sure interest will not be added if you are late in paying fees. Request that all fees be billed periodically. Insist that billing statements be supported by detailed and complete time records that include the number of hours (or partial hours) worked, a report of the people contacted, and the services rendered. Some lawyers may be reluctant to do this, but by receiving these documents and statements on a regular basis, you can question inconsistencies and errors before they get out of hand, be aware of the amount of the bill as it accrues, and pay for it over time. The sample monthly billing statement on page 312 is the kind of bill the author prepares for all his clients who are charged on an hourly basis. Insist on nothing less.

TIP: Most important, request the attorney to automatically and timely send you copies of all incoming and outgoing correspondence so you will be able to follow the progress of the case.

Understand what legal fees are deductible. Legal fees are tax-deductible provided they are ordinary and necessary business expenses. This means that the cost of legal fees paid or incurred for the "collection, maintenance, or conservation of income" or property used in producing income can be deducted. Deductions are also allowed for legal fees paid to collect, determine or refund any tax that is owed. Ask the attorney whether fees paid are deductible. Structure the fee arrangement to maximize tax deductions and ask for a written statement which justifies the bill on the basis of time spent or some other allocation to support the claim. Keep the statement in a safe place until tax time, and show it to your tax preparers. Accountants and other professionals often clip copies of the statements directly to the return so the IRS won't question the deduction.

The following is a summary of deductible legal fees:

- Attorney fees paid to negotiate severance pay and other post-termination benefits
- Attorney fees paid to obtain a tax ruling
- Attorney fees paid to negotiate an employment agreement
- Attorney fees paid to fight the enforcement of a restrictive covenant precluding you from earning a living
- Attorney fees paid to file a lawsuit to collect wages, commissions, or other compensation
- Attorney fees paid to oppose a suspension or disbarment of a professional license
- Attorney fees for services tending to increase or protect taxable business income (e.g., defending inherited stock)

OTHER ITEMS TO CLARIFY DURING THE INTERVIEW

Will the attorney be available?   Complaints often arise because of poor communication. At the initial interview, ask the lawyer what his normal office hours are. Advise him that availability is very important to you. Request that he return phone calls within twenty-four hours. Insist that his secretary or associate return phone calls if he will be unavailable for extended periods of time, but make it clear you will not call him unnecessarily.

Will the lawyer work on the matter immediately?   The legal system is often a slow process. Don't stall it further by hiring a procrastinating

Sample Modified Contingency-Fee Retainer Agreement

Law Offices of
Sack & Sack
135 East 57th Street, 12th floor
New York, N.Y. 10022
Telephone (212) 702-9000
Facsimile (212) 702-9702

Date

Name of Client
Address

Re: <u>Name of Employer</u>

Dear (Name of Client):

This letter will confirm the terms of my engagement as your attorney regarding the above. I have met with you several times and thoroughly reviewed your file to learn the pertinent facts with respect to your current problems. For those and additional services to be rendered, you paid a consultation fee of One Hundred Fifty Dollars ($150.00) and a retainer of One Thousand Dollars ($1,000.00).

I will now contact the above *in negotiations* in the attempt to collect additional severance and other post-termination benefits on your behalf beyond those monies directly offered to you in the proposed (Date) settlement agreement. For my efforts and in the event negotiations are successful, this office shall be paid a contingency fee of ONE THIRD (33.33%) of the gross amount of *any* money offered to me in settlement beyond said benefits and less the ($1,150.00) paid to me. Specifically included in the computation of my fee shall be a discounted value of any non-taxable monies, benefits, and outplacement assistance paid for by the employer that I obtain on your behalf.

All settlements will require your approval before I conclude same. Additionally, you understand that despite my efforts on your behalf there is no assurance of guarantee of the success of the outcome of my negotiations since the company may refuse to pay any additional compensation. Nevertheless, you have requested my law firm's intervention in this matter and I will promptly keep you posted with all developments as they occur.

The aforementioned contingency arrangement is not for any legal work rendered in formal litigation. In the event that negotiations are unsuccessful, we will discuss the possibility of my representing you in a formal litigation under mutually acceptable terms after our discussion and separate written agreement regarding fees.

I will personally handle all negotiations on your behalf.

If the above terms of this letter are acceptable and confirm our understanding and discussions, please sign below in the space where indicated and immediately return the original letter back to my office, keeping the copy for your records.

Thank you for your interest and attention and if you have any questions or comments, feel free to call.

Very truly yours,

Steven Mitchell Sack

I, Name of Client, have read the contents of the above retainer letter, discussed the terms with Mr. Sack, understand the contents and all of the terms thereof, and have received a copy of this retainer letter for my files:

Name of Client: _____ Date:_____

Lawyer's Sample Monthly Billing Statement

Date

Name of Client
Address

Final statement for all services rendered in the matter of the contract negotiation between (name of client) and (name of employer) at the rate of $200 per hour per agreement:

1. 1/05/99   Initial Meeting with Client
              10:30-11:15   NO CHARGE

2. 1/06/99   Review of initial proposed Agreement
              7:30-7:55 a.m.   25 min.

              Telephone conversation with Client
              9:05-9:15   10 min.

3. 1/07/99   Telephone conversation with Employer's
              Lawyer 9:40-9:45   5 min.

              Telephone conversation with Client
              8:45-8:50; 9:50-9:55   10 min.

4. 1/08/99   Draft of Revised Agreement including telephone
              conversation with client 6:50-8:05 a.m. 75 min.

              Fax agreement to Employer's Lawyer
              Final Discussion with Employer's Lawyer
              2:05-2:25   20 min.

Total time spent on Matter from January 5, 1999
through January 8, 1999:

              145 min. or 2.416 hours
              Amount earned: $483.00

lawyer. Insist that the attorney begin working on the matter as quickly as possible. Ask for an estimate of when the matter will be resolved. Include this in the retainer agreement for protection.

Are there hidden conflicts of interest? Lawyers must avoid even the appearance of impropriety. For example, when a lawyer represents you but previously represented your former employer in another case, there is an inherent conflict that limits his ability to zealously promote your best interests. Ask the attorney up front if he perceives any potential conflict of interest (e.g., is he related to or was he ever employed by the person you are suing?). An attorney must decline representing a client when his professional judgment is likely to be affected by other business, financial, or personal interests. If a lawyer is disqualified, his associates and partners are also forbidden to serve you.

How will funds be handled? Lawyers are obligated to keep client funds in separate accounts. This includes unearned retainer fees. The rules of professional conduct state that a lawyer cannot commingle client funds with his own, and bank accounts for client funds must be clearly marked as "Client Trust Accounts" or "Escrow Accounts."

A lawyer must notify the client immediately when funds are received. You must also receive an accurate accounting of these funds. This consists of a complete explanation of the amount of money held by the attorney, its origin, and the reason for any deductions. Be sure that you receive this. Ask for a copy of all checks received before the attorney deposits the funds into his lawyer's trust account. Tell the attorney to place your funds in an interest-bearing escrow account. Later on, when the funds are remitted, be sure the interest is included in the amount returned to you.

PROBLEMS ENCOUNTERED AFTER A LAWYER IS HIRED

You have the right to change lawyers at any time if there is a valid reason. Valid reasons include improper or unethical conduct, conflicts of interest, malpractice by the lawyer, etc. If you are dissatisfied with the lawyer's conduct or the way the matter is progressing, consult another lawyer for an opinion. Do this before taking action, because you need a professional opinion to tell whether the lawyer acted correctly or incorrectly.

Never fire the lawyer until a replacement is hired because you may be unrepresented and the case could be prejudiced or dismissed. If you fire the lawyer, you may be required to pay for the value of work rendered. You may also have to go to court to settle the issue of legal fees and the return of your papers since some lawyers assert a lien on the file. However, these potential problems should never impede you from taking action if warranted.

If you have evidence that the attorney misused funds for personal gain or committed fraud, you may file a complaint with the state grievance committee or local bar association. Don't be afraid to do this. All complaints are confidential. You cannot be sued for filing a complaint if it is later determined that the lawyer did nothing wrong.

Another alternative is to commence a malpractice lawsuit against the lawyer. Legal malpractice arises when an attorney fails to use "Such skill or prudence as lawyers of ordinary skill commonly possess and experience in the performance of the tasks they undertake." This doesn't mean you can sue if your lawyer gets beaten by a better attorney. You can sue only if he or she renders work or assistance of minimal competence and you are damaged as a result. You can also sue for malpractice when there is a breach of ethics (like the failure to remit funds belonging to a client) in addition to suing for breach of contract and/or civil fraud.

The following are examples of lawyer malpractice:

- Settling a case without your consent
- Procrastinating work on a matter (for example, neglecting to prepare will after being paid and before the client dies)
- Charging grossly improper fees and failing to provide detailed, accurate time sheets to compute fees
- Failing to file a claim within the requisite time period (the statute of limitations)
- Failing to keep you advised of major developments in a matter to your detriment
- Failing to disclose that a conflict of interest exists (such as neglecting to inform you that the lawyer or someone from his law firm previously represented your opponent)

Consult another lawyer before embarking on any of these courses of action to learn if you have a valid claim. An honest and unbiased lawyer will also tell you what steps should be taken to protect your rights.

COUNSEL COMMENTS: More lawyers are now willing to testify against each other. If your complaint to a state's disciplinary board is viable, it will be investigated (the process may take months). An investigative committee will decide whether the case should be given a hearing. After a thorough investigation, the board may make recommendations for disciplinary action against the professional, including a formal reprimand, suspension from practice, or revocation of the lawyer's license (which is rare). You may file a private lawsuit against the professional in addition to requesting that such an investigation ensue. In such a lawsuit, the lawyer will generally carry malpractice insurance and be defended by lawyers from his or her insurance carrier. Deciding whether or not malpractice has actually occurred is a question of fact to be decided by a judge or jury. Due to the complexity of most malpractice cases, and the fact that the lawsuit will typically be vigorously defended, it is critical to seek advice from a skilled lawyer.

Summary of Steps to Take
to Use a Lawyer Effectively

1. Speak to a lawyer before action is contemplated to determine if one is needed.

2. Schedule an interview if necessary; inquire if you will be charged for it.

3. Bring relevant documents to the interview.

4. Do not be overly impressed by plush surroundings.

5. Be sure the lawyer of your choice will be handling the matter.

6. Hire an experienced practitioner who devotes at least 50 percent of her working time to your type of problem.

7. Look for honesty and integrity in a lawyer.

8. Insist on signing a retainer agreement to reduce misunderstandings.

9. Have the agreement read and explained to you before signing and save a copy for your files.

10. If the lawyer cannot state exactly how much you will be charged, get minimum and maximum estimates. Include this in the agreement.

11. Be certain you understand how additional costs are calculated and who will pay for them.

12. If an hourly rate is agreed on, negotiate that you will not be charged for a few telephone calls to your lawyer.

13. Inquire if you can pay the bill by credit card.

14. Structure the fee arrangement to maximize tax deductions and savings.

15. Insist on receiving copies of incoming and outgoing correspondence and monthly, detailed time records.

16. Be sure the lawyer will be available, that he or she will immediately commence work on your matter, and that there are no potential conflicts of interest.

17. Insist that all funds received by the lawyer be deposited into an interest-bearing escrow account. Don't forget to ask for the interest later on.

18. Never allow the lawyer to pressure you into settling a case or making a rushed, uninformed decision.

19. Consult another lawyer before deciding to fire the present one, file a complaint with the grievance committee, or commence a malpractice lawsuit.

20. Do not expect miracles.

GLOSSARY OF TERMS

Abuse of process: A cause of action that arises when one party misuses the legal process to injure another.

Accord and satisfaction: An agreement between two parties, such as the employee and his or her company, to compromise disputes concerning outstanding debts, compensation, or terms of employment. Satisfaction occurs when the terms of the compromise are fully performed.

Action in accounting: A cause of action in which one party seeks a determination of the amount of money owed by another.

Admissible: Capable of being introduced in court as evidence.

Advance: Sometimes referred to as "draw," it is a sum of money that is applied against money to be earned.

Affidavit: A written statement signed under oath.

Allegations: Written statements of a party to a lawsuit that charge the other party with wrongdoing. In order to be successful, allegations must be proven.

Answer: The defendant's reply to the plaintiff's allegations in a complaint.

Anticipatory breach: A breach of contract that occurs when one party, i.e., the employee, states in advance of performance that he or she will definitely not perform under the terms of his or her contract.

Appeal: A proceeding whereby the losing party to a lawsuit requests that a higher court determine the correctness of the decision.

Arbitration: A proceeding whereby both sides to a lawsuit agree to submit their dispute to arbitrators, rather than judges. The arbitration proceeding is expeditious and is legally binding on all parties.

Assignment: The transfer of a right or interest by one party to another.

Attorney in fact: A person appointed by another to transact business on his or her behalf; the person does not have to be a lawyer.

At-will employment: See Employment at will.

Award: A decision made by a judicial body to compensate the winning party in a lawsuit.

Bill of particulars: A document used in a lawsuit that specifically details the loss alleged by the plaintiff.

Breach of contract: A legal cause of action for the unjustified failure to perform a duty or obligation specified in an agreement.

Brief: A concise statement of the main contents of a lawsuit.

Burden of proof: The responsibility of a party to a lawsuit to provide sufficient evidence to prove or disprove a claim.

Business deduction: A legitimate expense that can be used to decrease the amount of income subject to tax.

Business slander: A legal wrong committed when a party orally makes false statements that impugn the business reputation of another (e.g., imply that the person is dishonest, incompetent, or financially unreliable).

Calendar: A list of cases to be heard each day in court.

Cause of Action: The legal theory on which a plaintiff seeks to recover damages.

Caveat emptor: A Latin expression frequently applied to consumer transactions; translated as "Let the buyer beware."

Cease-and-desist letter: A letter, usually sent by a lawyer, that notifies an individual to stop engaging in a particular type of activity, behavior, or conduct that infringes on the rights of another.

Check: A negotiable instrument; the depositor's written order requesting his or her bank to pay a definite sum of money to a named individual, entity, or to the bearer.

Civil court: Generally, any court that presides over noncriminal matters.

Claims court: A particular court that hears tax disputes.

Clerk of the court: A person who determines whether court papers are properly filed and court procedures followed.

Collateral estoppel: See Estoppel. Collateral estoppel happens when a prior but different legal action is conclusive in a way to bring about estoppel in a current legal action.

Common law: Law that evolves from reported case decisions that are relied on for their precedential value.

Compensatory damages: A sum of money, awarded to a party, that represents the actual harm suffered or loss incurred.

Complaint: A legal document that commences a lawsuit; it alleges facts and causes of action that a plaintiff relies on to collect damages.

Conflict of interest: The ethical inability of a lawyer to represent a client because of competing loyalties, e.g., representing both employer and employee in a labor dispute.

Consideration: An essential element of an enforceable contract; something of value given or promised by one party in exchange for an act or promise of another.

Contempt: A legal sanction imposed when a rule or order of a judicial body is disobeyed.

Contingency fee: A type of fee arrangement whereby a lawyer is paid a percentage of the money recovered. If unsuccessful, the client is responsible only for costs already paid by the lawyer.

Continuance: The postponement of a legal proceeding to another date.

Contract: An enforceable agreement, either written, oral, or implied by the actions or intentions of the parties.

Contract modification: The alteration of contract terms.

Counterclaim: A claim asserted by a defendant in a lawsuit.

Covenant: A promise.

Credibility: The believability of a witness as perceived by a judge or jury.

Creditor: The party to whom money is owed.

Cross-examination: The questioning of a witness by the opposing lawyer.

Damage: An award, usually money, given to the winning party in a lawsuit as compensation for the wrongful acts of another.

Debtor: The party who owes money.

Decision: The determination of a case or matter by a judicial body.

Deductible: The unrecoverable portion of insurance proceeds.

Defamation: An oral or written statement communicated to a third party that impugns a person's reputation in the community.

Default judgment: An award rendered after one party fails to appear in a lawsuit.

Defendant: The person or entity who is sued in a lawsuit.

Defense: The defendant's justification for relieving himself or herself of fault.

Definite term of employment: Employment of a fixed period of time.

Deposition: A pretrial proceeding in which one party is questioned, usually under oath, by the opposing party's lawyer.

Disclaimer: A clause in a sales, service, or other contract that attempts to limit or exonerate one party from liability in the event of a lawsuit.

Discovery: A general term used to describe several pretrial devices (e.g., depositions and interrogatories) that enable lawyers to elicit information from the opposing side.

Dual capacity: A legal theory, used to circumvent workers' compensation laws, that allows an injured employee to sue his or her employer directly in court.

Due process: Constitutional protections that guarantee that a person's life, liberty, or property cannot be taken away without the opportunity to be heard in a judicial proceeding.

Duress: Unlawful threats, pressure, or force that induces a person to act contrary to his or her intentions; if proved, it allows a party to disavow a contract.

Employee: A person who works and is subject to an employer's scope, direction, and control.

Employment at will: Employment by which an employee has no job security.

Employment discrimination: Conduct directed at employees and job applicants that is prohibited by law.

Equity: Fairness; usually applied when a judicial body awards a suitable remedy other than money to a party (e.g., an injunction).

Escrow account: A separate fund where lawyers or others are obligated to deposit money received from or on behalf of a client.

Estoppel: Estoppel is a legal bar to prevent a party from asserting a fact or claim inconsistent with that party's prior position that has been relied on or acted on by another party.

Evidence: Information in the form of oral testimony, exhibits, affidavits, etc., used to prove a party's claim.

Examination before trial: A pretrial legal device; also called a "deposition."

Exhibit: Tangible evidence used to prove a party's claim.

Exit agreements: Agreements sometimes signed between employers and employees on resignation or termination of an employee's services.

Express contract: An agreement whose terms are manifested by clear and definite language, as distinguished from agreements inferred from conduct.

False imprisonment: The unlawful detention of a person who is held against his or her will without authority or justification.

Filing fee: Money paid to start a lawsuit.

Final decree: A court order or directive of a permanent nature.

Financial statement: A document, usually prepared by an accountant, that reflects a business's (or individual's) assets, liabilities, and financial condition.

Flat fee: A sum of money paid to a lawyer as compensation for services.

Flat fee plus time: A form of payment in which a lawyer receives one sum for services and also receives additional money calculated on an hourly basis.

Fraud: A false statement that is relied on and causes damages to the defrauded party.

General denial: A reply contained in the defendant's answer.

Ground: The basis for an action or an argument.

Guaranty: A contract in which one party agrees to answer for or satisfy the debt of another.

Hearsay evidence: Unsubstantiated evidence that is often excluded by a court.

Hourly fee: Money paid to a lawyer for services, computed on an hourly basis.

Implied contract: An agreement that is tacit rather than expressed in clear and definite language; an agreement inferred from the conduct of the parties.

Indemnification: Protection or reimbursement against damage or loss. The indemnified party is protected against liabilities or penalties from that party's actions; the indemnifying party provides the protection or reimbursement.

Infliction of emotional distress: A legal cause of action in which one party seeks to recover damages for mental pain and suffering caused by another.

Injunction: A court order restraining one party from doing or refusing to do an act.

Integration: The act of making a contract whole by integrating its elements into a coherent single entity. An agreement is considered integrated when the parties involved accept the final version as a complete expression of their agreement.

Interrogatories: A pretrial device used to elicit information; written questions are sent to an opponent to be answered under oath.

Invasion of privacy: The violation of a person's constitutionally protected right to privacy.

Judgment: A verdict rendered by a judicial body; if money is awarded, the winning party is the "judgment creditor" and the losing party is the "judgment debtor."

Jurisdiction: The authority of a court to hear a particular matter.

Legal duty: The responsibility of a party to perform a certain act.

Letter of agreement: An enforceable contract in the form of a letter.

Letter of protest: A letter sent to document a party's dissatisfaction.

Liable: Legally in the wrong or legally responsible for.

Lien: A claim made against the property of another in order to satisfy a judgment.

Lifetime contract: An employment agreement of infinite duration that is often unenforceable.

Liquidated damages: An amount of money agreed on in advance by parties to a contract to be paid in the event of a breach or dispute.

Malicious interference with contractual rights: A legal cause of action in which one party seeks to recover damages against an individual who has induced or caused another party to terminate a valid contract.

Malicious prosecution: A legal cause of action in which one party seeks to recover damages after another party instigates or institutes a frivolous judicial proceeding (usually criminal) that is dismissed.

Mediation: A voluntary dispute-resolution process in which both sides attempt to settle their differences without resorting to formal litigation.

Misappropriation: A legal cause of action that arises when one party makes untrue statements of fact that induce another party to act and be damaged as a result.

Mitigation of damages: A legal principle that requires a party seeking damages to make reasonable efforts to reduce damages as much as possible; for example, to seek new employment after being unfairly discharged.

Motion: A written request made to a court by one party during a lawsuit.

Negligence: A party's failure to exercise a sufficient degree of care owed to another by law.

Nominal damages: A small sum of money awarded by a court.

Noncompetition clause: A restrictive provision in a contract that limits an employee's right to work in that particular industry after he or she ceases to be associated with his or her present employer.

Notary Public: A person authorized under state law to administer an oath or verify a signature.

Notice to show cause: A written document in a lawsuit asking a court to expeditiously rule on a matter.

Objection: A formal protest made by a lawyer in a lawsuit.

Offer: The presentment of terms, which, if accepted, may lead to the formation of a contract.

Opinion letter: A written analysis of a client's case, prepared by a lawyer.

Option: An agreement giving one party the right to choose a certain course of action.

Oral contract: An enforceable verbal agreement.

Parol evidence: Oral evidence introduced at a trial to alter or explain the terms of a written agreement.

Partnership: A voluntary association between two or more competent persons engaged in a business as co-owners for profit.

Party: A plaintiff or defendant in a lawsuit.

Perjury: Committing false testimony while under oath.

Petition: A request filed in court by one party.

Plaintiff: The party who commences a lawsuit.

Pleading: A written document that states the facts or arguments put forth by a party in a lawsuit.

Power of attorney: A document executed by one party allowing another to act on his or her behalf in specified situations.

Pretrial discovery: A legal procedure used to gather information from an opponent before the trial.

Process server: An individual who delivers the summons and/or complaint to the defendant.

Promissory note: A written acknowledgment of a debt whereby one party agrees to pay a specified sum on a specified date.

Proof: Evidence presented at a trial and used by a judge or jury to fashion an award.

Punitive damages: Money awarded as punishment for a party's wrongful acts.

Quantum meruit: A legal principle whereby a court awards reasonable compensation to a party who performs work, labor, or services at another party's request.

Rebuttal: The opportunity for a lawyer at a trial to ask a client or witness additional questions to clarify points elicited by the opposing lawyer during cross-examination.

Release: A written document that, when signed, relinquishes a party's rights to enforce a claim against another.

Remedy: The means by which a right is enforced or protected.

Reply: A written document in a lawsuit conveying the contentions of a party in response to a motion.

Restrictive covenant: A provision in a contract that forbids one party from doing a certain act, e.g., working for another, soliciting customers, etc.

Retainer: A sum of money paid to a lawyer for services to be rendered.

Service letter statutes: Laws in some states that require an employer to furnish an employee with written reasons for his or her discharge.

Sexual harassment: Prohibited conduct of a sexual nature that occurs in the workplace.

Shop rights: The rights of an employer to use within the employer's facility a device or method developed by an employee.

Slander: Oral defamation of a party's reputation.

Small-claims court: A particular court that presides over small disputes (e.g., those involving sums of less than $3,500).

Sole proprietorship: An unincorporated business.

Statement of fact: Remarks or comments of a specific nature that have a legal effect.

Statute: A law created by a legislative body.

Statute of frauds: A legal principle requiring that certain contracts be in writing in order to be enforceable.

Statute of limitations: A legal principle requiring a party to commence a lawsuit within a certain period of time.

Stipulation: An agreement between the parties.

Submission agreement: A signed agreement whereby both parties agree to submit a present dispute to binding arbitration.

Subpoena: A written order requiring a party or witness to appear at a legal proceeding; a subpoena duces tecum is a written order requiring a party to bring books and records to the legal proceeding.

Summation: The last part of the trial wherein both lawyers recap the respective positions of their clients.

Summons: A written document served on a defendant giving notification of a lawsuit.

Temporary decree: A court order or directive of a temporary nature, capable of being modified or changed.

Testimony: Oral evidence presented by a witness under oath.

"Time is of the essence": A legal expression often included in agreements to specify the requirement of timeliness.

Tort: A civil wrong.

Unfair and deceptive practice: Illegal business and trade acts prohibited by various federal and state laws.

Unfair discharge: An employee's termination without legal justification.

Verdict: The decision of a judge or jury.

Verification: A written statement signed under oath.

Waiver: A written document that, when signed, relinquishes a party's rights.

Whistle-blowing: Protected conduct where one party complains about the illegal acts of another.

Witness: A person who testifies at a judicial proceeding.

Workers' compensation: A process in which an employee receives compensation for injuries sustained in the course of employment.

INDEX